**TRUST
MATTERS**

TRUST MATTERS

Parsi Endowments
in Mumbai and the
Horoscope of a City

LEILAH VEVAINA

Duke University Press   *Durham and London*   2023

Printed in the United States of America on acid-free paper ∞
Project Editor: Melody Negron
Typeset in Franklin Gothic and Arno Pro by Westchester Publishing Services

Library of Congress Cataloging-in-Publication Data
Names: Vevaina, Leilah, [date] author.
Title: Trust matters : Parsi endowments in Mumbai and the horoscope of a city / Leilah Vevaina.
Description: Durham : Duke University Press, 2023. | Includes bibliographical references and index.
Identifiers: LCCN 2023005406 (print)
LCCN 2023005407 (ebook)
ISBN 9781478025399 (paperback)
ISBN 9781478020578 (hardcover)
ISBN 9781478027515 (ebook)
Subjects: LCSH: Charitable uses, trusts, and foundations—India—Mumbai. | Parsees—India—Mumbai—Charities. | Religious trusts—India—Mumbai. | Trusts and trustees—India—Mumbai—Religious aspects. | Capitalism—India—Mumbai—Religious aspects. | Capitalism—Social aspects—India—Mumbai. | BISAC: SOCIAL SCIENCE / Anthropology / Cultural & Social | HISTORY / Asia / South / India
Classification: LCC KNS2168.5 .V483 2023 (print) | LCC KNS2168.5 (ebook) | DDC 346.54792/0642—dc23/eng/20230613
LC record available at https://lccn.loc.gov/2023005406
LC ebook record available at https://lccn.loc.gov/2023005407

Cover art: Tower of Silence, Bombay, India, 1903. Courtesy the Library of Congress.

To my Bo

ACKNOWLEDGMENTS

There are truly countless people to thank for their help throughout the long process of writing this book. I will begin with those who provided much guidance, support, and friendship in graduate school at the New School for Social Research. Carol A. Breckenridge taught me a great many things, above all her passion for the city of Mumbai. Carol's early inspiration encouraged me to join the Anthropology Department at the New School, which shaped and challenged me for many years. She was a true mentor and is dearly missed.

I am eternally grateful to Vyjayanthi Rao for guiding me throughout the process of my PhD, for her patience and insistence that I had something to contribute to the field, and her insightful understanding and teaching of the myriad potentialities of the urban. Janet Roitman was hugely influential from my first experience of her course on research methods to the moment during my PhD exams when she remarked how interesting the trust would be as an object of study, which refocused my project. I thank Hugh Raffles for his gentle humor, quiet guidance, and constant support. I treasure his advice to protect my writing time in the face of teaching and other distractions of graduate school and faculty life. Faisal Devji continuously supported and shaped my research with his thoughtful reading and critiques. The Anthropology Department was truly my home, and I wish to thank all the faculty that have graced the halls of the old "GF" building as well as at Sixteenth Street, with special thanks to Arjun Appadurai,

Hylton White, Ann Stoler, Nicholas Langlitz, Miriam Ticktin, and Sharika Thiranagama.

So many of my fellow graduate students were incredibly supportive and thoughtful critics of this research in its early stages. I would especially like to thank Amber Benezra, David Bond, Diego Caguenas, Brie Gettleson, Christina Kim, Soo-Young Kim, Smoki Musaraj, and Matthew Rosen, whose friendship and support throughout graduate school and beyond I will treasure forever.

This research was generously supported by the India China Institute, the Wenner-Gren Foundation, the American Institute of Indian Studies, the Irmgard-Coninx Stiftung, Cornell's Summer Institute on Contested Landscapes, and the Max Planck Institute for the Study of Religious and Ethnic Diversity from its initial through final stages. I would like to thank Emilia Bachrach, Ketaki Pant, Dinyar Patel, Shruti Patel, and Simin Patel for all your friendship and support in Ahmedabad and Mumbai. I am also immensely grateful for the guidance offered by Susan Wadley and Anand Yang during the AIIS Dissertation to Book Workshop.

My tenure at the Max Planck Institute for the Study of Religious and Ethnic Diversity in Göttingen, Germany, was truly remarkable for the time and exposure it offered for research. Peter van der Veer's scholarship and leadership were instrumental in creating an atmosphere of rigorous academic exchange as well as a familial one. Intense seminars would end with long and casual chats in the garden. At the institute, I was enriched by the various talks by world-renowned scholars and the intense workshop atmosphere with other doctoral students, postdoctoral fellows, and visiting fellows. I would especially like to thank Irfan Ahmad, Marian Burchardt, Derek Denman, Angie Heo, Nicole Itturiaga, Liza Wing Man Kam, Patrice Ladwig, Samuel Lengen, Tam Ngo, Salah Punathil, Jingyang Yu, Nathanial Roberts, Paul Sorrentino, David Strohl, Shaheed Tayob, Sahana Udupa, Xiaoxuan Wang, and Sarovar Zaidi. I hope to drink tea with you all again soon.

While in Göttingen, my understanding of India was greatly enhanced by the scholars of the Centre for Modern Indian Studies, particularly Srirupa Roy and Rupa Viswanath, and their mission to further critical caste studies. Their guidance and advice on academic and family life were essential at various stages. Göttingen truly became a home to me after I joined a writing group with Lisa Björkman, Radhika Gupta, Neena Mahadev, Aparna Nair, and Saikat Maitra. Reading their work and discussing mine over lovely meals, laughter, and true collegiality were invaluable.

Colleagues at the Chinese University of Hong Kong and beyond have provided me with such a stimulating and caring new home. I thank the Faculty of Arts for their support in the publication of this book. A special thank you to Ju-chen Chen, Sealing Cheng, Sidney Cheung, Christina Cheung, Andrew Kipnis, Venera Khalikova, Teresa Kuan, Minhua Ling, Gordon Mathews, Alastair McClure, Lynn Nakano, Jia Tan, Wyman Tang, Devika Shankar, and Kaming Wu, who have all encouraged and supported my research and life in Hong Kong. To my students, your intellect, curiosity, and bravery inspire me every day to be a better teacher and scholar.

Furthermore, my intellectual development and research have been greatly enriched by conversations with Sareeta Amrute, Debjani Bhattacharyya, Ritu Birla, Erica Bornstein, Thomas Blom Hansen, Jose Casanova, Sheetal Chhabria, Nathan Coben, Rohit De, Namita Dharia, Jatin Dua, Laura Elder, Joseph Heathcott, Matthew Hull, Jane Guyer, Riaz Khan, Howie Kislowicz, Catherine Larouche, Hirokazu Miyazaki, Nada Moumtaz, Gustav Peebles, Nikhil Rao, Sanam Roohi, Sanjay Ruparelia, Levent Soysal, and Katherine Verdery.

I am enormously indebted to Mitra Sharafi, not only for her excellent scholarship but also for her patient and constant guidance, particularly about issues of Parsi and Indian colonial law. As I continue as a scholar, I hope to emulate her institution-building and mentorship of junior scholars. I would also like to deeply thank Bill Maurer for how his work enlivens the discussion of econo-legal instruments. His encouragement and support of my research have been so enriching at various points throughout the process.

I am so grateful for the enthusiasm and support from my editor at Duke University Press, Elizabeth Ault. From our first conversations, I gained much confidence and insight into what this book could be. I am deeply thankful to the anonymous readers for their close attention and care. You have renewed my faith in the peer review process as you elevated this book with your thoughtful suggestions and expertise at every turn.

A huge thank you to the many people in Mumbai and Hong Kong who took the time and effort to speak with me about trusts, their personal disputes, and their lives in the city. I genuinely remain grateful for their hospitality and graciousness. Special thanks are due to Muncherjee Cama, Noshir Dadrawala, Behram Dastur, Anahita Desai, Goolrukh Gupta, Jamsheed Kanga, Homi Khushrokhan, Firoza and Khojeste Mistree, Jehangir Patel, Neville Shroff, and the many others who preferred that I not mention their names. Staff and officials of the K. R. Cama Oriental

Institute and the Bombay Parsi Punchayet and other trusts, were invaluable to this research.

I consider myself so fortunate to know many scholars whose work I admire and whom I count as close friends. I thank Ajay Gandhi, Mateusz Halawa, Randi Irwin, Kadija Ferryman, Sabine Mohammed, and Scott MacLochlainn for their many hours of conversations and time spent with parts of this manuscript.

I am so grateful to those in my extended family whom I got to know better in Mumbai and Germany during fieldwork and writing. I am enormously thankful to my grandfather, Phiroze Driver, with whom I lived throughout my fieldwork. His generosity, kindness, and humor are cherished and deeply missed. Huge thanks and love to Kalpana and Cyrus Driver, Mahrouk and Sohrab Kapadia, Anke and Werner Rosenkranz, Mahrouk and Feroze Vevaina, and Shirin and Cyrus Vevaina, who hosted me during various stages of the process. Their hospitality, understanding, and encouragement were so vital during this time. I deeply want to thank Reema Dodin, Rachel Fomalhaut, Annie Kirby, Jane Kirst, Garance Stettler, and Maryam Zomorodian for the friendship, laughter, and support you have offered me since I have known you.

I owe everything to my grandparents, Homai and Dinshaw, Zarine and Phiroze; my parents, Tinaz and Soli Vevaina; and my brother, Yuhan. I would not be the person nor the scholar I am, without your sacrifices, hard work, and guidance. Thank you for your love, unwavering support, and encouragement. To my Kai and Zarina, who instilled a new drive into finishing this book, thank you for all the love, delight, and joy you bring to my life. Most of all, I have depended on the love, support, encouragement, and editing of Tim Rosenkranz. Thank you for listening, reading, and helping me bring this book to life.

During the tenth month of my fieldwork in Mumbai, I had scheduled an interview with an advocate and law professor who was very involved with minor property disputes in the Court of Small Causes.[1] As I walked through the complex, the stony structure of the courthouse was punctuated by a series of arched porticos lined with typists and benches of petitioners waiting for their matters to be called. As with such old buildings, the ceilings were very high, and while this dissipated the heat, all windows and doors remained open, making for an acoustic nightmare in the courtrooms. I was instructed to the Bar Room in the newer concrete building attached to the older stone court. The halls were quieter here, with several men sitting at typewriters typing on the now-familiar pistachio green court document paper. They barely glanced up as I walked by and continued their work, providing a soundtrack to the courtrooms with their manual typing. In a sharp but muted black-and-white sari, "Dr. Pandey" invited me to meet in the upstairs advocate's lounge, a plain hall with a few long tables and plastic chairs, keeping with the functional theme of almost everything in this lower-level court. "So," she asked me, "you said on the phone that you wanted to know about property. Is that true? Or do you want to know about people and property?" Her query got to the heart of the matter theoretically and literally; I was very interested in this relationship between social and religious life and materiality like housing, urban real estate, and the endowment form. I felt like her question had quickly pulled these strands together.

My research, while focused on the charitable trust as a legal form, is per-haps more accurately a study about the trust as a technology of property relations for Parsis (Indian Zoroastrians) living in Mumbai. In its simplest form, a public charitable trust is inaugurated when a person, the settlor, en-dows an asset for a particular charitable purpose, a residence to house the poor, for example. The trust is then managed by trustees for its beneficiaries into the future. As the state often wishes to encourage such endowments, it grants them tax exemption and perpetual life bound to the original wishes of the settlor. My book asks not what trusts are but what they do; how they were historically utilized and how these nineteenth-century technologies spill over their original purviews and become entangled in the fraught and overburdened landscape of built spaces in the city; how the residues of trust matters help to constitute Parsi property relations, their communal life, obligations, struggles, and death in Mumbai today.

As is often the case with fieldwork, I did not begin my research on Par-sis with the trust squarely in my focus.[2] Instead, I was very interested in Parsi intracommunal governance and the institution of the Bombay Parsi Punchayet (BPP), the apex community organization, and its extensive land holdings in the city in the face of a community that was seen to be dwin-dling. While numbering less than fifty thousand in a city of over twelve million, the Parsis are said to be the largest private landowners in Mum-bai through trusts like the BPP.[3] I asked myself, what would happen if one of Mumbai's biggest landlords no longer had any tenants? Implicit in this question are notions of temporality, and of rapid changes in growing urban space in conflict, perhaps with the endurance of a legal technique. In this megacity, to say that living space is scarce is at once an understatement and yet also slightly misleading. Many of Mumbai's ultra-elite residents enjoy large flats, bungalows, and even entire high-rises.[4] However, just as income is unequally dispersed through this and virtually any city, the density of liv-ing is as well (V. Rao 2007). It is quite striking to traverse a neighborhood like Lalbaug in Parel, the old mill district, with its bustling streets, flyovers, street hawkers, pavement dwellers, and unending vehicular, human, and bovine traffic, to pass through a gate and enter Nowroze Baug, a Parsi hous-ing colony, with its open green spaces, low-rise, quiet yellow buildings, and one or two people in its lanes. So how can we account for this disparity? What is communal life like in these spaces, and what happens to the social life of these spaces if they are slated for redevelopment?

A Horoscope of the City

This begs the question of how we may comprehend a city, an already complex spatial arrangement teeming with sociality, with often deep histories and even more vast imaginaries, ethnographically. Some have tackled the city through infrastructure, housing, specific communities, and food—all different vectors into understanding the city through a partial yet no less critical vantage. Many scholars have offered the metaphor of the city as a palimpsest, wherein the traces of older-built forms remain visible even as they are replaced with newer buildings and construction (Huyssen 2003). This metaphor says much about how the built form of a city accrues over time and is an excellent reminder to urban ethnographers that the city within which they traverse and research is one of just the present moment, having differed before, with a promise to change soon after that.

Formerly preoccupied with rural life, the urban turn within South Asian studies pushed away from viewing the city as colonial, in contrast to the "pure" native hinterlands, and toward understanding what it reveals about colonial and postindependence logics of space, sociality, and power (Glover 2007; Ring 2006; Searle 2016; Dharia 2022). Very recently, there has been a slew of excellent ethnographies on Bombay-Mumbai itself, capturing the politics and sociality around infrastructure, its street-food culture (Anjaria 2016), the history of informal settlements (Chhabria 2019), water politics (Björkman 2015; Anand 2017), and the lives of those living in postindustrial spaces (Finkelstein 2019). This book engages with these works and wishes to explore the distinct conjunction of time, law, and capital that arises when a charitable trust manages communal giving, keeping, building, living, and dying.

Being very interested in housing typologies in Mumbai, I saw that while there were several built forms like slums, cooperative housing societies, and heritage structures that were being dutifully attended to by diligent scholars (N. Rao 2013b; Ring 2006; Adarkar 2011; Chhabria 2019), the entire unevenness of landscapes held in trusts was being overlooked. This immense amount of land and spaces managed by charitable trusts is another landscape in great need of study. What is so particular about this landscape is its endurance. Offered in perpetuity because of charitable mandates, these spaces are allowed to live forever because they are obligated to do good. Yet these spaces perdure in time with a different circulation than other types of built forms in the city. My field research entailed extensive and repeated visits and interviews at trust offices, with residents of trust housing, lawyers, accountants, Mumbai's municipal offices, and within the Charity Commission, the arm of the state that defines the good. During a visit to the latter, my interlocutor presented an answer to how one might comprehend the city. On passing me a copy of the directory of trusts, which described every single public trust holding in Mumbai, he declared, "This is the horoscope of the city!"

A horoscope might seem a strange term to label a thick directory that lists in detail every trust, every trustee, and annual reporting of funds, but I had an idea of what he meant. On each page of the directory were the details of trusts, their locations, and assets; that is, all their real properties in greater Mumbai. My interlocutor intimated that a horoscope might offer a unique frame for reading the city and its future potential, one framed around the timescale and spatial geography of the trust. This was a much more expansive understanding of the timescale of trust than a bureaucratic document might express. It pushed me to ask, what kind of relationship among urban space, time, and modes of action might a horoscope offer?

How can we understand the ways in which trusts represent this horoscope or a mode of seeing time? We can think of a horoscope both spatially and temporally: forecasting a temporal order through the relative position of a spatial one. A horoscope usually denotes a forecast based on the aspect of the stars and planets; I argue that this horoscope of Mumbai assumes a constellation of trust housing, temples, and other spaces that provide a possible future based on their relative positioning in the present. This horoscope, the directory of trusts, is one prognosis of time based on the relative positioning of perpetual trust assets in the city. Each line marks the historical inauguration of particular modes of action to achieve this possible future.

In 1910, the art critic Karl Scheffler memorably described Berlin as a city "condemned forever to become and never be." This provocative indictment of a place as never being complete in the present but continually reaching to fulfill its future potential may not resemble the city of Bombay-Mumbai itself, but instead the urban subjunctive mode of the trust and what it imagines for the city. By looking at the trust directory as a horoscope of the city, we are invited to understand this legal arrangement through its historical and current spatial constellations, but most importantly, what those past arrangements promise for the future. We are encouraged to understand the city in the subjunctive: what it should be.

The subjunctive mood has often been used within anthropology to describe the dissonance in practices and beliefs surrounding health (Good et al. 1994; Mattingly 2014; Hardin 2021). The subjunctive here expresses a condition of wishing or "an irrealis mood describing actions or emotions that have not yet occurred" (Hardin 2021, 433). Within urban studies, this wishing for an alternate future is often understood through the concept of aspiration (Appadurai 2004; Anand and Rademacher 2011; Van der Veer 2015; Goh and Van der Veer 2016), which we may understand as hopes for the future based on specific cultural and historical values. Yet, what the subjunctive adds to hope is a mode of being based on acting *as if* a wished-for condition should, in fact, be a reality. We will encounter several moments of acting as if, from residents who act as if they were legal tenants, to trustees who give out charity to high earners as if they were poor, flats sold as if they were legally owned, and women who are "deemed" as if they are no longer Parsi-Zoroastrian. Legal techniques incorporate the subjunctive mode in legal fictions, which are facts understood to be untrue yet useful because they allow for an understanding or an action as if they were true.[5] Developed through precedent within the common law, legal fictions are often remedies to changing circumstances. The trust directory as a horoscope of the city encourages us to act as if the promises of settlors have come to be in the present and should continue in the future. They are thus apt instruments to deal with perpetual promises in an ever-changing cityscape.

Looking through the lens of urban space or development, the real estate managed by a charitable trust can be seen as a negative space, as it forecloses most possibilities of sale or alternative use. Once registered with the commission, these lands are potentially held outside market circulation and forever for a certain purpose. If one imagined a cadastral map of Mumbai with all its various trust properties marked, it would create a very particular property regime (Verdery 2003) with little or languid circulation: a kind of negative print that is meant to last in perpetuity versus the faster velocity of real estate on the open market. These presents, gifted in the nineteenth century to communal groups, the public, and the city, have enabled and constrained possible futures.

Studying the Trust Ethnographically

My ethnographic research explores this contingent connection among past, present, and future. Field research for this project was conducted in Mumbai from 2009 to 2018 in multiple phases and later extended to Hong Kong. The research entailed extensive and repeated visits to trust offices with residents of trust housing, lawyers, accountants, and numerous lay Parsis. My interlocutors spent much time with me describing their relationships with these unique financial and legal instruments they encountered daily. The research extended into the heart of Mumbai's charity commission, municipal development authorities, and even the High Court. Trust secretaries and building managers were invaluable interlocutors for my study, as they had the in-depth knowledge and institutional memory of trust operations and policies.

Being Parsi has given me a distinct advantage in accessing these resources. I found that the unsettled state of being considered a native anthropologist is much more complex than an insider–outsider dichotomy (Narayan 1993). I found it to be more situational than dual. Being born in Bombay but growing up abroad also allowed me at moments to be seen as someone with no stake or involvement with local disputes but familiar enough to be told everything about them. Very often, trust was extended to me by an interlocutor who knew my distant relative in the city. Other times news of my inquisitiveness had been passed around within this small community. I was surprised and heartened by how openly and honestly my interlocutors shared stories of family disputes over property, their financial hardships, and estrangements caused by cleavages in religious practices.

I have no formal legal training, which often made me feel at a deficit, especially when reading legal texts or in conversations with legal professionals about how the trust should work, tenant rights, or property taxes. Sometimes during fieldwork, this was an advantage, as I could ask my interlocutors who were lawyers and accountants very basic questions because learning how trusts work in context was my ethnographic object. But other interlocutors, especially those financially or legally disadvantaged, often saw me as "the expert" and invited me to intervene in their family conflicts over property issues. Due to the sensitive nature of these disputes, I have used pseudonyms unless given explicit permission to use real names or the person is a public figure, elected trustee, or legal litigant.

Listening to stories of litigation, whether within interviews or in courtrooms, became a large part of my fieldwork. It seemed that just about everyone I spoke with was a trustee, suing a family member, or was being sued themselves over trust assets or property. Hence, far from being nineteenth-century relics of property management, trust matters really matter to contemporary Parsis, to this megacity, and to the issues of contemporary Indian secularism. My aim with this book is not to study public charitable trusts in Bombay-Mumbai for their own sake but to ethnographically show how people utilize them, build lives and homes, support rituals, and dispute through them.

When I began a fieldwork interview with a trustee or trust manager, they would often skeptically ask me precisely what I wanted to know. I would simply reply, "Can you tell me how your trust works?" On many occasions, the vehement response would be, "Trusts don't work, Leilah!" This was followed by a much-welcomed long explanation of the struggles and issues the trust engendered or encountered in Mumbai: the frequent trips to court, the paperwork, and the accusations of corruption. In one meeting, an expert in trust law, answering the same question, assured me, "The law does not allow trusts to fail." This book will be an exploration of people's relationship with a legal instrument that does not work and yet cannot fail. As the following chapters will show, trusts are contentious and contingent forms of social relations through property. They are gifts and obligations connecting the past and the future in perpetuity, and they prompt us to question notions of reciprocity, continuity, change, and crisis; that is, they push us to rethink the relationships among giving, capital, law, and temporality, and how an instrument coming out of a system of equity can move through time and the city and produce deep inequalities.

While some, like Piketty (2018), have explored the relationship between capitalism and inequality, Katharina Pistor (2019, 2) asks how wealth is created and then accumulated in the first place. She reminds us that capital is created through an asset and the legal code, the latter being critical to how the asset may generate wealth (3). Since assets and the established legal regime differ so much over time and space, the big question remains, which assets are selected to be coded, by whom, and for whose benefit (3)? The trust is one such technique of the coding of capital, requiring extensive legal and financial knowledge from its inception. As will be described in more detail, Parsis were early and experienced coders of capital. The book will explore how, by whom, and for whose benefit the endowed assets come to be accrued and then distributed wealth. Through its chapters, it will examine the social and material relations that emerge from the trust's paradoxes of ownership, dissected between trustees and beneficiaries; how this tenacious instrument pushes up against the changing cityscape; and how the objects of trusts begin to take on a (half)life of their own.

The Trust's Inheritances

The contemporary form of the charitable trust has inheritances from three modes of giving (Zoroastrian, Islamic, and English) from distinct historical backgrounds, which merge in a contingent and piecemeal fashion.

Charitable giving is one of the pillars of the Zoroastrian tradition still maintained by Parsis. The acquisition of wealth is considered righteous if earned honestly and shared liberally (Cantera 2015, 315–22).[6] In Zoroastrian theology, Ahura Mazda is the all-knowing but not all-powerful supreme deity. He is opposed to Angra Mainyu, his chief rival, who is responsible for bringing suffering, pollution, and evil into the world (Y. Vevaina 2015, 211–34). Humans are entrusted to make the right choices and follow the Prophet Zarathustra's teachings by deploying "good thoughts, good words, and good deeds" (*humata, hukhta, huvareshta*) to eventually vanquish evil. The aspiration to this credo is central to how contemporary Parsis describe their everyday relationship with their religious tradition. While large-scale philanthropy by the wealthy was often mentioned, all class levels of my interviewees detailed their small-scale acts of charitable works. Giving is further incorporated into several ritual practices such as thanksgiving liturgies, or *jashans; ghambars,* or community feasts; funerary rituals; and *muktads,* annual remembrances for the dead.

Pious endowments were common in the Zoroastrian tradition well before the migration to India. During the Sasanian period (224–651 CE) and after in Iran, pious foundations were established by individuals for the benefit of deceased souls and the performance of religious rituals and charitable acts. Divided into three types, a whole category of inherited property was reserved for the "preservation of the soul" (Macuch 1991, 380–82).[7] This fund set aside by the settlor of the foundation was called the "property of the soul." Maria Macuch relates how specific formulas within wills allowed for different uses and rights of trusteeship within these practices. The assets set apart consisted of a principle, *bun* (foundation or origin), which was usually some productive property, and the income, *bar* (fruit), generated from the *bun.* Only the *bar,* or surplus, could be used for the foundation's expenses, while the principle itself could never be alienated. Endowments, like temples, which could generate no income, had other productive assets attached to the original principle and could not be separated from it. Critically, these endowments were registered and secured from government confiscation or debt repayment. In Sasanian legal terminology, there was no distinction between family endowments and those designated to benefit the public (Macuch 1991).

During the Islamic era (seventh century onward) in Iran, a single person, if converted to Islam, was entitled to inherit the entire family estate, so to retain the family property, many Zoroastrians, now a minority, settled foundations and registered them with the Muslim authorities (Macuch 1991). The foundation in this period was utilized to preserve and protect assets within a community that had newly become a minority. This new status and other religious and economic persecution encouraged many Zoroastrians to flee Iran. During this period, Zoroastrian foundations became subsumed under the law as *waqf,* the second historical antecedent to the contemporary trust, and were often used by Zoroastrians to protect their property.[8]

Waqf, the Muslim endowment form, stems from the Arabic root word, *waqafa,* to stop, hold, or tie up. When referring to a piece of land, that property is stopped or held outside market realms of circulation (Kozlowski 1985, 1). The *waqif* divests themselves of formal rights of possession of the moveable or immoveable property but retains the right to appoint a custodian, or *matuwalli* (one who is trusted), to manage the property. The waqif designates beneficiaries who may enjoy the waqf's yields. A waqf could be established for myriad reasons that cut across strict divisions of public and private use, and familial or charitable benefit. In practice, a waqf was often founded as a means to protect an estate from confiscation by the state or disintegration due to succession by strict following of sharia (Qadir 2004, 147).

Once a waqf was instituted, it was in most cases safe from seizure by authorities and became a favored instrument during times of political turmoil. In India, this practice was often used in opposition to Muslim personal laws of succession that emerged in conjunction with colonial rule. Due to the British enforcement and reification of textual sources for Islamic law, which provided for a consistent property division among rightful heirs, the waqf was often used to counter this strict division. For example, an estate owner with only wives and daughters would pass his property on to male first cousins by Quranic law. In contrast, an endowment allowed for the transmission of the income of an intact inheritance to his direct descendants (Qadir 2004, 147). The property could still be in the family name with its concomitant status associations, while family members could remain beneficiaries in perpetuity. This practice of giving to prevent the division of family property is critical to the work of all endowment forms.

A third ancestor of the contemporary trust is the introduction of English trust law into colonial India. Trusts are based on the concepts of guardianship and obligation; they are today the legal foundation of mutual funds, provident and pension funds, and of course, more explicitly for the endowment of assets for a particular purpose. From the British legal tradition's perspective, trusts were quintessentially British legal innovations that blossomed in the late eighteenth century.[9] However, as we have seen, parallel traditions can be found between the Zoroastrian endowment and the Islamic waqf. So often were trusts utilized in English and colonial courts that they were "like those extraordinary drugs curing at the same time toothache, sprained ankles, and baldness sold by peddlers on the Paris boulevards; they solve equally well family troubles, business difficulties, religious and charitable problems" (Lepaulle 1927, 1126).

The corporation is the other form of common property management that we are more familiar with. While trusts and corporations are similar in that they are instruments of common property, have perpetual succession, and have some form of legal personality, they are different in some fundamental ways. Legal historian Frederic William Maitland analyzed mechanisms that could offer groups a continuous life beyond the natural lives of their members (2003; Getzler 2016). Along with the corporation, he looked toward the English trust form, an endowment settled by a founder and managed by trustees, with beneficiaries reaping its fruits. Under common law, trusts with a religious or charitable purpose have indeed achieved this immortality, both from death and taxes. Unlike corporations, which began by being chartered by the state, unincorporate bodies were created on their own terms.[10] I argue that this makes the trust a particularly apt mechanism for those who found it beneficial to follow colonial rules while insisting on managing their own communal affairs.

Trusts are bound by their deeds and original objects, and in cases of charitable trusts, by the laws governing charities. Corporations are organized under bylaws and may shift these regulations under certain circumstances. They each manage generated income and profits differently. A public trust must deposit its income into its corpus and is only allowed certain expenditures, while a public corporation is bound to distribute its profits among its shareholders. The trustee must be, again, at least in theory, disinterested. That is, they should not be receiving any gain from the trust. The beneficiaries are not stakeholders in the general sense either and therefore cannot make any claims to profit,[11] but only to the original objects of the trust. Shareholders, instead, are active and interested members of a corporation and share the tax burden of the income. The beneficiary of a public charitable trust may choose to receive and enjoy its assets and obligation but need not; they have no burden of duty or responsibility within this relationship (Maitland 2003). As Maitland insists, "Those who would understand how our 'unincorporate bodies' have lived and flourished behind a hedge of trustees should understand that the right of the destinatory [beneficiary], though we must not call it a true *dominium rei*, is something far better than the mere benefit of a promise" (Maitland 2003, 95–96). The beneficiary is not simply the receiver of a promise but the owner of an obligation.[12] These obligations are legal, financial, and temporal relations. These forms of obligations make giving through the trust such a distinct social form.

In India in the colonial period and beyond, we have a confluence of all three endowment inheritances. Ritu Birla (2009) traces the legal and discursive production of notions of community and temporality through the institution of legal infrastructure. Birla has shown how the British colonial government in India began to carve out preferred avenues of philanthropy through legal regulations on giving (and keeping) and market interventions like the legal contract. These legal interventions constructed the "market," attempting to disembed it from the "native" customs of family and community. The market then "becomes a stand-in for 'the public,' a site of modernity and a space distinguished from the private realm of ancient and anachronistic 'native culture'" (Birla 2012, 1018). Many scholars have noted the persistence of this dichotomy and how it obscures the workings and influence of vernacular forms of kinship and caste on contemporary Indian society (Mosse 2020; Gandhi et al. 2020). My work is influenced by Birla's insistence on moving from the relationship of law and economy toward understanding the "law as economy" (Birla 2012). Instead of viewing the two as distinct, Birla shows their mutual embeddedness in colonial governance in India.[13]

Haynes (1987) has traced the shift of native giving "from tribute to philanthropy" as the colonial rulers encouraged giving to become more public and formalized. Yet, as Birla (2009) has shown, this shift was not a clear unidirectional one, as many forms of traditional or customary giving remain alongside more formalized and legalized philanthropy, although the former were coded as irrational or "nonmodern." My work will deepen this articulation by showing how long-held endowment practices in the Zoroastrian tradition have enabled the deployment and convergence of more recent colonial legal forms within Parsi practice. The book will show that these practices remain deeply ingrained in customary Parsi kinship and ritual performances while being thoroughly formal and financialized through the public charitable trust.

Rethinking Trusts: From the "Dead Hand" to a Hinge in Time

Many scholars refer to the trust as the "dead hand" (Maitland, Runciman, and Ryan 2003; Friedman 2009; Birla 2009). This stems from the Roman legal term of mortmain, *manus mortus,* which in certain historical legal contexts assumes the unproductive uses of the asset after it is settled (Birla

2009, 68–73). The rules against perpetuities, known as mortmain laws, were first established in feudal England. The Church and other ecclesiastical bodies were the early targets of the rules, enforcing an end to the perpetual ownership of property unless exempt by decree of the Crown (Stebbings 1989, 5). These laws were enacted to curb the extensive property holdings of the Church by King Edward I in the thirteenth century. The big exception was the charitable trust. Perpetual status was given by royal charter to institutions of education, guilds, and some cities, and only later to business organizations.[14] It was only in the mid-nineteenth century that groups could incorporate without a royal decree. The Mortmain and Charitable Uses Acts of 1888 and 1891 saw that land given in perpetuity without authorization was forfeited to the Crown. This law was never implemented in British India but was in other parts of the British Empire, like Hong Kong (L. Vevaina 2019).

Understood to be one of the fundamental techniques of the trust, to hold and tie up assets for a particular purpose, this emphasis or evocative metaphor of the dead hand often elides the way trusts work in practice and in the context of the way settlors deploy them, beneficiaries enjoy them, and legal infrastructures manage them. What this book will emphasize is the binding of the obligation attached to these properties; that is, what is critically kept perpetual. Secondly, while trusts hold assets like real estate in their tight grip, the continuing quest to make the property more "productive" pushes to animate the dead hand (Moumtaz 2021). My research shows that such reanimation is not the endgame of the trust itself but a latent possibility from its very inception.

The birth of a trust is temporal, spatial, and material. Within three months of establishment in Mumbai, a new public charitable trust must submit a copy of its deed to the charity commissioner and register it in the Directory of Public Trusts. Since the directory was compiled after the Bombay Public Trust Act in 1953, many of the Parsi trusts settled in the nineteenth century have 1953 as their date of establishment. Once registered, a copy of the deed is kept at the Charity Commission, and the original is usually held in the trust office. In the case of the BPP, the original documents are kept in their library and not handled often, as they are older documents. Their deeds, with pages yellowing, have several small holes that betray many years of consumption by insects. The original documents then serve as a security of a promise once made.

In contrast, the commissioner's office keeps the trust deed in an open file, ready to accept the annual financial reports, addendums, and other documents that keep the trust "alive." Since recent high-profile cases are under litigation, copies of the general trust deeds of the BPP have a new life too; they circulate via email, and one was handed to a nosy anthropologist over tea. While trusts are a central part of Parsi life, from managing sacred spaces, to housing, medical care, and education, trust matters do not affect community members in the same ways. Instead, they produce communal divisions and alliances and raise economic opportunities and lifelong dependencies.

Therefore, I will show throughout the book how the trust should be understood as a hinge structuring the temporal, spatial, and material lives of persons and things. This was inspired by Biagioli (2006), who described scientific names as a hinge between two moments of scientific production. Pedersen and Nielsen discuss the transtemporal hinge as that which "holds together otherwise disparate elements . . . in a manner that serves to maintain an optimal balance of distance and proximity between them" (2013, 124). They utilize the hinge concept as a methodological device based on symmetry. What the trust does, however, is hinge the donor and beneficiary asymmetrically by inserting the role of the trustees. It can be imagined more like a hinge on a scale between the weight and the object being weighed, easily tipping to one side but continually establishing a relation between the two entities. Trustees have fiduciary rights over the assets but not rights of complete alienation. They are bound by the settlor's wishes and the deed. The recipients of charity have beneficial rights but have no duties to the trust or the deed. The representatives of the wish, the trustees, as the givers, are bound. Therefore, the trust, like the hinge, binds the trustee to the wishes of the settlor but also splits obligations, allowing for an opening and closing of the relation.

The settlor of a public charitable trust relinquishes their ownership right over the assets to obligate the trust to a particular purpose and for a certain but indefinite number of people. While divesting their ownership rights over the trust assets, the settlor preserves their charitable intention in perpetuity. That is, while the original ownership relation (settlor–asset) is lost at the moment of endowment, a trust's obligation to fulfill its objects endures in perpetuity. Trustees may buy and sell assets to pursue the trust's objects, although, for charitable trusts, these decisions are closely regulated by charity laws and the tax code.[15] It is only when these objects fail that the trust's perpetuity is in danger.[16] If the objects are not upheld, the assets do not return to the settlor but may be captured by the state if the trust is dissolved. This threat of capture or the loss of tax-exempt status for charitable trusts raises the stakes and intensity of the obligation the trust holds to its objects.

Furthermore, the trust structures obligations as hinges in time: connecting the beneficence of the settlor to all beneficiaries through time. This time-work will be discussed much further in the book's first two chapters, using the concept of the horoscope. Just as the horoscope encourages circumscribed action in time, so too does the trust allow for circumscribed giving in space. The constraint of a horoscope is one's birth, as it is the configuration of the stars at that particular moment that ordains one's fortune, and so too, the trust is constrained by the original wish and intent of the settlor. The deed lays out the trust's character or attributes, if you will, for future action. These chapters will explore how formal endowments change the temporal compass and reach of charity, past the immediate and individual giving of the wealthy, into perpetual and communal giving, through the medium of real estate, into the cityscape. Once endowed, real estate becomes subject to a much slower velocity of circulation as it is obligated toward a specific purpose or to a distinct group. Again, here time is hinged asymmetrically. The trust privileges the donor's intention to choose who may enjoy a particular asset or service, and its self-perpetuation favors the future over the present. This makes for uneven temporality between the trust as a legal mechanism and the trust as a bureaucratic and charitable organization. The intense debates and litigation that stem from these dueling chronotopes will be explored throughout the book as they exemplify how the Parsi community is struggling with its hinged past and future, in the present.

Communal Imaginations: A Pinch of Sugar or a Coin

Parsi historical identity is synchronous with the arrival of boatloads of Zoroastrian settlers seeking refuge from Iran after the tenth century.[17] "Parsi" became the ethnic term used to refer to Iranian Zoroastrians who had come to India's west coast.[18] Zoroastrianism, one of the world's first revealed religions, began in the second millennium BCE in central Asia and Afghanistan, and at its peak was the state religion of the Achaemenid (550–330 BCE), Parthian (247–224 CE), and Sassanian empires (224 BCE–651 CE). While still a lived religion today, its practitioners are not only few but also increasingly scattered around the globe. The first substantial diaspora was formed when Zoroastrians fled Iran from the seventh century onward after the Arab invasion and settled in medieval India, forming the Parsi community. Due to merchant trade over the nineteenth and twentieth centuries, Parsis settled in various entrepots of the British Empire, creating a second diaspora, with India as the new homeland.

Although historically unsubstantiated, the story of how this settler group gained permission to step on the shores of Gujarat continues to be critical to the contemporary self-identity and self-understanding of this group.[19] The commonly told narrative relates how the rajah of Sanjan, Jadi Rana, summoned the Persians at his shores to his court and demanded to be told how they could prove that they would not be a burden on nor a threat to the indigenous Indian communities. They responded that they wished to till the land and practice their religion. In response, the rajah showed the Persians a jug full of milk, saying that India, like the jug, was full. In one version of the story, a high priest of the Persians, or *dastur*, added a coin to the milk and said that, like the coin, no one would be able to see that they were there, but they would enrich the milk, nonetheless. The more common version claims that the priest added a pinch of sugar to the milk and contended that, like the sugar, the Persians, while remaining invisible, would sweeten the lands of Sanjan. In both versions, the rajah approved their settlement and then addressed their conditions of entry: The newcomers were to explain their religion, promise not to proselytize, adopt Gujarati speech and dress, surrender their weapons, and only conduct rituals after nightfall.[20] The new migrants were allowed to maintain their sacred fire and began to build infrastructures to support their ritual practices.

It is worth noting that the assimilatory metaphors found in this narrative of rural Gujarat are essentially held and followed by the contemporary Parsi community in India. Most Parsis today continue to insist that cultural assimilation to some degree has been vital for their historically peaceful coexistence in India, often echoing the model minority narrative. I argue, however, that the coin and the sugar offer different modes of assimilation and integration through their respective materialities: the coin remains intact but raises the level of the milk, while the sugar dissolves and changes the composition of the milk itself. These metaphors of assimilation are apt ways of describing the two main strands of contemporary Parsi debate between the orthodox, who, like the coin, wish to remain ethnically intact, and liberal or reform Parsis, who wish to blend in with the rest of Indian society while claiming to sweeten it. One of the main disagreements between these two factions is over what constitutes proper religious practice, especially marriage choice and funerary rites. The lines of the debate reflect not only differing views of correct religious practice but also an ongoing tug-of-war between lay Parsis, the Punchayet, and the priesthood.

As detailed in the following chapters, Parsi real estate in Mumbai is deeply imbricated in the formation of the original Bombay Settlement in the seventeenth century. After much success in shipbuilding and trade in rural Gujarat, many wealthy Parsis were bequeathed lands by the British in the island city. By the nineteenth century, several Parsis in Bombay were prominent natives within the colonial system and were heavily influenced by British models of education and law. By 1865, lay Parsis in the community even drafted a Parsi communal code recognized by the British (Sharafi 2014). These early settlers constructed some of the city's foundational infrastructure, such as water tanks, schools, and hospitals. They built housing colonies called *baugs*, sanatoria, and funerary grounds reserved for their community. Upon their deaths, these wealthy benefactors often endowed their properties to the Parsi Punchayet or settled their eponymous endowments. Parsi settlers to the city tended to settle near older migrants to enjoy the closeness to temples and access to communal living spaces (White 1991).

Another large migration took place from Gujarat to Bombay in the middle of the nineteenth century, spurred on by the existence of these endowments, which supported subsidized homes and employment with public works projects. While many Parsi surnames denote their origins in southern Gujarat—"Bardoliwala," "Amroliwala," and "Billimoria" all denoting small villages—no one would dispute that they are also thoroughly "Bombay Parsis." This designation contrasts with others from around India. It strongly contrasts with later Zoroastrian immigrants from Iran, who still call themselves Iranis although their families have been born in India for generations. Under the law however, Iranis are counted as Parsi Zoroastrians and may avail themselves of all trust benefits.

As per the trust agreements, these properties were reserved for inhabitancy and use by Parsis only and were instrumental in increasing Parsi migration from rural Gujarat to Bombay, making contemporary Mumbai the city with the largest Parsi population in the world, even to this day. The social prominence of wealthy Parsi merchants in India and their ties with colonials further eclipsed the authority of the Parsi priesthood, which continued to lose influence as more significant numbers shifted to Bombay, attracted by housing and other support structures sponsored by such philanthropy (Ringer 2011, 32–37).

As Bombay lore goes, and this is true of many academic accounts of the city as well, the Koli people are "natives" of the area that we now call Mumbai. Small communities of Koli still live in the city today, in Koliwada and other places, and some continue to practice fishing as their subsistence. Sheetal Chhabria (2018) describes the ways in which Kolis were granted this aboriginal status in the first place and had their varied practices and occupations fixed as a fisherman's caste over the eighteenth and nineteenth centuries. She argues that many other communities deploy this lore for their own narrative purposes. As Parsis and other merchant communities and cultivators were given incentives to settle in Bombay first by the East India Company and then the colonial authorities, many Parsis today claim a kind of nostalgic autochthony as well. This goes along with a strand of their discourse of "we built this city" often followed by a list of Parsi-constructed public works.

Due to this early access to prime real estate, a large number of Parsi residential settlements like baugs and sanatoria are in central locations in southern Mumbai. They remain subsidized at nominal rents compared to the market value of the land. The Doongerwadi or "Towers of Silence" funerary complex alone is about sixty acres of real estate in the exclusive downtown neighborhood of Malabar Hill. Some baug residents even pay as little as one dollar per month rent in a city with real estate prices that rival Manhattan. Apart from the enticingly low rent, most baugs have fire temples, ritual wells, playgrounds, parking, medical and dental care, facilities for festive events, and are relatively safe. Given the high value of these properties and their restricted use for this population alone, the question of who counts as a Parsi, and thus who can gain access to the material and social benefits of membership in the community, has become increasingly critical in the context of a rapidly growing megacity and a rapidly shrinking community. As my ethnography shows, the access and distribution of space and resources are far from settled but are ongoing sources of the struggles over class, gender, religiosity, and ethnicity within and beyond the Parsi community; it remains an unsettled state.

Parsis and Baug-Parsis

I sat down to dinner at an ultra-exclusive country club at the invitation of "Dinshaw," a descendent of one of Mumbai's oldest and wealthiest Parsi families, who had endowed many institutions in the city. Dinshaw sat as a trustee on several trusts, as did many of his family members. When I told him of my project on trusts and my particular interest in Parsi housing, he quipped, "Well, first you must understand that there are Parsis and then baug-Parsis," referring to Parsis who live in trust-managed housing colonies. Dinshaw enunciated this distinction as a joke about the social class and parochial attitudes of baug-Parsis, which made the rest of the guests at our table giggle or wince. But as I learned, the everyday lives of those living within Parsi colonies were distinct from others who had to or could afford to live in private housing.

While it is often complex to talk about social class in any context, in postcolonial India, this is one of many categories (like caste) that have blurry boundaries, regional diversity, and layer upon layer of congealed histories that complicate easy classification. However, the distinction that Dinshaw made was often repeated in my fieldwork from both "categories" of Parsis. Unlike some early Parsi settlers who received grants of land from the British as rewards for being "good" natives, many Parsis did leave the very earliest settlements in Gujarat, in the second migration of the nineteenth and early twentieth centuries, because of the availability of subsidized charitable housing in baugs, managed by various charitable trusts like the Punchayet. Due to municipal regulations such as the Rent Act (1947), however, these families became tenants and remained in subsidized flats regardless of the growing income levels of their descendants.

It is estimated that about 50 percent of Parsis in Mumbai live in some form of trust housing like baugs and sanatoria. The other 50 percent would be spread over private arrangements: those who own their flat outright or through cooperative societies or those like Dinshaw who might reside in a private villa in the city. As is true of many cities, locating oneself and others by neighborhood and type of residence is very common and often a shorthand for denoting class, race, religion, or ethnicity. Describing someone as residing on Park Avenue or within the Marcy Homes of New York City, respectively, could denote completely different lifeworlds. Neighborhoods are used as markers of difference by those who deploy them in these ways, and clearly, Dinshaw was attempting to mark out the social class of those who live in baugs, as well as reaffirming his own.

Within the Parsi Zoroastrian tradition, there are divisions among family lineages that were strict in terms of marriage endogamy in the past. Some descend from priestly, *navar* families whose sons are the only ones sanctioned to become Zoroastrian priests. Lay Parsis are known as *behdins* (those of the Good Religion), and non-Parsis as *juddins* (those of other religions). These terms do not correspond directly to social class in the sense of income or educational levels. Some more orthodox members still frown upon marriage between *navar* families and *behdins*. Marriage between Parsis and *juddins*, while an increasing occurrence, is one of the most controversial issues within the community and further complicated due to the specific legal arrangements of many trusts. These marriages reveal the cleavages of access to trust assets as they trouble the beneficiary status of female Parsis who might be "deemed" to no longer be Parsi after marriage. Hence not only are intermarriages purportedly threatening to community demography, but they have also become central to understanding the stakes of trust matters.

In terms of levels of education, most Parsi girls and boys would have completed primary and secondary schooling with either English or Gujarati as the medium. One of the earliest schools for girls in India, the Alexander Girls' English Institution, was founded by a Parsi in 1863, and almost all other Parsi educational institutions established since are funded and managed by charitable trusts. Women's education has been a priority for the community since the mid-nineteenth century. I claim that education levels do not map neatly onto Dinshaw's binary categories. Regarding employment, trusts have served to keep most Parsis within white-collar jobs as several offer educational funds for college, study abroad, and the high fees for medical, dental, and law schools. While most elite Parsis attend convent schools and universities, schooling and higher education are highly regarded within the community and, with the aid of charitable trusts, are attainable for almost all.

Religiosity also differs quite a bit among these categories. Other terms that cross-cut Dinshaw's binary would be the self-description of many Parsis as orthodox or liberal, who are split on some of the community's most controversial topics such as intermarriage, proper disposal of the dead, conversion, and the validity of priestly authority, further discussed in the following chapters.[21] While it is a stereotype that non-baug Parsis are all rich and more religiously liberal, plenty of conservative and orthodox Parsis live in private homes. Because of the historical geography of Parsi settlements, many baugs are located close to Zoroastrian temples, or *agiaries*, if one is not directly on the premises, making them at least convenient for pious baug residents to visit.

However, those living within baugs are surrounded by other Parsis in these enclaves. This style of segregated living is assumed to have contributed to the flourishing of specific communal ways of life often depicted in novels and other media.[22] Furthermore, I argue that a critical difference is the greater involvement of trusts in the lives of those within their walls. As singular authority, either from priests or other community leaders, has splintered, more and more often, trust housing has been utilized to enforce "proper" Parsi behavior and practice. Aspi, a lifelong baug resident in his sixties, who spoke with me one sunny afternoon, frustratingly remarked how "grossly unfair" it was that he had to abide by specific rules like marrying within the community for fear of being evicted while "those that can

FIGURE I.1. Bhika Behram Well. Photo by author.

afford it do whatever they want." Hence, for many baug residents, being a tenant of the BPP comes with both incredibly subsidized housing in an extremely expensive city and specific rules and norms of behavior. It is, therefore, no accident that Parsis, who successfully and publicly challenge community codes and mores, tend to live independently from trusts.

Another and perhaps most vulnerable subset of Parsis are those who reside in various sanatoria or widow residences managed by trusts. Originally meant as temporary rest homes after medical treatments, most of the former have become permanent housing for the poorest Parsis. This shift is discussed further in chapter 1. Many sanatorium residents also benefit from trust welfare programs. On my third visit to the famous Bhika Behram Well (see figure I.1), located on the west side of the Oval Maidan in south Mumbai, I met Freni, an elderly Parsi woman. The well is just off the main road at the southern end of Cross Maidan and has been open to passing travelers since 1725 when it was built and endowed by a Parsi traveler from Gujarat. Freni could barely speak clearly; her teeth were rotted out, and her eyes were a milky grey, betraying her lack of medical care. She lived in the widow *chawl* on Modi Street, a walking distance from the well.[23] She sat in disheveled clothes and asked all visitors for a bit of help by nodding and putting out her hand, palm up. She and others walk here daily to receive alms from other community members who often bring food or offer small amounts of money. They would press their gifts into her palm and then hold her palm in both hands while whispering a blessing. Therefore, while there are reportedly no Parsis living in slums or informal housing in the city, primarily due to the availability of charitable housing, there remains a wide range of Parsi lifeworlds in Mumbai.

There are also "Bombay Parsis" who don't live in the city permanently. Many Parsi college-age children are able, again often with trust scholarship funds, to go abroad for college or university, most often within the boundaries of the former British Empire: the United States, Canada, the U.K., Hong Kong, Australia, and New Zealand.[24] While many end up settling abroad, they are a floating population in Mumbai, especially during the cool winter, the season for weddings and *navjote* celebrations. Even within the global Parsi Zoroastrian diaspora, being a Bombay Parsi carries a connotation of authenticity, assumed traditionality, and even orthodoxy in practice. Among diaspora Parsis, Bombay-Mumbai is now the new homeland that evokes a return to an authentic form of practice and religiosity. I do not believe this is due only to Mumbai currently holding the majority of Parsis in the world, but rather the intimate connections that Parsi life and traditions have with the city itself, ties that Parsis and others see as slowly fraying in the twenty-first century. Since the 1990s, their foreign capital has been welcomed back to India within the particular legal category of the Non-Resident Indian (NRI). The BPP is especially fond of this group and courts them as prime consumers of the trust's redeveloped apartments. Since 2008, these Parsis are also allowed to vote in BPP elections if they are physically present to cast their ballot in Mumbai, an attempt to make the Punchayet the apex body of the global Parsi community. Hence, while most Parsi trusts have a relatively small population of beneficiaries, this population may be shrinking or expanding through various legal and enforcement mechanisms.

The trope of the Parsi *bawaji* was quite vivid at one time, brought to life in Parsi theater and often in Indian films (Desai 2019).[25] The character would most likely be portrayed in traditional Parsi dress as old, middle-class, eccentric, and almost always benign. These portrayals were often held up proudly by Parsis of an older generation as gentle teasing: "All Parsis end up being eccentric because we live so long." This trope is rarely seen in more contemporary popular culture. It is even seen as embarrassing by some younger Parsis, who strive to talk, dress, and comport themselves like other residents of Mumbai, or New York or London, for that matter. Portrayals of Parsis in contemporary media often center around intense community infighting, often with a tone of ridicule, or are preoccupied with the "extinction" of Parsis in India, with their decreasing demography. Many Mumbaikars today, especially those who have migrated to the city themselves, often have no recognition of who Parsis are or, if they do, assume that they have already died out. This shift from being renowned natives of a city to being slowly erased from its memory is felt acutely by many Parsis. It is acknowledged as a crisis and mobilized by many Parsi trusts. As trustees strive to be guardians of lands and wealth, they must ensure that beneficiaries, properties, people, and things have perpetual life in the city.

Hinging Time: Why Trusts Matter

The following chapters will retheorize trusts and their structured obligations as hinges, both spatially and materially, through familial and religious property. It is assumed that an endowment of any kind hinges together productive and unproductive capital in pursuit of an obligation, for instance, using trade profits to support a temple or investing dividends to fund a school. The settled property is considered unproductive because it is stopped and tied up by the trust and must be supported by attaching itself to productive property to attain perpetuity. As a tool of finance, a trust generates wealth and benefit by managing its liquid assets over time (Hertz 2010, 807). An important distinction here, illuminated throughout the book, is that what is being hinged together are forms of liquid finance capital with solid, immovable assets like land and material infrastructure, in pursuit of the objects of the trust. Both forms of assets circulate but at different tempos and can be enabled or constrained by regulation at different choke points. The issue of productivity is also at large. The two asset forms must produce goods or services of general public utility; that is, they must provide for the good.

By acting in the subjunctive mode, that is, what should be, this econo-legal form privileges obligation and certainty rather than precarity, and perpetuity rather than circulation. It is only through seeing its effects over time that we see the paradox of how the law facilitates capital to accumulate and be distributed in particular ways. As the trust comes out of the framework of Equity, it is a legal instrument that attempts to address the inflexibility that results from strict adherence to the law. This allows the trust to circumvent taxes to fund the public good, avoid strict inheritance, and even have a person's wishes fulfilled after death. Yet the perpetual nature of the charitable trust in relation to urban space and communal history serves as a constraint on the space of a developing city and on shifting gender and religious norms of a community. Therefore, *Trust Matters* explores an alternate imagination of the workings of capital.

This book speaks to broader scholarship linking faith and fortune (Weber, Wells, and Baehr 2002; De Goede 2005; Maurer 2005; Birla 2009). The literature relating ideas of the supernatural and notions of the economic have been long-standing within anthropology compared to other disciplines more concerned with theories of secularization. The latter theories held that the more untangled these two domains were, the more a place or time had achieved modernity.[26] By analyzing the trust as an econo-legal mechanism that serves as the infrastructural backbone of religious giving and practice, my research shows how there is no opposition between these two but examines instead how this legal mechanism hinges them together in charitable giving. Our understanding of this supposed separation of religious from economic life has marked our inherited genealogy of finance, resulting in finance's apotheosis in the West. In contrast, the book will show that communities like the Parsis have historically harnessed finance with the endowment form to shore up and nurture their religious and communal life, offering an alternate genealogy to finance.

De Goede reminds us that "financial instruments and practices are discursively constituted and firmly rooted in cultural, moral, political, and religious history" (2005, xvi). There has been a growing body of work in this vein that firmly historicizes rather than exoticizes colonial and postcolonial India's tryst with financialization (Searle 2016; Bear 2015; Bear, Birla, and Puri 2015; Bear 2020; Goldman, Gidwani, and Upadhya 2017; Upadhya 2020; Bhattacharyya 2018, 2020) with a particular focus on the work of speculation in India's various constellations of capitalism.

These works argue that speculation, also a form of seeing, enacts the relation of uncertainty to value production. Deeply grappling with temporality, "[speculation] does not reckon risk and probability or tame uncertainty; it is a practice that aims to realize incalculable possible futures" (Bear, Birla, and Puri 2015, 388). I will argue that the trust is the obverse of speculative practice, distinct but not separated from it, dwelling in the mode of the subjunctive. To endow or entrust is a formal legal attempt to fix a particular obligation and attach it to an asset. By focusing on what should be, those acting in the subjunctive mode attempt to gain or maintain value (economic or moral) through tying up and preserving; this is the act of endowment. As a mode of action, the trust intentionally acts against the *what if* and instead acts *as if*. Emerging out of a philosophy of equity, it is remedial rather than anticapital. It is only through time and the cityscape that trust matters reveal the stakes and conflicts of acting as if, as they run up against urban development, a divided community, and their own historicity.

Structure of the Book

Trust Matters will explore how nineteenth- and early twentieth-century deeds seem to spill over their original purposes and are contested both from within the community and from the spatial pressures of a growing megacity. As a document and legal mechanism, the trust serves as a hinge connecting the temporalities of religious giving, which helped build Bombay and maintains an almost glacial landscape of communal real estate in Mumbai. The following chapters trace the transformative process by which these trust assets shift from being objects of property relations to being subjects in property relations (Moumtaz 2012; Verdery and Humphrey 2004). That is, they shift from objects through which social relations, like charitable giving from donor to beneficiary, are managed to assets with perpetual obligations.

Chapter 1 takes up the provocation from my interlocutor within the Charity Commission that the trust directory might offer a horoscope of the city. It will explore the historicity of trusts and how they capture and utilize time in urban space. This chapter follows the trust as it traverses the timescape and municipal regulatory constraints of Bombay-Mumbai. It will show the early transformation of Parsi property into real estate during the colonial period and then discuss some critical figures who founded the trust landscape in the city. It will end with a discussion of how the doctrine of *cy près* allows the trust to work within "the meantime" (Riles 2011, 173), the temporality of the subjunctive, rather than allow its objects to fail.

In chapter 2, "Presents and Futures," I will further explore issues of temporality through charitable giving with the story of Jerbai Wadia, the widow of a hugely wealthy family. She endowed several plots to the BPP as communal housing for Parsi beneficiaries. While greatly benefiting her coreligionists and encouraging Parsi migration from rural areas to the city, Wadia's communal beneficence came from partially disinheriting two of her sons, who had converted to Christianity. Her current descendants are now in a battle with the BPP over the management of her charitable gifts. The chapter will examine how the trust troubles the giver–receiver binary of reciprocity in terms of the obligations owed and the temporality of those obligations. I show that the trust's tripartite structure (the settlor, trustee, beneficiary) reorganizes religious giving into an intergenerational relation of obligation and accountability and challenges assumptions of the centrality of reciprocity to social life.

Chapter 3 examines how contemporary Parsi family and marriage practices intersect with trust bureaucracy and organizational practice. With current demographics deemed to be in crisis, this chapter explores what this designation entails and calls forth. The BPP's obligations to distribute its assets to its beneficiaries can only be maintained in perpetuity if beneficiaries exist; therefore, reproducing its beneficiaries through methods like enclave housing, marriage bureaus, and IVF becomes the object itself. Maintaining the trust structure has become the purpose. While housing, for decades, has been offered to encourage endogamous marriage, a new and controversial fertility scheme entangles the knot of ethnic and religious subjecthood in particularly gendered ways.

More than just a framework for disputes and the maintenance of justice, the law is "an element in political strategies—especially strategies for destroying old options and creating new ones" (Asad 1993, 335). As all religious endowments formally circumvent established rules of inheritance and property transfer by attaching specific (religious) obligations and naming beneficiaries (worshippers), the laws governing them have the capacity to radically shape the form and even content of religious practice. Chapter 4 further explores how "one of the most effective ways of making proper subjects is by managing proprietary objects" (L. Vevaina 2019, 261). Through the analysis of landmark Parsi legal cases over beneficiary access to trust-managed sacred spaces, this chapter will show how the role of trust beneficiary both enables and constrains notions of ethnoreligious identity and to what degree a secular court will interfere in religious trust matters.

Chapter 5 explores the relationship between trusts and Zoroastrian mortuary ritual practice. Atop the glitzy neighborhood of Malabar Hill in Mumbai rests the poetically named "Tower of Silence" funerary complex wherein Parsis still leave their dead to be excarnated by carrion birds. The endowment of this mortuary space augured the first governance structure for the community in the city, with the BPP, remaining the apex body for Parsis in India. Chapter 5 examines the role of mortuary ritual infrastructure and its relation to critical disputes in the community over the form and content of death rituals and who may participate in them. A newly built prayer hall attached to a cremation ground has offered a ritual alternative to some. To others, the idea of a corpse, the ultimate in Zoroastrian impure material, being placed into the purest fire is an outrage. This chapter shows how the trusts supporting and managing mortuary infrastructure first oblige and then enable ritual transformation. From excarnation to ashes, this chapter shows the entanglement of ritual infrastructure, created and managed by the trust, and the property and propriety of Parsis.

After a deregulation of land markets in India in the 1990s, many trusts, historically large landowners, had the opportunity to redevelop open plots on their existing properties. Chapter 6 explores how new development projects, while filling their coffers, may undercut and fragment the charitable obligations of the trust. As accusations of corruption and breach of trust plague the BPP, other smaller Parsi trusts with lands are receiving donations from Hong Kong to undertake development projects. This chapter places Parsi trusts and built spaces in the city within global networks of philanthropic capital flows and blockages. As several trusts in Mumbai struggle to maintain their assets as their corpus funds run out, monies have been sought and secured from wealthier coreligionists. With this beneficence often come differing views on how charitable funds should be spent. This chapter offers an analysis of the liquidity of capital outside the world of private finance and into the communal worlds of religious charities. It explores how the charitable trust, and the circulation of its obligations, generate new geographies of community across the city and the global diaspora.

The book concludes with a broader reflection on the expansive ways the trust mechanism allows one to rethink notions of time, obligation, kinship, and capital. Within the constant transformation of Bombay-Mumbai, the trust's endurance and particular material, social, and legal constructions push toward new potentials for the ways in which religious groups may manage their lifeworlds in cities today. It will reflect on how the trust, as a time-keeping device, has been pivotal as a mechanism of finance and communal connection across generations.

CHAPTER 1. **IN PERPETUITY**

The Trust and Timely Obligations

A colleague once gave a talk on "serendipity in the field," and meeting "Mr. Sodawala" could be seen as such a "happy accident." This kind octogenarian, dwarfed by his large desk, was one of my key interlocutors who spent much time with me describing the trust he manages. One of the largest Parsi trusts after the Bombay Parsi Punchayet (BPP), Mr. Sodawala's trust ran several housing colonies and funds for medical care and education. Founded by a wealthy Parsi at the turn of the twentieth century, this trust was now run by five trustees, men and women of renown in the community who decided on larger matters, with Mr. Sodawala running the day-to-day affairs. While the medical and educational funds were distributed to "cosmopolitan" beneficiaries, all the housing was reserved for Parsis only.[1] Like other Parsi housing trusts, the trust was plagued by the high maintenance costs versus the low income generated from heavily subsidized rents. "I answer to two higher authorities," Mr. Sodawala said. "To the founder," whose portrait he motioned to behind his desk in a very reverent manner, "and to the Charity Commission," while emphatically pointing his index finger to his desk.

After relating the beneficence of the trust's settlor or founder with much reverence, and the forms of uses of all the assets and properties he managed, Mr. Sodawala related the accounting he and all other charitable trusts were bound by law to give to the Charity Commission. Annually, the trust filed multiple reams of paperwork, including all assets, credits, and liabilities. He recounted these to me as he showed me some of the documents from the previous year. One simmering afternoon as we sat under the fan of his office and were concluding our meeting while tying up the stacks of papers with string, the party for his next meeting arrived. "What luck!" Mr. Sodawala exclaimed as he enthusiastically introduced me to "Mr. Naik," who was the former public relations officer of the Charity Commission and who now consults with trusts on how to maneuver and comply with the office's red tape. Like many Indian government bureaucracies, the charity office is notorious for not being terribly open and helpful to young researchers poking around and asking odd questions, so I was thrilled to have an introduction, and Mr. Naik kindly gave me his business card.

I met Mr. Naik at the Charity Commissioner's offices for a promised tour in September 2011. A previous visit in 2009 had left me with the same impression as any other government bureaucracy in India: piles and piles over stacks and stacks of papers, either bound by string or in weathered, dusty folders, the sounds of ringing telephones and the greatly welcome whirring of fans above. The occasion of that visit was to accompany 104 petitioners seeking redress from the charity office against the BPP regarding how flats were allotted. At that time, what seemed like at least thirty people, some journalists, and I, were crammed into the commissioner's office. Most were yelling and accusing the BPP representative of corruption while the commissioner sat at his desk, asking each to take their turn or to allow one representative to speak for them. The visit was very intense, with emotions running high, as many of the petitioners had been waiting for years for a flat allotment.

This second visit led by Mr. Naik was like stepping into an advertisement for "the New India." The second floor opened onto a large open office with cubicles, the spaces marked by bright yellow pillars and uniform lavender-hued office chairs. Instead of fans, air conditioners provided the cooling and perhaps relieved the older paperweights from their sense of purpose. There was only a trace of paper files in sight. Instead, many of the desks supported computers. The most significant change was the new architecture of transparency, as all the senior officers were enclosed in glass along the perimeter, allowing the light from the windows in and sending the rumors of corruption and back-door deals out.

At the end of the visit, Mr. Naik walked me downstairs to the record room to see that I received a copy of Section C, the Parsi section of the Public Trust Directory, wherein all Parsi charity trusts must be registered.[2] We proceeded to the back of the office, and a large door was opened onto an almost warehouse-like space with dozens of rolling shelves, often seen in large libraries. Within these were vertically stacked paper files wrapped in jute. I imagined that the decades of information wrapped there must finally leave its trace on one line of each page of the directory. Before passing me the office's copy of the directory, Mr. Naik held it up and exclaimed, "This is the horoscope of the city!"

A horoscope might seem a strange term to label a thick directory, but I had an idea of what he meant. On each page of the directory were the details of trusts, their locations, and assets; that is, all their real properties in greater Mumbai. Mr. Naik intimated that a horoscope might offer a unique frame for reading the city and its future potential, one framed around the timescale and spatial geography of the trust. He provided a more expansive understanding of the timescale of trusts than this bureaucratic registry might typically provide. Mr. Naik brought my inquiries about public charitable trusts and this worldly document into the astral plane, into seeing and understanding urban real estate and assets as part of larger constellations of capital and time and the techniques of law. His proclamation shifted my attention to the subjunctive tense, what the city should be.

Another document for reading the city's future might be the urban development plan. The city plan, a supposedly hyperrational tool, also offers a prophecy of the future, one purportedly based on expert knowledge on what the city needs and where it should go (D'Monte 2002).[3] The most recent Mumbai development plan released in 2015 had much of the city up in arms as it seemed to include many errors and was later scrapped until a newer version was approved in 2018. The new plan forecasts development for the city until 2034. The development plan must contend with varying velocities of real estate, from the mercurial construction of informal housing to the staid and often decaying endurance of colonial-era properties.

Scholars of South Asian cities view urban planning as never fully realized and always unevenly laid out or highly contested (Hull 2012b; Roy 2005, 2009; Chatterjee 2004; Weinstein 2008; Benjamin 2008). Most go further to highlight the myriad overlapping authority structures that govern urban life as one of the causes of the stillborn nature of the plan. Mumbai has fifteen agencies managing urban planning and built spaces at various government scales: municipal, state, and national. This constellation is further imbricated with a host of nongovernmental organizations (NGOs), think tanks, heritage groups, and landlord and builder lobbies. The future it envisions is one full of aspiration and, simultaneously, one of inevitable disappointments, as its timely projects are rarely fulfilled.

This book nestles within the vast literature on the anthropology of time (Gell 2021; Munn 1992; Bear 2016), particularly Gell's framing of social time. I take inspiration through the chapters from authors like Bakhtin (1981) and his concept of the chronotope, a specific and often conflictual relationship between time and space, and Bear's (2016, 2020) analysis of the movement and circulation of capital to view the time contradictions produced. Returning to Mr. Naik's provocation, how can we understand the ways in which a directory of trusts represents this horoscope or seeing of time?

A horoscope serves up a daily or monthly guide to action based on the "verdict of the stars." Instead of being resigned to one's fate, which is decided upon by other forces, one is given a choice to act, but in a circumscribed manner, in that the horoscope has laid out parameters for that action, narrowing possible potentials. No person is left out of the timescale of a horoscope, which is the supreme guiding mechanism for all life. The horoscope lives thoroughly within the subjunctive mode, being concerned with what should and could be for the best outcome.

As mentioned in the introduction, we can think of a horoscope both temporally and spatially: forecasting a temporal order through the relative position of a spatial one, it offers a specific chronotope with a prescriptive element. While a horoscope usually denotes a forecast based on the aspect of the stars, I argue that this horoscope of Mumbai assumes a constellation of trust housing, temples, and other spaces and provides a possible future based on their relative positioning. This horoscope, the directory of trusts, is one prognosis of time based on the relative positioning of perpetual trust assets in the city.

Following the directory of trusts as a guide to these assets marked by obligations in perpetuity, this chapter will explore the trust's timely obligations. It will trace the ways in which formal endowments change the temporal compass and reach of charity past the immediate and individual giving of the wealthy into perpetual and communal giving through the medium of real estate, into the cityscape. Unlike the inheritance of property through generations of kin, the perpetuity of trusts has a guiding prophetic element—that is, the donor's intention, which obliges the trustees through time and is enforced through the law with institutions like the Charity Commission and the courts. Therefore, while the donor transfers their will into a future obligation for the trust, these obligations are further bound together with legal mechanisms for achieving those futures. The following will show how Parsis were early recipients of land in the colonial city, but it was the utilization of the endowment form with early donors and architects that helped orient their horoscope, marking their constellation of property ownership into the future. The chapter will end with a discussion of the meantime and how the trust manages to navigate its perpetual obligations within the city today.

Making Real Estate in Colonial Bombay

By the time the British had acquired Bombay from the Portuguese in 1661, the original seven islands had been joined into four through land reclamations (Dossal 2010, 5). The Portuguese were the first colonials in Bombay, and the British Crown acquired the islands as a dowry for a royal marriage. Historian Mariam Dossal (2010, 30) stresses that from its beginnings as a Portuguese outpost, the peninsula had several overlapping land tenure systems, which the British then tried to dominate and administer by requiring land to be registered. To promote trade, the colonial Bombay government developed incentives for industrious natives to settle by allowing construction wherever they chose "as long as the houses they built did not interfere with the defense of the island or adversely affect the commercial interests of the [East India] Company" (Dossal 2010, 34). Under these conditions, various skilled Parsis from Gujarat were enticed to the city. Dossal suggests that from the very early settlement, patterns were ad hoc, never conforming to any kind of zoning we would recognize today. This haphazard development, coupled with multiple and overlapping property regimes (native, Portuguese, Company, and Crown), has led to an incredibly diverse and complex entanglement of built spaces and ownership in the city today.

Parsis were early settlers to the city, and through their beneficial ties to the British as brokers, shipbuilders, and traders, by 1812 they were dominant in the Fort district, where other natives were not allowed. As the Fort plots were later acquired for defense or commercial purposes by the government, Parsis were given plots in Salsette (what is today the northern suburbs of Bandra and Andheri) in exchange. Already we begin to see the two poles of contemporary Parsi settlement emerging: the most prominent in south Bombay, in areas like the Fort and Colaba Island, and to the north in Salsette. These areas functioned to orient later Parsi settlements in housing and sacred spaces and remain two of the most lucrative poles of real estate in contemporary Mumbai. Until 1839 and the Act VI of 1851, all lands were technically held by the colonial government and then leased by others, but the Act established the existence of private property on the island. Land could henceforth be held in "fee simple" and quickly bought and sold, effectively creating private property that could be alienated and hence a market in land (Dossal 2010, 97). In 1839, the Court of Petty Sessions recognized the value held in land, which was to be calculated by the Land Revenue Surveyor and adjudicated by the court if disputes arose (Dossal 2010, 109–10). Lands thus registered as private property were then available for entry into the government's tax revenue schemes.

Dossal states that one main impetus of the 1839 and 1851 legislations was the need to acquire land for the rail system. To do so, the government had to evaluate and compensate the existing landholders for the acquisitions. Since many wealthy Parsis had leases on lands needed to establish the rail lines, Dossal (2010, 123) documents the many cases in which juries were required to settle differences between the government and proprietors. These cases mark not only the prominence of such individuals and their landholdings in mid-nineteenth-century Bombay but also the willingness and the ability of wealthy Parsis to use the court system to maintain their rights or secure compensation, a kind of legal literacy that continues to this day. The rail system and the accompanying growth of the textile industry "spread the regime of wage labor, clock work, and time discipline" in the city (Krishnan 2013, 8). Expanding the railways into the cotton-producing Deccan also helped cement the port of Mumbai as a critical site in the ever more lucrative international cotton trade (Dobbin 1972; Farooqui 2006).

In the mid-nineteenth century, the colonial government, through land surveys, effectively transformed the island's multiple property regimes into one system of saleable plots of land, which "made possible the transition from a nascent to a full-fledged capitalist land market" (Dossal 2010, 133). Stimulated by the closure of Confederate ports, Bombay's cotton boom financed much city-building and investment in centers of art, hospital, road construction, and grand buildings. Ninety-nine-year leases were utilized to maintain some sense of stability in prices in the Fort area that was now invested in as the central business district, as "long term leases but not absolute sale was the best way of encouraging urban development at the same time safeguarding the interests of the government" (Dossal 2010, 149). The government had learned lessons from the speculative bubble of the cotton boom and its burst after the end of the American Civil War, which sunk cotton prices, causing much volatility in Bombay's land market. Thus, from Bombay's very inception as a colonial settlement and port, its real estate market has always been stimulated or contracted by global processes. The city's horoscope was intimately tied first to the distribution of opium, then cotton, and later finance.

Charity in Perpetuity

Let us remain in the mid-nineteenth century for the moment. Many of the civic institutions initiated by Parsis and other commercial elites always required the permission and cooperation of the colonial government but also sometimes received matching funds. A common practice in this period was funding philanthropic works through the subscriptions of various donors. A pioneer in infrastructure in Bombay was Khan Bahadur Muncherji Cowasji Murzban (1839–1917). Architectural historian Preeti Chopra shows how colonial Bombay's spatial and structural formation was not solely a task of the British but cooperatively formed through negotiations between the British and native engineers and architects like Murzban (Chopra 2011b, 100). He is also the figure who established the first communal charity housing in the city. Chopra recounts how Murzban was not only a well-educated Parsi engineer with good negotiating powers but also a freemason and "visionary" philanthropist. Murzban stands out not only for his community status as a Parsi, which enabled much of his work, but critically he was a committee member on various charities. He received his title of Khan Bahadur for his "loyal conduct and services" (Chopra 2011a, 88). His role within these charities connected him intricately to a network of powerful Parsi industrialists and philanthropists, who were willing and able to finance city improvement projects for Parsis and the rest of Bombay's inhabitants.

Murzban's pattern was to approach the government for permission to establish what he saw as a needed institution and then finance it through the backing of philanthropic Parsi families like the Camas and Allblesses, who would fund it.[4] Chopra notes that Parsi philanthropists financed a majority of the public buildings designed by Murzban. In this way, he made himself indispensable to the colonial elite and wealthy Parsis, who could see their philanthropic visions immortalized in stone through his design.[5] Another example was The Alexandra Native Girls' English Institution, founded by Manockjee Cursetjee, designed by Murzban, and jointly funded by the government and the trustees of the school, on Hornby Road. It is one of the first girls' schools in India and continues to enroll and educate Parsi and other Indian girls to this day.

Influenced by housing models in Britain, Murzban also set up the Cheap Rental Quarters for Parsis in 1887, which is now known as the Gilder Lane or Murzban colony, depicted in figure 1.1 (Chopra 2011a, 103). The pattern of British philanthropists convincing their government to intervene in working-class housing to uplift those members of society was repeated

FIGURE 1.1. Gilder Lane Colony, near Mumbai Central. Photo by author.

in Bombay and received fresh incentive after the plague of 1896 ravaged the city's poorer sections. The early Parsi housing colonies at this time were considered superior housing configurations as they were relatively low density and had adequate clean water supply in wells required for religious rituals. After the plague in Bombay, it was noted that not one of the 123 families living in the colony was sick (Murzban 1915, 109). Murzban was influenced by the Peabody's Homes in England, which were constructed from funds entrusted by a wealthy banker for the poor of London. Unlike earlier philanthropic models, these homes and the trust were not meant to profit but were "self-perpetuating so that future generations might gain some benefit" (Chopra 2011a, 106). Murzban's shift to organize giving through the Cheap Rental Quarters, harnessing the subscriptions of his coreligionists, extended the time-scape of his constructions well into the future. Here again, we see the endowment hinging liquid funds and solid properties together.

With another innovation in philanthropic style, Murzban founded the Garib Zathoshtina Rehethan Fund (GZRF), or Poor Zoroastrians Building Fund, in 1890, which was funded through numerous donations from Parsis from a range of backgrounds "from wealthy and famous baronets and leading families to other individuals of modest means" (Chopra 2011a, 107). By 1899, about three hundred families were housed by Murzban (Hinnells and Williams 2007, 277). Each building, although not aesthetically dissimilar from the next, had a plaque memorializing the donor family or group of donors. Beyond their charitable purposes, the "promotion of charity and the development of 'cooperative' institutions may have aided the development of commercial networks," especially in light of the fierce competition in Bombay in the mid-nineteenth century among Parsis, Khojas, and other native communities who were vying for profitable alliances in overseas trade (Wadia 2008). Many early trust deeds list several powerful industrialists and barristers as trustees who would jointly decide on the fate and financing of their trusts. These very networks of family and communal ties, while later delegitimized by colonial legal interventions focusing them more on the public (Birla 2009), were imprinted into the histories of trust documents as financial and legal instruments. Wealthy families like the Petits, Jeejeebhoys, Camas, Wadias, Adenwalas, Sassoons, Shankersetts, and Chinoys endowed lands, buildings, and funds to their communities and the public and have their philanthropic legacies inscribed in plaques all over the city.

The British introduced a formal legal mechanism that aided these practices in India in this period. For the Parsis, this British legal instrument mapped particularly well onto existing Zoroastrian practices of charitable giving and allowed property to be endowed for particular social or religious purposes beyond the inheritance practices of an individual family.[6] As Birla (2009) has shown, the colonials were eager to funnel native giving (private and religious) into public and charitable uses. She analyzes how corporate and tax interventions and the standardization of financial instruments organized capital in the colony by slowly delegitimizing certain vernacular practices and offering up advantageous (read colonial) alternatives. In the beginning of the 1880s, the distinction between private and public trusts was introduced in India, a shift that, Birla notes, directly discredited certain forms of vernacular giving and exchange within the private realm of natives.

Birla focuses mainly on the concept and practice of the Hindu Undivided Family, a legal and financial entity that was slowly relegated to being outside of "good" market practice. While Parsis were clearly liminal figures in this period—not quite colonials and not quite natives—they indeed were quick to abide by the new guidelines set by the British for "proper" capitalist practices. Critical for my study, Birla shows the slow shift to a new definition of what constituted charity in Indian practice. From a broad definition of giving, which encompassed several vernacular practices and modes of circulation, charity became circumscribed to forms of giving that were meant to advance general public utility.

Through acts like the Charitable Endowments Act (1863) and the Income Tax and Companies Act (1886), only charitable giving that fell under the rubric of general public utility was considered tax exempt. With the Income Tax Act, nonagricultural lands became targets for tax revenue, bringing in lucrative taxes from soaring urban properties. The Companies Act clearly defined the not-for-profit limited liability company as distinct from a public charitable organization as the benefits of the former were only directed at its members, while the latter was for the public (Birla 2009, 78). As trust laws evolved in India, this concept became the yardstick against which all charitable trusts should measure, moving away from older practices where private and public intentions were mixed. This division of purpose was further strengthened with the Income Tax Act of 1961, which did not allow tax exemption for any mixed trusts established after the Act. As most Parsi trusts predate 1961, they still enjoy tax-exempt status while maintaining mixed objects.

Apart from its objects, what is critical about the trust is how ownership, a status clear in other property relationships, becomes occluded. The settlor or donor of a trust, while completely alienating their rights over the trust assets, preserves their charitable intention in perpetuity. Unlike a company or corporation, which has an obligation to provide profits in the present, the trust is at once a future-oriented device for maintaining the donor's past obligation in perpetuity—that is, while its original ownership relation is lost at the moment of endowment, a trust's obligation to fulfill its objects endures. Full ownership with alienation never transfers to the trustee, who is simply to remain the guardian of assets and is charged with maintaining the original obligation. Once endowed, the trust takes on some characteristics of legal personhood; although it is not a legal person, it has only a half-life. Through the trustees, who are only vested with ownership, the trust may buy and sell assets to pursue its objects. The assets themselves have objects in the sense of obligations to fulfill. Thus, assets like real estate that were once objects to be bought and sold now achieve a kind of subjecthood as they are bound with obligations to fulfill.

Even the liquid assets of trusts are bound. Corpus funds must be maintained and increased through prudent investments, while any profit must be rechanneled into the objects of the trust. Both a charity commission and the beneficiaries provide audits and oversight, respectively. Charity commissions must approve any asset transfer of the original settled objects, and laws on charities regulate investments, especially regarding risk. Beneficiaries also offer a check on the trust and trustees; as chapter 4 and my other work explore, beneficiaries are increasingly aware and mobilized to sue the trustees if they deem a breach of trust (L. Vevaina 2021).

Murzban's Objects: Gilder Lane

I visited the Gilder Lane and Murzban colonies a few times during my fieldwork from 2010 to 2012—the first time with a person associated with the GZRF trust that Murzban founded. Murzban's charitable objects have succeeded in that his perpetual intent remains. Over one hundred years later, his schools and housing units are still in existence. Unlike some more prominent and more famous *baugs*, these structures are smaller in scale with narrower streets and paths. One of the fund's trustees gave me a tour of the colony. As we turned into the drive a little bit away from Bombay Central Station and off a bustling road, I noticed much construction, piles of debris, scaffolding, and the eruption of dust clouds from our car passing through. Because the buildings are very old and even considered low-grade heritage structures, the trust repairs them one at a time while temporarily rehousing all the tenants. The Gilder Lane blocks are also unusual in the chromatic scape of Mumbai's Parsi colonies because they are light blue rather than the usual pale yellow of other colonies. The buildings are two-story with gabled roofs, verandahs, and wooden grillwork on the façade, giving them a quaint Victorian aesthetic. The widow's *chawls*, one-room spaces reserved for poor widows, are small, but the tenants pay very little per month to the trust. New applicants for vacancies must earn less than ten thousand rupees ($130) per month, and few residents own cars.[7]

On later trips to Gilder Lane, I visited with an older Parsi couple. The wife, Meher, lived in Rustom Baug until she was married and then shifted into the small flat in Gilder Lane.[8] She welcomed me into her front room, which was relatively small and made even more cramped by a large daybed on one side and a table on the other. The space was decorated with what seemed like several lifetimes' worth of curios. Beyond the front room was the bathroom and then a small bedroom. "When I shifted here, it was a big change for me," Meher remarked, relating that after being newly married, she lived with her husband and his parents and another relative in this small space. "But now it seems big since it is just the two of us." The couple never had any children. "Where would we have put them?" she asked with a chuckle. She took me to the kitchen, which was not attached to her flat, but must be accessed by leaving her rooms and going through the main hallway. This style of communal living and the almost *chawl*-like configuration (Adarkar 2011) is not seen in later-colony architectural styles, which shifted to a more bourgeois style of private bedrooms and attached kitchen and leisure spaces. Meher spoke fondly of Murzban and his accomplishments as if she knew him, but not of the current trustees. She had clashed with the trustees over delayed repairs and who would bear the costs of those repairs. Like Mr. Sodawala, Meher's fealty lay with the deceased settlor, not with the living managers of her trust.

Chopra recalls that at the Murzban colony at Gilder Lane, there stands a bust of Murzban and an inscription in which he is described as the "originator of the idea of colonization among Parsees and Indians." She writes that Murzban is given much credit for this housing scheme for his own community, which is differentiated from other Indians, but then goes on to claim that "Murzban is thus a leading architect of the idea of community segregation, both at the level of public institutions . . . and the private domestic realm" (Chopra 2011a, 109–10).[9] Endowing property in a trust for a particular set of beneficiaries is one way to exclude access to it from all others, and for a charitable trust, forever. A trust is, in effect, a discriminatory mechanism. It privileges the donor's intention to pick and choose who may enjoy a particular asset or service. I argue that while Parsi colonies do have segregationist settlement patterns with their legal restriction to Parsi residents only, what was groundbreaking here was their very establishment in perpetuity through the use of trust agreements. In terms of housing, this exclusive use was counted on to perpetuate and nurture minority life in the city.

The Colony and the Covenant

After Murzban's initiatives in 1890, the BPP first entered the charity housing game in 1910, with trustee Sir Cowasji Jehangir I establishing the Hughes Road Colony, later known as Khareghat Colony, which still stands today near the Babulnath Temple. The other institution that changed the nature of Parsi settlement and concretized it in Bombay was the Parsi Central Association (PCA), founded in 1919, which helped construct the Dadar Parsi Colony.

Unlike a baug, the Dadar Parsi Colony is not enclosed by walls but has several wide tree-lined streets with large multifamily bungalows. The colony today has fourteen gardens, two schools, an *agiary* (fire temple), a *gymkhana* (community center), and one of two remaining Zoroastrian *madressas* (seminaries) left in Mumbai. As part of the scheme planning, it was designed to have large open spaces and included five gardens and a park designed as a radial, which still serves as a verdant respite for many residents and visitors. It is known to be the largest Zoroastrian enclave in the world, with about ten thousand Parsis in the neighborhood. Since many Parsis have migrated northward in the city, the colony has become a second nodal point of concentrated Parsi life. Many weddings and other ceremonies are held at the *gymkhana*, which also hosted several heated campaign meetings I attended during the Punchayet elections in 2008 and 2011.

I met and learned much about the colony's history from the granddaughter of its founder and Goolcher, a resident very involved with the colony association. When one mentions the Dadar Parsi Colony within the community, everyone mentions Goolcher's name. She had been very difficult to make an appointment with due to her being so busy for the big Navroz celebration that March. What helped immensely was that I was not just another foreign researcher learning about the colony but that Goolcher knew my aunt, who lived a few buildings away from hers. Goolcher's residence is also close to Della Towers, a redeveloped property that one can only describe as an outlier for the colony, incredible for its enormous size and intensity of its façade of neo-Persian architecture in an area that is mostly three to four stories. Upon meeting Goolcher, who seemed to be in her sixties, and her husband, whom she insisted I meet, I was struck by the veracity of her claims of busyness. The doorbell, her mobile, and her landline rang intermittently during our discussions, and at one point when she was occupied, I was turned over to her husband, who also grew up in the colony. They both recounted the history of the colony as well as the current issues of redevelopment and concerns over it remaining a Parsi enclave.

The history of the colony begins in the early twentieth century. While primarily focused on informing and representing Parsis within the emerging independence movement, the PCA formed the Parsi Central Association Cooperative Housing Society, PCACHS, in 1920. Some influential PCA members like M. E. Joshi were able to secure lands for Parsis in Dadar and formed the Dadar Parsi Colony in the northern neighborhood of the same name. Joshi and others petitioned the British for this plot (440 acres) under the Dadar-Matunga-Wadala-Sion scheme, the first planned scheme for Bombay.[10] The scheme was under the management of the Bombay City Improvement Trust (BIT) to relieve congestion in the city center and to spread out settlement after the devastation of the plague in the 1890s (Rao 2013b). Rao notes that among the projects of the BIT, its suburbanization projects "unyoke[d] lands in Bombay from the variety of tenures under which they had been held" and "stabilized the meaning of 'property' in land," producing parts of Bombay as "commodified and fungible spaces" (Rao 2013b, 24). In constant disputes with the Bombay Municipal Corporation (BMC), the BIT had its assets and projects subsumed into the latter during the 1920s (Rao 2013b, 25–27).

The Plan also built the Hindu Colony in Dadar and the Tamil Colony in Matunga. This kind of segregated living went through cycles of being a preferred choice in land development and was highly contingent (Rao 2013b). It was given legal support by the 1904 Cooperative Credit Societies Act, which allowed for discrimination based on community. This allowance was overturned, in theory, by the Maharashtra Co-Operative Societies Act in 1960, which sought to pursue the postindependence spirit of secularism by promoting associations based on factors other than caste and community (Rao 2013a, 416). The 1960 Act held that the earlier provision violated the 1872 Indian Contracts Act, which stipulated the right for any person capable of a contract not to be excluded by any association.

In terms of its property regime, the Dadar Parsi Colony is entirely mixed. At least seventeen different trusts own and manage several plots in the colony, including the Parsi Central Association, the Parsi Punchayet (thirty buildings with 246 flats), and the Zoroastrian Building Fund. For instance, with the PCA, the Improvement Trust leased land to the PCACHS, which then signed covenants to keep the plots for Parsis only. In some cases, one trust will own the land while a separate trust manages the building upon it. Other plots are managed through several Parsi housing societies. One hundred eleven buildings are under the "Parsi covenant,"—agreements that they will remain Parsi, but the other buildings with about 250 flats can be sold or leased to anyone.[11]

By the 1970s, the Parsis of Dadar Parsi Colony began to push back against more and more non-Parsis moving into the area and, through lawsuits, attempted to enforce the covenants that the colony remain Parsi only. The area of the colony in Dadar was attractive to builders as there was much unused Floor Space Index (FSI) on most of the plots, and the area was seen as not as "productive" or densely settled as possible.[12] Builders would approach the building owners, who were mainly receiving low rent-controlled rents, with attractive offers to add floors to the existing structures, which would be sold at market rates. Walking through the colony today, one notices several plots where it seems like two floors of a different architectural aesthetic have been plopped onto an existing old bungalow.

Often the residents of these added floors were not Parsis. The PCACHS brought several lawsuits forth in the late 1970s. It stressed in these suits that the covenant was critical not only to retain the Parsi character of the plots but to support the middle-class and weaker sections of the community, the original purpose of the land scheme (Rao 2013a, 429).

In 2003, the Parsi Central Association filed suit against a developer over three buildings sold on the covenanted plots. The developer had already torn down one old bungalow and had planned to sell flats to non-Parsis in his newly constructed medium-rise building. The PCA Housing Society took the developer to court, claiming that the "covenant runs with the land" and even if Parsis lawfully sold buildings to non-Parsis, only Parsis were allowed to live in them. The Society maintained, "Various institutions and organizations of Parsis have grown up catering to the needs of the community in the reserved area for over 75 years. The reserved area has been sort of a nucleus for bringing up children in religious practices in the formative years and inculcate in them religious teachings. A right atmosphere is created in the reserved area which is conducive to the upbringing of Parsi Zoroastrian children in their way of life and to preserve their culture. Breach of covenant would adversely affect the religious, social, cultural and traditional continuity, solidarity and advancement of the small community."[13] The developer had claimed to the court that the covenant was old and now out of date and should be illegal under the Transfer of Property Act, as it was not based on the bylaws of the Housing Society, which was not allowed to discriminate.[14] The developer had offered to resell only to Parsis at the market rate but came to an impasse when the Society refused, maintaining that the flats were meant to be subsidized for the community as per the original intent of the colony. The court upheld the covenant and granted an injunction restraining the developer from letting out the flats to anyone other than a Parsi.

Right before ending my fieldwork, I finally met retired lawyer "Mr. Sohrabji" of the Parsi Central Association, and instrumental in the above covenant case, at his home in one of the famous art deco buildings at the Oval Maidan. I entered the main room, which was humming to the low volume of the television, which was left on throughout my visit. I sat amidst antique furniture, mismatched chinoiserie, and European sculptures.[15] As we both sipped tea, I asked about the Association and its legal battles. When talking about the PCA, Mr. Sohrabji, now in his eighties, seemed lost in thought as to an answer to a question. He would think silently and say, "*Mona per che,*" which could translate to "it's at the tip of my tongue," perhaps belying his age. At other moments he was sprightly and playful. "I am literally the founder of the covenant," he said with a smile. When I looked confused, as he was certainly not, he continued with a chuckle, "I *found* them all together in a cupboard!" He chuckled on and continued, explaining that the PCA looked after these restricted-use covenants, which ensured that while the building may belong to anyone, the residents of the flats may only be Parsi. "Our mission is to keep the colony for Parsis," he maintained. "It is the covenant that constitutes the colony." Here again, the covenant's structure becomes its purpose.

Historian Nikhil Rao insists that rather than seeing such communal housing societies "as a 'traditional' communally-homogenous arrangement, they are rather, a quintessentially modern response to the housing crisis, using instruments such as leases and co-operative societies to protect (but also transform) community" (Rao 2013a, 431). This covenant's promise was a further obligation added to the early trust deeds of the Dadar Parsi Colony and was allowed by the courts to perpetuate into the future. Even though the court buttressed the covenant, the multiple property regimes of the colony and the willingness of many residents and developers to build leaves the DPC in an unsettled state at the current moment.

Cy près and Other Legal Fictions

As the charitable trust is perpetual, it has no end time for its objects, but only the meantime, the time after its inception. Once established, a charitable trust is irrevocable, even by the original settlor but can be amended after extensive evidence is presented to a court using an argument known as *cy près* (as near as possible) that the original object is no longer possible.[16] The certainty concretized in settling the trust is then shifted to the subjunctive in the life span of the trust. The concept stems from the English courts of equity. Indian court rulings are clear that cy près cannot alter the original objects just because something else is preferable or even more beneficial. Objects can only be altered if they cannot be executed (Setalvad 2009, 285). So only under the conditions of the impossibility of its objects is a trust allowed to shift to a new purpose.

I had so many questions about this concept, and several interlocutors referred me to one legal practitioner, "Mr. Vakil." I managed to secure a meeting during the court holidays in his offices in Prospect Chambers, perhaps at one time a glorious art deco building in Fort but now in disrepair. Upon entering his office, I was amazed at the walls of books, primarily legal volumes and some others. There was a large portrait of a famous Parsi barrister on the wall, whom he mentioned was his grandfather and was famously a trust secretary of the BPP. When I explained that I was interested in trusts, he showed me his copy of the Directory of Charitable Trusts from 1979. I found out later that this was the last time it was published as a single volume. He had an incredibly sharp mind, quoting me passages and page numbers from legal texts and cases. Vakil had been involved in community issues from a young age but remarked that he steered clear of certain legal disputes. When I asked if he thought that Parsis were too litigious, he responded that most legal suits involved petty disputes because Parsis had no communal arbitration like the Khojas, for example.[17] I was coming to see that much of the legal conflicts of the community were due to the structure of trusts and the lack of singular authority in the community, unlike perhaps the Khojas. When I asked about trusts, he gave mostly legal definitions, citing references from memory from legal volumes as he spoke. He would often correct my question and my imprecise use of legal terminology before he would answer, which made the meeting exasperating and fascinating at different moments.

What struck me most was his assertion that "the law does not allow trusts to fail." As discussed in the introduction, this committed stance by the law to maintain the workings and objects of charitable trusts is quite remarkable. The reasoning for this stance is the work of good that charities are supposed to perform; therefore, they are given tax and time incentives to perpetuate. Trusts may only shift their mandates if the original objects or obligations cannot be fulfilled. Mr. Vakil explained to me how deploying the cy près argument could allow the trust's once immutable obligation to shift to new possibilities; it could act *as if*.

The perpetual drive of the trust and the equally ossifying consequences of the 1948 Rent Act, fixing prices at those levels, left trust flats in languid circulation and led to a gradual increase in the waiting list for charity flats. Before the updated Rent Act in 1999, the trust's "temporal sensibility" was only that of the "long-run," cast into the distant future, beyond the horizon of short-term political or economic gains (Guyer 2007). Many trust managers I spoke with bemoaned this permanence. Since many of the older trust deeds were written in the late nineteenth and early twentieth centuries, they have stated provisions for now outdated technologies. One manager related how the trust had to go to court to be able to provide funds for light bulbs instead of the oil lamps listed in the trust deed. Therefore, many property lawyers I spoke with said there was an art to formulating trust deeds. Being overly specific could force the trust to go constantly before the Charity Commission to propose even minor changes, yet they had to be clear enough to prevent abuse. The main issue for many trusts with built spaces and housing is that the price of upkeep of these spaces far exceeds the minimal income they receive from residents as rent prices were fixed by rent control legislation.[18]

For many public charitable trusts, the mechanism of the trust itself and its fidelity to its original objects sometimes stood in the way of new projects that could develop or enrich the trust's corpus. These constraints often force trustees to construct other curious legal fictions, a legal tool of workaround, firmly in the subjunctive mode. Annelise Riles (2011) defines a legal fiction as "a statement that is consciously understood to be false, and hence is irrefutable" and as a "technique for working with and in the meantime" (173).[19] Far from being meaningless, this technique has real effects: "From the point of view of those who deploy them, legal fictions are more like machines than stories—they are practical interventions with concrete consequences" (173). In the context of trusts, it seems we have many instances of such fictions precisely because the trust instrument has such a particular relationship to time and tenaciously holds or stops property's ability to circulate into the future. After the moment of settling, the trust resides in this meantime as its objects are meant to be upheld in perpetuity. In the meantime, trustees and beneficiaries often are forced to act *as if* to temper the strong fidelity of the trust to the wishes of a past settlor.

The Sanatoria Circuit

Very close to the Doongerwadi funerary complex in Cumballa Hill are the extensive grounds of B. D. Petit Parsi General Hospital and Petit Sanatorium. After seeing the ravages of bubonic plague in Bombay at the turn of the nineteenth century, Seth Bomanjee Dinshaw Petit, enriched by the cotton trade, along with his son Jehangir, gathered donations for a Parsi hospital in 1905. The Petits approached the Parsi Punchayet to create a trust for the property and act as trustees.[20] A deed was executed in April of 1906. While the property is vested with the Punchayet, all the administration and management of the grounds and hospital remain with a managing committee headed by a president and registered under the Societies Act of 1860. This makes the managing committee a separate and more flexible legal form than a trust. It is headed by a president who is to remain a member of the Petit family. While the hospital's main goal was to serve poor Parsi patients, it did so by accepting richer Parsi patients to subsidize costs. While the hospital was a great success

FIGURE 1.2. Sanatorium at Parsi General Hospital, Cumballa Hill. Photo by author.

story of an effectively run trust, the plot also holds a sanatorium and a controversial newer high-rise ownership building, both of which have shifted their original purpose with the successful use of cy près.[21]

One might recognize the Petit Sanatorium building that abuts the road (see figure 1.2), as the old Victorian Gothic building has been used as a location in several Indian films. I had been trying to get in touch with someone from the Petit trust via telephone for quite a while when one of my interlocutors, an architect who knew the manager, encouraged me just to tell the security guard that I was there to meet "Madam," the trust manager, and I would be let through. The large locked front gates and the languid guards usually were my last stop, but one day I asked, "Is Madam there?" They surprisingly ushered me through the gates and into the building. "Shireen," the trust manager, in a dazzling emerald-green silk blouse, greeted me warmly as if she had been expecting me and beckoned me into her office. She was trained in textiles and then later a friend at a housing development company had offered her a chance to "cut her teeth" with a new development project. She got to know contractors and had hands-on experience with higher-end real estate with that employer before joining the trust. Although the paint was weathered, her office was bright and still looked grand with its high ceilings, large windows, and original fixtures.

Shireen offered to take me on a brief tour of the sanatorium grounds, now almost empty, as I learned that most residents had been paid to leave. The architecture was grand but in much need of maintenance, as there weren't just chipped paint and ceilings but also spaces where archways were near collapsing and supported by steel reinforcements. The building façade is a Grade III heritage, but the interiors could be renovated. Most rooms were four hundred square feet with their own kitchen and bathroom. In 2005 a garden was finished for both the sanatorium and the tower complex. Knowing that the trust was under litigation, I began slowly with my questions about the building and its architecture. She related proudly that the original structure was built 110 years ago as a sanatorium. At that time, the sea came right up to the edge of the compound, so in the true sense, it was a place to rest and reenergize.[22] After the hospital was built, the sanatorium was constructed to be where the family members or those discharged could stay for about two months to convalesce. At the time, many Parsis came from *bhargaum*, or out of town, to get treatment, so they needed a local place to recuperate. She seemed to elaborate on these times with great nostalgia, in abrupt contrast to how she later described the current period at the sanatorium.

There are three large sanatoria in Bombay (run by three separate trusts), "Panday at Colaba, Bhabha in Bandra, and ours," Shireen related. Once the city's housing crunch became acute, people realized they could just stay. And those residing in the sanatoria began to make permanent plans to remain in their rooms. Adapting to the new resident clientele, the trustees allowed people to stay for four months, with a new scheme that they would shift to the next sanatorium for four months and move about in a kind of circuit from one to the other. This short cycle would disallow anyone from claiming tenancy status. All three trusts were dipping into their corpus funds for upkeep as barely any of the residents were paying rents or any fees while the structures, all about one hundred years old, were deteriorating. She explained further that Panday had roof leaks and constant quarreling among the trustees, and then from 2000 to 2009 a few occupants at Bhabha just decided to stop the circuit and stayed put. They acted as if they were permanent tenants. Therefore, those at Petit stayed as well, as they had no place to go.

On a second sweltering day in March, I braved the traffic to again go to Bandra-West to visit Bhabha Sanatorium. A Parsi caterer living in Godrej Baug had once lived "like a nomad" through this circuit of sanatoria and had put me in contact with "Keki," a practicing mobed and person "in the know" at Bhabha sanatorium. I didn't mind the trip since the area can only be described as gorgeous with its palm-tree-dotted ocean view and cool breeze close to a luxury hotel and Bollywood megastar Shah Rukh Khan's residence. Keki greeted me in his *sudreh*, the Zoroastrian holy vest, an almost sheer muslin undershirt, and quickly and informally introduced me to his wife sitting under a fan. I was offered hot tea and biscuits as they began to tell me about the sanatorium. Keki assured me that the tea would make me sweat more and help to cool me down.

The property was owned by Sohrabji Behramjee Bhabha. It was left in his will to an eponymous trust along with an agiary, a *chawl*, hospital, dispensary, and funds for communal feasts, called *ghambars*. The land was leased in 1936 from the collector for seven rupees per square yard and has been since renewed. Bhabha's will stated that the purpose was at the discretion of the managing trustee, who is now his nephew. Sohrabji Bhabha wanted the estate to look like Buckingham Palace, and indeed, the older sections are quite grand in the same style.

In 2000, residents of buildings one and two formed a group and pushed for tenancy rights, saying they had nowhere to go and didn't want to rotate to other places. In December 2000, they went to court. Keki described some in the group as thug-like in their approach as they went to Petit Sanatorium and threatened everyone there to stay put. The thinking was that if everyone stayed put, the rotation would have to stop since there would be no vacant rooms. The cases were complicated because the current managing trustee had emigrated abroad and had difficulty appearing in court. The BPP in 2001–2002 took over the trust, fearing that otherwise, the land would return to the government collector. Some residents were still there as the case was ongoing in the City Civil Court. Of the agitating few, some had non-Parsi spouses and were therefore refused by Petit. "Some are *khandias* [corpse bearers] and have even been in jail," Keki said, attempting to relate his moral disdain for this group, whom he thought ritually impure. According to Keki, some residents were now monied and had cars and other property in the city but continued to stay without paying any rent.

As we walked the grounds and into a few empty buildings, the rooms he showed me were huge, six hundred to seven hundred square feet, and again, many had sea views. All the rooms were originally furnished with Burma teak and even kitchenware. The occupant simply had to show up with their personal items to convalesce. All the taps were brass made in England, he boasted. Now almost nothing was left; he mentioned that many previous occupants had left with the furniture and stripped the fixtures.

As we continued the tour, Keki admitted that he was previously on very bad terms with the BPP and therefore was very hesitant to meet me in the beginning. He earned the title of "Mr. Bombay" in his youth, had won many titles in bodybuilding, and now trained younger men. He boasted that in his time, the estate had also had a few film shoots of his "neighbor," Shahrukh Khan. Keki mentioned that the BPP had plans to redevelop some spaces, but the buildings soon earned heritage status, so even those plans were put on hold.

He then gave me a tour of the oldest building, modeled on Buckingham Palace, a grand English-style hallway with a ballroom and library. It must have been breathtakingly beautiful when kept up, but it was now empty, dusty, and cobwebbed. Some rooms were still occupied, and a few people peeped out of their curtained entrances, curious about my presence. As I left, I noticed that I had been watched by a few women out of their windows. I was hoping I could leave slowly and perhaps talk to someone else, but Keki escorted me directly to the gate and closed it behind me. His would be the last word on the matter.

This experience at Bhabha informed my questions when discussing the Petit Sanatorium in Kemps Corner. Shireen had joined the administration at the Petit trust in 2004, and at that time, some residents had been moving through the rotation for about thirty years.[23] As she described this, her tone also circulated from empathy with the resident families and their plight to the frustrated tone of a harried landlord. The three sanatoria trusts insisted that they rotated rooms so the residents could never legally claim an address, but the application forms were not redone each time. This slip into informality became a point in the legal proceedings against the trusts. Shireen claimed that many trustees had the "benevolent attitude of *kaha jase?*" ("where will they go?") if the families were simply to be kicked out. According to Shireen, by then, many residents had cars and washing machines, signs to her that they had exceeded their justification of being poor and needy. "Some even sold their other properties outside the city" and stayed on here, she exclaimed, clicking her tongue in disapproval. In 2003, a few eviction cases were brought to the small causes court, and then in 2009, the Petit trust decided to settle, paying the remaining occupants to leave. In 2011, only one occupant was left, allegedly holding out for more money, but Shireen declined to comment further as the case was still under litigation. The status of the sanatorium was still held in the meantime.

The Meantime

Cy près is the mechanism for the trust to deal with the present time, denoting a close enough substitute. This kind of legal fiction is "not really so much an epistemological claim as it is a special kind of pause, for the moment" (Riles 2011, 173). If the law does not allow trusts to fail, as Mr. Vakil noted, it does allow them a workaround. Riles reminds us that while we might think of them as lies, legal fictions "begin to serve as pathways, scripts, private constitutions for a particular kind of action" (Riles 2011, 180). Therefore, beyond their truth, what is crucial, especially to those who deploy them, is what kinds of possibilities for action are created or foreclosed (Riles 2011, 175).[24]

"But the deed is clear: the trust must build and manage a sanatorium, so what happens now?" I asked Shireen. Yes, she said, "but it is not stated in the deed that it must be on this plot. We have gotten permission to build a new sanatorium further to the north within other properties of the F. D. Petit Trust." By that, she meant that the trust petitioned the charity commissioner with cy près to allow the shift northward. Since the existing sanatorium was no longer functioning as a sanatorium, the original object of the trust, but instead as permanent housing, the trust had a substantial legal advantage not only in its eviction cases but also with its proposal to rebuild elsewhere. The following section will detail a success story from the point of view of trusts with the deployment of cy près.

Within the same compound as the sanatorium and the hospital stands Petit Towers, a luxury high-rise built in 2004. Shireen related that it was vacant land with unused FSI, and the building was constructed to support the trust's income. Here again, a once dormant landscape was reawakened by FSI and the financial potentiality of untapped capital. She exclaimed that the building was set askew so that residents would have an "amazing view," east and west, of both of the city's shorelines. The original structure was stone on stone with lime, with no cement. When they tore it down, they numbered each stone and rebuilt it exactly. The cladding on the tower was done to look weathered. "It just needs a wash; it never needs to be repainted," and the towers are the first residence with a solar paneling system as well as cooling and heating systems that run on water, Shireen exclaimed proudly. The trust's goal was "a truly luxury clientele," but following the original deed, the trustees could only sell these flats to Parsis. They tried everything they could to market the ownership flats to wealthy Parsis but only got about eleven to twelve families willing to buy at that time and at the advertised rates. Caught between the trust's mandate and losing on their investment, the trust petitioned the charity commissioner with cy près, showing evidence that they could not find enough Parsi buyers and proposed "going cosmopolitan," opening the sales to all communities. Currently, the building is at full ownership occupancy (Parsi and non-Parsi). The trust received enough funds to maintain the sanatorium building and fund the hospital for a time. The commissioner's condition was that the trust must build a Parsi-only building somewhere else. Shireen related that the trust planned to buy a plot in Borivili in the north of the city and build three hundred Parsi-only charity flats but has not done so yet. While the trust continues to thrive with the earnings from the tower, many within the community see this project as a massive failure since it lost its Parsi-only character. During the 2008 BPP trustee election, this case and its outcome were among the lightning-rod issues that riled up the more orthodox voters who insisted that the trust should have lowered the price of the flats rather than go cosmopolitan to non-Parsis. From the perspective of the Petit trust, the construction of the tower and the future shifting of the sanatorium was necessary for its most important object, the hospital, to endure. The destiny of the hospital eclipsed the future of the sanatorium and its residents.

For the Petit trust, this deployment of cy près denoted that time was out of joint, a disjuncture of the "real" present and the one guaranteed in perpetuity. Therefore, while the deployment of cy près does not alter the time horizon of a trust, it does offer a shift or a deferral of its objects in perpetuity. In the cases above, cy près enabled a spatial shift as well; the trust and its objects would continue in a different location. Like a legal fiction, it offered "a technique for working with and in the meantime . . . it defines and manages the near future—the time for which this particular commitment holds true" (Riles 2011, 176). It allowed for the Petit trust to set in motion a detour from the supposed doomed inevitability of the near future, the insolvency of the hospital, and toward possible alternate futures for the trust in Mumbai.

The cy près doctrine allowed the trust to reorder its constellation and amend its horoscope, temporally and spatially shifting its forecast. Set against the unruly development of Mumbai driven by the great profits of development, trust property is continually prophesying, enabling, and constraining certain futures, much as the city development plan means to do. It offers a different horoscope because it is not bound to the mandates of a planning corporation but sometimes to the century-old wishes and beneficence of a private individual. Decaying structures and low rental incomes threaten to weaken the hinge function of the trust, to maintain its original objects into the future, but the cy près doctrine allows for the navigation of the present, the meantime. It maintains the integrity of the hinge while deploying a new potential future. The technique of cy près assures that the law has not allowed the trust to fail. It renews the durability of trust capital as it allows the once-fixed objects to shift rather than have capital released from its charitable purpose.

CHAPTER 2. **PRESENTS AND FUTURES**

The Trust and Obligation's Asymmetries

I met Tanaz, a Parsi woman, at a dinner party with some common friends in Mumbai. She had heard that I was researching Parsis and trusts and wanted to learn more about my work. Sitting next to me on a sofa, she sat on the edge of the seat and asked eagerly, "You work on trusts? My mother just established one!" She explained that her mother was widowed relatively young and remained very wealthy. Tanaz was an only child in her forties and was dating Sunil, a Hindu man she had met through work. We all sat on the sofa and exchanged stories about graduate school, traffic, and the current controversies over trust real estate in the city. "Can you believe her mother just wants to give all her money away?" exclaimed Sunil, at one point. Tanaz shot him a look with her eyes widened, making me aware that this was part of an extended disagreement between them. "Well, it's her money, and she can do what she likes," said Tanaz, who seemed to have a good income as a professional woman. "This way, her money goes to poor people and can really make a difference," she said, mostly to Sunil. "She is setting it up for medical funds for Parsis who can't afford operations and such. This is important to her." While Tanaz affirmed her mother's decision, her partner seemed to question the entire enterprise. He quickly insisted that immediate family were the ones who should inherit a person's fortune. I imagined that I was meant to arbitrate somehow but decided to stay out of the disagreement, at least at that moment.

Per her mother's wishes, Tanaz would not gain the immediate wealth of her mother per the succession laws of her community.[1] But she was named as one of the trustees of the newly settled public charitable trust named after her family. Rather than directly bequeath certain assets, her mother planned to bequeath her obligations to Tanaz and the other trustees. In this way, the trust served as a way of bypassing the norms laid out by succession laws in which Tanaz, as an only child, would have inherited all her mother's wealth. By setting up the trust within her lifetime, Tanaz's mother also avoided any future conflict between her legal will and her charitable intention, a cause of numerous disputes among many descendants of trust settlors. She might have thought that her only daughter might not have any children or that they would not be counted as Parsi if their father were non-Parsi.[2] Endowing the trust was a way of transmitting her family name and fortune into the future for her community, past the natural lives of her blood relatives.

However, this begs the question of trust in another form: does it not display a lack of trust in Tanaz to fulfill her mother's wishes of helping poorer Parsis without a formal legal mechanism? One can only speak in the abstract without knowing more about the specifics of their relationship or her mother's "true" intentions. Yes, scholars have shown that at least one reason to endow property is to abate the uncertainty of one's legal heirs not being able (in terms of being a minor, for example) or willing to manage the property wisely or carry out certain intentions (Friedman 2009, 118). Embedded in the purpose of the trust is the fulfillment of a particular intention to be carried out over time, but embedded in the practice of endowment itself are also values of what constitutes good or proper relations toward these assets. By opting for this form of wealth transmission, Tanaz's mother gave to her community over her immediate kin and privileged perpetual giving over immediate direct giving. Her wish would be congealed in a trust while her wealth would be invested and then slowly disbursed over time by trustees.

While many other Indian communities employ trusts or trust-like endowments to manage their religious institutions and charities, I argue in this chapter that charitable giving through the mechanism of trusts is a qualitatively different phenomenon within the Parsi community as it permeates almost every aspect of their communal life, governance, and history in the city. I will show how the trust replaces the circulation of personal assets through customary inheritance within a family with the circulation of communal obligations in perpetuity and the effects that are brought to bear on urban space.

Deriving from the Latin *ligare*, "to bind," "both obligation and bond can imply constraint and captivity, but both can also imply an act one performs on oneself," a term "shot through with an unruly combination of capaciousness and selective precision" (Guyer 2012, 493). In line with the trust's tying up and stopping property, obligations are bound to these assets. The trust binds social relations with material assets, and within those assets, it further constrains capital, tying it to social relations.

The settlor of a trust, while divesting their ownership rights over the trust assets, preserves their charitable intention in perpetuity. That is, while its original ownership relation is lost at the moment of endowment, a trust's obligation to fulfill its objects endures. The written deed is a unique kind of document as it not only serves as a "script for the collaboration between two parties" (Riles 2011, 50) but is also an obligation not from one party to another but to an object—a purpose or ideal. Legal texts refer to a trust document as the first material instantiation of the "obligation attached to the ownership of property" (Rajaratnam, Natarajan, and Thangaraj 2010).

As a legal mechanism, the trust may buy and sell assets to pursue its objects, although charity and tax laws regulate these decisions for charitable trusts.[3] Laws governing charities as endowments have explicitly framed how charity is defined, to whom it may be owed, and what constitutes a legitimate and hence tax-free philanthropic purpose (L. Vevaina 2019). The law encourages endowing property for charitable purposes by allowing it to be exempt from tax, and secondly, exempt from the rule against perpetuities, a legal rule that prevents people from exerting control or ownership of private property beyond the natural lives of the people involved.[4] They are allowed these two exemptions as they are seen to be for the public good. Therefore, this legal obligation is fundamentally also a moral one, as it is framed by and through very particular understandings of charity and who deserves a charitable gift. This obligation cannot be separated from the property once the trust is established. It is only as moral instruments to promote the good that charitable trusts have a perpetual nature.

This chapter will examine how the trust troubles the giver-receiver binary of reciprocity, what Mauss discussed as "the power of obligation to set up the precise conditions of repayment" (Guyer 2012, 495), both in terms of the obligations owed and the temporality of those obligations. I argue that the trust structure reorganizes religious giving into an intergenerational relation of obligation and accountability. Like our understanding of the gift, charitable giving through the trust brings specific obligations between the giver and receiver through time. Yet, this chapter will show how the social relations it engenders are firmly asymmetrical and may trouble our notions of reciprocity.

Jerbai's Wish

Many wealthy Parsis endowing trusts for the benefit of other Parsis in Bombay fulfilled both a religious duty to give charity and a social role in nurturing and protecting this microminority in a growing colonial city (Palsetia 2017). Earning their fortunes through the lucrative China trade and then in cotton production, some wealthy Parsis of the eighteenth century endowed hospitals, schools, housing, and sanatoria to their coreligionists in perpetuity using the instrument of the public charitable trust.

Jerbai Wadia (1852–1926), the widow of wealthy industrialist and mill owner N. N. Wadia,[5] endowed five enormous properties and accompanying funds in the name of her husband and sons in place of her children directly inheriting the assets.[6] The five estates were dedicated as Parsi housing colonies in the 1920s and 1930s through separate trust agreements. The first, in the name of her husband, the Nowrosjee Nusserwanjee Wadia Trust Buildings for Parsees, was endowed in 1916 after his death as "residences exclusively for the use and occupation of poor and middle-class Parsees professing the Zoroastrian faith."[7] This housing colony was named Nowroze Baug (see figures 2.1 and 2.2) and still stands in the Lalbaug section of Parel in central Mumbai. Rustom Baug, another of her endowments, named after her youngest son who died in 1919, had as its objects "the provision of clean, comfortable, and inexpensive residential quarters for poor and middle-class members of the Parsee Community professing the Zoroastrian faith and in connection therewith to afford to such persons, facilities and conveniences for the performance of funeral and other ceremonies, medical relief instruction and recreation and for such other purposes as the Trustees may think directly or indirectly conducive to the comfort and well-being of the said persons and upon further trust to maintain, improve, develop, control, and manage the said Institution."[8]

I argue that Jerbai's trust deeds are constitutional documents, constructing and inaugurating social, legal, and financial relations among the settlor, the trustees, beneficiaries, and ultimately the city. Furthermore, their "structure [becomes] the purpose" (Friedman 2009, 119) in that they transform the property relation between owner and asset into a bifurcated

FIGURE 2.1. Gate at Nowroze Baug, Lalbaug Parel. Photo by author.

FIGURE 2.2. Aerial of Nowroze Baug, Lalbaug Parel. Photo by author.

relation of obligation and possession with the trustees and beneficiaries. Each deed constructs two distinct sets of people: trustees who hold the obligation and beneficiaries who are recipients of that obligation. Jerbai, as a settlor of a public charitable trust, relinquished her ownership right over the assets in favor of obligating the trust to a particular purpose and for a certain but indefinite amount of people. Hence, unlike immediate giving, which defines a person as a giver or receiver at one moment, the charitable trust's beneficiaries are indefinite not only because they are a subset of the public but also indefinite (successive generations of Parsis) through time. While divesting her ownership rights over the trust assets, Wadia preserved her charitable intention in perpetuity. That is, while her original ownership relation is lost at the moment of endowment, her trust's obligation to fulfill its objects endures. This legal obligation is transformed into a moral obligation of care and guardianship and cannot be separated from the property once the trust is established. Her immortal wish survives her mortal life.

Jerbai remained the managing trustee of all the funds and endowments, and each deed stipulated that her sons and their heirs would remain trustees. They further maintained "that if there shall be any difference of opinion among the Trustees for the time being of these presents that of the majority shall prevail but this proviso is subject to the express condition that the wishes of the said Bai Jerbai N. Wadia during her lifetime shall prevail."[9] Hence, through these legal agreements, Jerbai's wish and charitable intent remained paramount. She further ensured her obligation would be carried out by placing her kin as trustees. As per these original deeds, the estates were then handed over, or donated, to the BPP in the 1950s when it was seen that the properties were best managed by the more extensive bureaucracy of the Punchayet, albeit with the guardianship of the Wadia Committee of Management, which still includes her descendants. Today, her endowed properties are comanaged by the BPP and the Wadia Committee.

While Jerbai clearly went out of her way to donate to the needy of the community, a manager at the Wadia Committee of Management intimated to me that Jerbai might have had a double purpose with her generous donations. Firstly, she saw the need at the turn of the century to encourage more Parsis to emigrate from rural parts of Gujarat to the city for better economic prospects and deemed that providing subsidized housing would be the proper incentive. The second factor in her beneficence was the controversial conversion to Christianity of her two sons, Sir Ness and Sir Cusrow. Endowing the assets allowed Jerbai to remove the possibility of her

FIGURE 2.3. Parsi woman at well in Nowroze Baug. Photo by author.

sons inheriting her estates and assets directly from her as per the succession rules of her community.

Again, enter the trust, the perfect mechanism for such circumvention of inheritance. Using the trust, Jerbai could maintain her estate for the needs of her community and honor her husband and three sons. The circulation of her assets through inheritance to her kin was supplanted with the circulation of her wishes and charitable obligation to her community. By channeling her good wishes through the trust instrument, Jerbai expanded the reach of charitable assets to successive generations of her kin and community. Her sons were not only honored by name, but their descendants, now recognized as Parsi Zoroastrians again, will remain trustees and guardians of her wishes.[10] Rather than the hundreds of receivers of charity she could have reached through direct giving in the 1920s, by financializing her giving, Jerbai is still able to aid thousands of Parsis in each successive generation into the future. The next sections will detail how in the fast-paced and changing legal and urban environments of Mumbai, the endurance of past obligations into the future produces ongoing problems in the present, often due to the opposing and asymmetrical interests of trustees and beneficiaries.

In honor of her late husband, Naoroji Nusserwanji Wadia, Nowroze Baug was completed in 1908 as part of Jerbai Wadia's wish to house poor Parsis. Jerbai oversaw the building of the flats according to Parsi custom with a hearth fire (*chulaa waati*) and a well (see figure 2.3) within each colony to secure fresh water for ritual purification. In the first decade of the *baug*, she allotted the flats and set the rents (Rs. 9–11) herself. In 1917, she established the N. N. Wadia Building Trust Fund to maintain and build additional housing colonies to encourage further migration of Parsis from Gujarat. The N. N. Wadia trustees, after the death of her son Sir Ness Wadia in 1957, then turned over partial management of the five Wadia baugs to the Bombay Parsi Punchayet.

The Bombay Parsi Punchayet (BPP)

The BPP offices are on Dadabhai Navroji Road, near the Chatrapati Shivaji Terminus, one of Mumbai's main train stations. The building is imposing with wide, curving staircases, a large lobby, and high ceilings. The trust occupies the third and top floor as the large staircase opens onto a lobby area with a massive sign for the BPP with its insignia of Persianate winged bulls flanking the trust's initials. The main office space is ample, with high ceilings, the ubiquitous whir of ceiling fans, and rows of desks with piles and piles of paper files. The "cabins," or enclosed offices, are along the perimeter and primarily serve as offices for the CEO and upper-level management. The seven trustees do not have their own offices on the premises, as they do not work there full time. The BPP offices look like any older bureaucracy in India: rows of desks with stacks and stacks of papers, accompanied by the rings of telephones, with many office clerks moving from desk to desk. Many beneficiaries wait restlessly in the lobby for their name or case number to be called. On the other side of the lobby area is the conference room, which holds the BPP's library and hosts the weekly trustee meetings. Among the multitude of Parsi trusts in Mumbai that provide a variety of subsidized housing for Parsis, the Bombay Parsi Punchayet, a trust and an amalgam of *kathas* (smaller funds), has the most significant presence in Mumbai. It claims to be the second-largest landowner after the Bombay Port Trust in Mumbai and has the premier role as a governance structure for the community.

Besides the laws governing trusts and endowments, another piece of legislation that critically impacted housing trusts was the Rent Act of 1948. All trust assets are meant to be held in perpetuity; hence, even if well maintained, trust buildings tend to be of older building stock than the rest of the city's fast-moving development. While there has always been some movement of trust assets through generations, this landscape in Mumbai was further ossified with rent-control laws. In its immediate aftermath, the 1948 Rent Act had indeed served its purpose of aiding postindependence migration to the city. Still, its own endurance had, by many accounts, taken a devastating toll on Mumbai's real estate market (Pathak 2008). This freezing of rental values greatly favored those who were tenanted and had already settled into the city before the advent of the law.

For trusts like the BPP and other landlords, the Rent Act had grown to have some devastating effects: the subsidized rents that charity tenants enjoyed before 1947 were then forever frozen by the Act. Even when a resident died, the frozen rents perpetuated through generations, as the 1948 Act had very liberal regulations about family members inheriting rent certificates. The BPP housing manager related how after the death of a baug resident, it was typical for close kin to turn up and sit vigil in the flat through four days of the traditional death rituals and then claim tenancy as inheritors of the rent certificate. Furthermore, because of the Act, the trust had no way to remove successive generations of tenants from charity flats even if they became millionaires. Flats only became available if the tenant died with no successors or if a resident voluntarily gave up their flat to go elsewhere, which was very seldom.

While trusts are defined by their deeds, the changing legal and municipal environments of their assets significantly affect their circumstances. While perpetual endowments oriented and somewhat ossified settlement in Bombay, the 1990s deregulation of financial markets and the legalization of transfer fees, called *pugree*, drastically changed the conditions of possibility for this once-dormant scape of real estate in Mumbai. This municipal intervention and market liberalization saw real estate prices climb and sped up the velocity of property circulation all over Mumbai. For trusts like the Bombay Parsi Punchayet, new redevelopment projects on its extensive lands suddenly had great potential to increase its vulnerable cash corpus, maintain its current housing stock, and attract richer Parsis' wealth.

Givers and Takers

I met recent trustee "Ardvan" in one of the early months of my fieldwork, at his home in an ownership building within a BPP housing colony.[11] I was warmly greeted with tea and biscuits by him and his wife, "Dinaz," both of whom have spent the last decades devoted to community affairs. Upon my entering the study and explaining the focus of my research, the conversation moved into historical examples of community philanthropy, specifically, about Jerbai Wadia. Dinaz remarked that she [Wadia] was one of the last great Parsi philanthropists who put funds toward the community and helped build it into what it is today. Ardvan then mournfully remarked that things were different now. "As a trustee, I have seen that Parsis are a community of takers," he exclaimed. Charity, he noted, was always important, but now people acted as if charity was a birthright. He asked in a sarcastic tone, "Would a Parsi ever dream of taking a loan from the bank?"[12] In some sense especially the way the trust deeds are written, charity, or assistance, is a birthright since one just has to be Parsi to receive it.[13] Furthermore, there is never any suggestion of repayment or reciprocal duty that goes along with receiving funds or living in a baug. Hence, Ardvan intimated that taking charity from a trust was somehow an unreciprocated gift, as nothing was ever returned, while taking a loan from a bank was seen as a financial transaction.

The work on prestations and counterprestations in Indian contexts, especially on *dān*, has much to say about reciprocity and the binary of giving-receiving that Ardvan discussed.[14] Parry's (1986) intervention pushed against the notion of the gift and reciprocity, pointing toward the relationship between the gift and the commodity form. He insisted that gifts might exist without reciprocity but not without spirit. This corresponded to specific social forms that have separated the disinterest and interest in exchange—that is, the gift and the transaction (Sanchez et al. 2017). But what might we learn about giving through the trust mechanism? The following will examine the relations the charitable trust engenders with its gifts and how it structures asymmetries between the giver and receiver, leaving reciprocity aside altogether. Hence, while there remains certainty of the givers (settlors and trustees) within the trust relationship as they are named entities, the receivers are uncertain, an indefinite category within public charitable trusts, as they are, in this instance, any Parsi, into perpetuity. Here we see the trust constituting objects into subjects in social relations, as the connection between being Parsi and being a beneficiary is created through access to these trust assets and the tripartite structure of the trust. These relations strive to define community boundaries and relative categories of rich and poor, which are especially acute in a city like Mumbai with its high poverty levels and informal settlements.

Later in my fieldwork, I met another of the trustees elected in 2008. One could say that "Firdaus" was an ideal candidate for BPP trustee, as he had extensive experience with trusts. Yet Firdaus's tenure on the board was highly tenuous and political, perhaps due to his expertise. I met him in February of 2011 in his office in south Mumbai. The office was small and very modest, with the surrounding offices and floors filled with other charities and funds. Firdaus explained that in the sense of a charitable cause, housing does not qualify unless it entails housing the destitute to alleviate poverty. He insinuated that this was not the case with the BPP anymore, but that is precisely why the community's definition of poverty (more in chapter 3) seems so absurd relative to accepted definitions. As long as a community member is deemed poor, any charity to that person comes under the rubric of general public utility. Referring to a recent sale of a flat in Cusrow Baug, he asked me, "How is the transfer of a six crore [$985,000] flat still considered charity?"[15]

The various individual endowments managed by the BPP establish the trust beneficiaries as "Parsis and those that practice the Zoroastrian faith" and "poor or needy" Parsis. Hence when the BPP announced its expansion plans for colonies like Nowroze Baug, a few advocacy groups, including the Alert Zoroastrian Association, were up in arms that BPP monies would now be invested in building housing for rich Parsis, as they would be the only ones who could afford the ownership flats, which typically would sell for four to five crores ($650,000–$820,000). As per the BPP's claims, even though it sells flats for crores of rupees, the monies go into managing and providing housing for poor Parsis. As one Mumbai developer, who was familiar with charitable trusts, exclaimed to me, "Poor housing is expensive!" That is, the BPP, like other older trusts, is short on liquidity and must maintain large estates of old building stock in need of repairs for the benefit of charity recipients. The BPP employs the language of other Mumbai developers and claims that it cross-subsidizes charity housing with its transfer schemes.[16] Profits earned from selling new ownership flats are meant to directly fund charity or subsidized housing. This asymmetry of income and expenditure is the standard scheme for most welfare programs.

When I asked about the cross-subsidy scheme, Firdaus nodded his head and stated that the scheme was deemed necessary by many of the trustees, even of the older generation. He estimated that the BPP's corpus at that time was about 120 crore rupees ($19.5 million), which was just in liquid assets and did not count the real estate value, which he admitted was priceless yet mostly inalienable. Like the other trustees I had spoken with, he explained that maintenance costs were draining the corpus at a higher rate than it could replenish through the very low-risk investments the trust could make by law. Hence, the cross-subsidy was needed, but he warned,

"What if the trust is found to be in breach of its duty to support general public utility? Would it lose its tax-exempt status?" As he wondered aloud, he worriedly shook his head to indicate that the whole system could come crashing down. Because of his cautious take on the cross-subsidy, he insisted that he was left out of trustee meetings. He claimed that the other trustees, two of whom were quite zealous about redevelopment, withheld financial reports from him until he approached the Charity Commission to receive them.

Nowroze Baug: "Redevelopment Is in the Air"

Nowroze Baug is an enclave in Parel, a neighborhood that was once famous for its textile mills and, in recent decades, several public-private redevelopment projects. The baug has about a dozen low-rise buildings and a playground on approximately five and a half acres. Compared to the bustle and crowded streets outside its gates, the baug is quiet with large lanes and the familiar pale-yellow painted structures. In 2009, the BPP announced its new development plan to demolish several buildings in various baugs across the city and build newer high-rise ones in their place. To the horror of many current residents of Nowroze Baug, all 358 tenements within the colony were slated to be replaced with this plan. In its own words, the BPP's plan was proposed: "With zeal to provide housing on a large scale, in order to redress one of the most vexing issues assailing the community, the BPP has embarked upon a Rs. 450 crore development plan . . . to create over 3200 new flats" (BPP Review, October 2009, 21). To assist the BPP, the trustees had put together a housing committee that included high-profile Parsi developers. Taking on the rhetoric of Mumbai planners, the BPP referred to the scheme as its "Master Plan for the community's much-needed housing requirements . . . to permanently remove the chronic housing shortage" (BPP Review, 1). Even though the community is dwindling in numbers, the BPP retains a considerable waiting list for its subsidized flats, a paradox that will be analyzed further in the next chapter. The committee was optimistic with the new proposal as it assumed that the majority of baug residents, who would all eventually receive new flats, would be in favor of the project.

The BPP proposal further situated its communal plans on par with the highly discussed plans for the redevelopment of Bhendi Bazaar in central Mumbai by the Dawoodi Bohra Muslim community. This plan was initiated directly by Bohra community leader Syedna Mohammed Burhanuddin and approved by the Indian central government's Smart Cities initiative.

It promised to "uplift" the Bohras living in cramped spaces in central Mumbai to better living quarters through cluster redevelopment. Most of the existing 245 structures were mixed-use and quite dilapidated, with one even collapsing in 2017. The plan involved replacing these existing mid-rise structures with seventeen high-rise towers while preserving the community's sacred spaces. Four of the seventeen would be sold at market value to recover costs. Unlike other cluster redevelopment schemes, this one is led by a charitable trust, the Saifee Burhani Upliftment Trust, settled in 2009. The scheme was mostly welcomed by the inhabitants of Bhendi Bazaar and slowly received approvals from existing tenants. In contrast, the BPP scheme was met with deep suspicion from many in the community who felt that their present condition was better than what was offered for the future.

I met Peshotan, a middle-aged Parsi man, at his flat in Nowroze Baug on a balmy December day in 2010. He briefly introduced me to his wife, and then we sat in the gallery outside his front door, thankfully under a fan. All the blocks at Nowroze Baug had small galleries outside; most were used for hanging laundry, with a few having chairs and tables for sitting, particularly in the cooler winter weather.

Peshotan first wistfully told me stories of baug life, about how he grew up feeling like his neighbors were extended family, how he met his wife in the baug, and how central life in the colony was to his work in the mills nearby and his social world. Later in the conversation, with a tone of doom, he explained how all of it was at risk with the possible redevelopment of the baug. To prove to the BPP that Nowroze Baug was of value just as it was, Peshotan had gone door-to-door in the colony, asking residents about their childhood, marriages, and children, assured that he would find evidence that baug life contributed to "intact families" and low incidents of intermarriages as compared to the averages.[17] He explained to me that even though residents were lower-middle class and mostly gained income from the mills, they used to have three to five children per family. As he handed me his data, written on page after page of a ledger, I was struck by his intense effort and persistence. Peshotan hoped that his data would oppose and trump the financial data used by the redevelopers and the trust.

Peshotan then pointed to the next building and the looming view of Hilla Towers, a Parsi-only, ownership high-rise in the background (see figure 2.4). "Redevelopment is in the air," he noted with resignation as I rose from my rattan chair to take a photograph. Peshotan and a few other residents in Nowroze Baug formed a group to discuss the advantages and disadvantages of redevelopment. For them, projects like Hilla Towers, a neighboring

FIGURE 2.4. View of Hilla Towers from Peshotan's flat, Nowroze Baug. Photo by author.

building that literally casts its shadow over the baug, represented expensive ownership flats that would be out of their grasp. While the tower soars over the six-story height of the baug, the two structures are strange foils of each other. On the one side, Nowroze Baug, named after Nowroze Wadia, the patriarch of the family who was to completely transform the landscape of Parsi life in Bombay by giving migrant Gujarati Parsis a new and relatively affordable place to live; and, on the other side, Hilla Towers, also Parsi-built, but a private residence to a more moneyed set of Parsis, perhaps a sign of things to come for the entire community. Peshotan remarked over and over how different the sociality of such a building would be in comparison with the baug. He passionately spoke of how much everyone enjoyed how neighbors shared the front gallery space for a game of cards, hanging laundry, or children playing. The promise of redevelopment was anticipated with dread by many of the baug residents. The BPP and the Wadia

Housing Committee began to get some pushback from the group. Often when I visited the Punchayet offices, I would see a member of the Nowroze Baug committee waiting patiently in the lobby for a time to advocate with a trustee for the baug's survival. They wished to remind the trustees of their obligations to Jerbai's wish and to themselves as beneficiaries.

On one visit to the N. N. Wadia offices in Ballard Estate a few months later, the offices of the Wadia Management Committee that runs the five Wadia baugs, I sat in the office of one of the housing managers and noticed a sizeable architectural rendering leaning up against the wall. The manager saw my glance, nodded, and smiled: "Yes, these are some of the proposed plans for Nowroze Baug." "Pretty fancy," I responded. "It's all very hi-fi," he agreed, a shorthand for high finance. If I had not been told that the rendering corresponded to Nowroze Baug, I would not have guessed it. Gone were the pale-yellow low-rise buildings, all replaced with twenty-story luxury towers of glass and steel. The one area of green space in the rendering included a large swimming pool with white-skinned, bikini-clad female figures sunbathing around it. The only remnant of the current baug was the ornamental gate, which stood at the front of the image. To me, this image was highly dissonant with the current architecture and atmosphere of the baug.

The Nowroze Baug plans lay at a standstill for many years while the residents continued to come together in opposition to the proposals. For a charitable trust and any large redevelopment project in Mumbai, the landlords and developers cannot simply evict or force the current residents to move out, even temporarily. Thanks to many hard-won battles with slum redevelopment, now, at least 70 percent of existing residents of any kind of housing must approve of the project and must be rehoused or compensated according to MHADA regulations.[18]

Much focus on redevelopment projects lies in their assumed policy successes or failures. The rhetoric of most redevelopment projects entailed the successful removal of a certain number of people, moving them from dilapidated housing into shiny new high rises. This rhetoric leaves out any losses of sociality, access to work, or other less tangible forms of value. Peshotan's sentiment of loss in the face of potentially nicer real estate was very palpable in contrast. He and others also pointed to a more individual meantime, a time horizon that the trust cannot well account for. What would happen in the decades between demolition and rehousing? While the trust could protect its objects using *cy près*, what of the residents? Where would these newly evicted tenants go if the BPP already had a long waitlist for its flats? This sentiment of the uncertain meantime in Mumbai is vividly captured by

Finklestein (2019). In her poetic ethnography, Finkelstein pushes back on the narratives of Mumbai as a postindustrial city, particularly regarding its mill industry. By examining the lives and stories of current mill workers, who work within spaces of "lively ruination," she explores the notion of the anachronism embedded in understandings of *chawl* housing (Finkelstein 2018), what she calls "queer chawl time" (2019). This landscape is directly adjacent to Nowroze Baug, with many of its residents housed in *chawls* through the once-paternalistic care offered by mill owners to their laborers. Once slated for redevelopment, most of these *chawl* residences were demolished for high-end commercial and residential real estate, leaving these workers in this lively ruination. The workers in Finkelstein's research did not have the degree of protection offered to beneficiaries of Jerbai Wadia's trusts, who still had to be convinced and approve of the new redevelopment projects.

Hence, what was left to do for the BPP and the developers was to win the hearts and minds of the residents of Nowroze Baug. In March 2013, in an unusual move, Jerbai's great-grandson, Nusli Wadia, and his son Ness visited the baug along with developer Hafeez Contractor and the BPP trustees. According to the *Times of India*, the Nusli Wadia encouraged the residents to "look at this project in a positive and objective way; not in a combative way. . . . We want to give you something better than you have" (Bharucha 2013). The baug residents were then treated to a PowerPoint presentation that unveiled the plans to demolish the old structures and build four forty-story buildings, a promise to make Nowroze Baug a "new deluxe Parsi colony." According to the 2013 proposal, every current resident of the baug would first be temporarily rehoused by the trust and then provided a new apartment between 400 and 1,250 square feet in the new towers on an ownership basis, where they would continue their residence. Another estimated five hundred new flats would be allotted to priests and young couples per the BPP's merit-rating scheme, and any remainders would be sold at market rates to other Parsis to cover costs.[19]

Besides the residents' general suspicion and fear of the plan to demolish the baug as it existed, the proposal contained another snag that could hold up the redevelopment. In its current incarnation, what is now an open playground space is slated to house one of the tower buildings. Many critics of the plan point out that Mumbai civic authorities would be unwilling to approve it as the city is already so lacking in recreational space. The baug has one of the only undeveloped green spaces in this highly congested part of the city.[20] The residents informed the BPP of their plan to form an independent body to liaise with the trust and represent the baug and formed the Nowroze

Baug Residents Redevelopment Committee (NBRRC). Their first agenda item was to request a detailed written proposal from the BPP, the Wadia committee, and the developer to begin negotiations. This request was submitted in May of 2013, yet the project has been stalled in the meantime.

As mentioned, at least 70 percent of baug residents must agree to any redevelopment scheme, and the trust promises to house them in the interim. Yet at a baug meeting I attended, many seemed afraid they would never be rehoused in the new facilities nor be able to pay the much higher property tax on their flats.[21] There was a further worry about the class difference. "How will we fit with those people?" one older resident remarked. "They come from abroad with money and have gone to fancy universities; we are the children of workers." This assumed class or social schism had actually been taken into account by the developers, one of whom wanted to assure me that ownership residents and former charity residents would be in separate buildings to avoid any "social awkwardness." While landholding trusts like the BPP risk their cash corpus on large redevelopment schemes, I argued in L. Vevaina (2015) that what might be at risk are their original objects: to care for the poor and needy of the community, who felt neglected by this new proposal, which would also create more class schisms.

At the 2013 meeting between Jerbai's descendants, Nusli and Ness Wadia, and the residents of Nowroze Baug, upon hearing the hesitancy of the latter to agree to the redevelopment, Nusli Wadia implored them to "please trust us; if you don't, you should." Yet mistrust of the trust's intentions was rife. At the beginning of this chapter, I discussed how settling a trust perhaps displayed a lack of trust on the part of the settlor toward their progeny, who would generally inherit their wealth. A trust is, in its creation, a mechanism to mitigate the uncertainty of an obligation moving forward faithfully to the next generation. Historically established in times of financial or social uncertainty, it was a technology to stop the circulation of property in the open market or within strict rules of succession, a way to foreclose crisis: losing property to the government or to heirs, who might not carry out the designated purpose. Once legally endowed, the "dead hand" of the settlor was to rest firmly over the lands or funds in perpetuity. From its origins to today, the Parsi trust in contemporary Mumbai is caught between two opposing ethics: one highly speculative ethic marked by high risk to earn profits to enlarge its corpus and perhaps the pockets of some trustees, and the other one of disinterest, following an ethic of subjunctive philanthropic care, what the trust should owe to its beneficiaries to achieve the good (L. Vevaina

2015). Here we see a growing lack of trust between beneficiaries and trustees to maintain the settlors' original wishes and bound obligations.

The charitable trust is a very particular fiduciary relationship. The triangular structure of the (a) settlor, whose intentions become embodied in the trust deed,[22] (b) the trustee, and (c) beneficiary, makes for a unique actor in the real estate market. The trustee must be, again, at least in theory, disinterested—that is, they should not be receiving any gain from the trust. The beneficiaries are not stakeholders in the general sense either and therefore cannot make any claims to profit, but only to the original objects of the trust (subsidized housing, medical care, education, etc.).[23] For example, if a beneficiary rents a trust property for a hundred rupees per month (less than two dollars), they should technically have no rights over any profit from transferring that property to another beneficiary.

While they have no legal ownership claim over the flat, a tenant's claim of possession is powerful enough that it is *as if* they do. I have heard repeatedly that even those in charity flats receive a portion of the *pugree*, or transfer fees, when the flat is moved to another tenant. The trustees and the beneficiaries see a potential in these cases to exploit their dual ownership rights in the trust flats. By harnessing this potential, they push the flats back into slow circulation. In Mumbai, this seems to be the only incentive for a tenant to leave a property they act as if they own. Currently, when tenanted flats are sold to other Parsis, the trust and the outgoing tenant negotiate the division of the sale price, which is set by private auction. The interested parties meet in the boardroom, and then slips of paper with amounts are exchanged back and forth. Within the BPP, this is done with the CEO, the tenant, and the interested buyer. If the sale involves one of the Wadia trust flats, a person from the Committee of Management from the Wadia side is also present. This attempt at transparency of the pugree payment is still seen by many as violating the objects of the trust itself on two levels. Firstly, as profits are gained from charity, many see this as a threat to the trust's tax-exempt status. The second critique is that the BPP, desperate for liquidity, has become less interested in serving the needs of poor Parsis than in enticing the purchasing power of richer ones, therefore moving further toward the ethic of interest and profit making (L. Vevaina 2015).

Perhaps most troubling to the critics of the cross-subsidy plans and the building of ownership flats are the various ways in which they have begun to privilege the wealthy Parsi over the poor and destitute, the original intended beneficiaries of the trust. Many BPP trustee meetings are now held with high-end residential developers. They are all jockeying for the chance to propose redevelopment and the new look of the baugs, pieces of land and real estate that in their consideration have been "lying fallow," unproductive for so many decades. As developers of some of the most central and expensive real estate in the city, they would not only profit from the square-meter price of the land but also the additional transfer development rights (TDR), which would give them the incentive to build in the more northern parts of the city.[24] The existing trust real estate in Nowroze Baug was not seen to be financially productive enough for the trust, in contrast to the sentiments of social value that Peshotan insisted upon.

Jerbai's Obligation

Almost a year later in 2014, the baug redevelopment was assuredly further stalled by a stunning move by the Wadia family in May. According to the *Mumbai Mirror* (Sadhwani 2014), the family had been in talks with the BPP to regain complete control over their five namesake colonies (Nowroze Baug, Jer Baug, Cusrow Baug, Rustom Baug, Ness Baug) and manage them through their trust, effectively reverting to the arrangement before these trusts were given over to Punchayet management—that is, back to Jerbai Wadia's founding wish that her family members manage the properties. Industrialist Nusli Wadia, head of the Wadia family and trustee of the N. N. and R. N. Wadia trusts, respectively, was reportedly unhappy about the BPP's slow pace and handling of baug issues. He cited several issues, most of which included immense litigation against the BPP, within the BPP board, and particularly with one of the BPP's most public and popular schemes.

The Punchayet's liquidity has always been an issue as it claims its outgoing expenses for welfare schemes and baug maintenance continually eat away at its liquid funds. Earlier that year, in a controversial move, Chairman Dinshaw Mehta oversaw the withdrawal of Rs. 100–200 crores ($160,000–$320,000) from fixed deposits from baug tenancy transfers to be shifted into paying for the Mobed Amelioration Scheme, which gives out payments to Parsi priests to subsidize their living costs. A source from the Wadia camp explained to the *Mumbai Mirror* that there was no provision that the monies from tenancy transfers could be used for anything other than the maintenance of the colonies. Hence, the withdrawal was a misuse of the trust's funds, a breach of trust. Chairman Mehta responded that nowhere was it written that the trust could not use these funds for other purposes and, in his characteristically frank manner, claimed, "We cannot give up five colonies which house needy Parsi families. The Wadias are giants in real estate industry and we believe they are eyeing the five colonies for commercial gains. Under no circumstances will we give up. We have been told that the Wadias might approach a court soon, but we are willing to put up a fight."[25] The article claimed that four of the Punchayet trustees had sided against Mehta and were in support of the Wadia decision. The BPP remained fraught with infighting since the trustee election campaigning in 2011 exposed weak loyalties and personal vendettas among the trustees. The Wadia group made no official statement or response to Mehta.

The willingness of the BPP to undertake litigation is itself part of the reason for the lack of liquid funds. Parsi periodicals often relate how costly the cases like *Kanga v. BPP* (described in chapter 4), which have reportedly cost the trust over three crore rupees ($555,000), are a drain on the cash funds of the trust. The tussle with the Wadias had stalled the payment of some of its other funds. This cash-flow problem caused the BPP to halt two popular schemes, the Mobed scheme, which supports priests, and the second-child scheme, which paid out funds to support Parsi couples with a second child.

While the Wadia announcement had no doubt stirred up panic and desperation for the BPP, which stood to lose five of its biggest and most prominent baugs, would Wadia have a right to take the colonies back? Technically, even the settlor of a trust, the person or persons who endow funds or assets into a trust, has relinquished their right to it later; that is, they have entirely alienated these assets but have ensured, through the trust, that the original objects be maintained in perpetuity. Nusli Wadia might have a case through two other avenues: First, as a Parsi, he is a beneficiary of the trust and may take the BPP before the charity commissioner if he deems the trust to be in breach of its objects as per the deed.[26] The court would need to interpret the deed to adjudicate the misuse of funds. Second, a stronger case could be made because the Wadia family retained some control over the five colonies through their arrangement with the BPP to manage them through the Wadia Committee of Management. Nusli Wadia, as trustee of the Wadia trusts and the Wadia Committee of Management, retains some discretionary power to uphold his great-grandmother's wishes that the baug be kept "as residences exclusively for the use and occupation of poor and middle-class Parsees professing the Zoroastrian faith." Jerbai's wish at the trust's founding remains legally and perhaps morally for her great-grandson an obligation he must fulfill. The BPP holds, in its defense, that providing material support for struggling Parsi priests is also part of its trust objects and that it had the obligation and discretion to distribute its funds. Both parties, therefore, were burdened and enabled to give by their present and future obligations.

Obligation's Asymmetries

Through the formalization of Jerbai Wadia's wishes, the trusteeship of her descendants, the management of the BPP, and the reception of her gift by people like Peshotan, the trust has structured many obligations for Parsis in the city. The trust mechanism transforms the property relation between owner and asset into a split relation of obligation and use with the trustees and beneficiaries. Ownership is bifurcated into the fiduciary owner, the trustee(s), and the beneficial owner, the beneficiaries. Thus, the circulation of material assets, once endowed, and from then onward, becomes replaced with the circulation of this moral obligation through successive generations. The obligation, however, is not held by the trust's beneficiary but actually by the trustees. The beneficiary may choose to receive and enjoy the trust's assets and obligations but need not; they have no burden (tax or otherwise) of duty or responsibility within this asymmetrical relationship. For example, even though a Parsi is born a beneficiary of many trusts, they need not attend any fire temple, live in any kind of trust housing, nor avail of any of the welfare programs available to them. They must just be recognized as a Parsi. The trust, therefore, seems to trouble the giver-receiver binary of reciprocity, both in terms of the obligations owed and the temporality of those obligations.

Marcel Mauss held that the necessity of reciprocity was the basis of social relations creating a never-ending flow of gift exchange (Mauss 1990). For him, these cycles constituted the boundaries of a society by the very spirit imbued in the *res*. In his discussion of ancient Roman law, the giving of the *res* creates a legal tie to the original family or house of the giver; the receiver then feels this obligation to return. "It remains bound to him and binds its present possessor until the latter is freed by the execution of the contract, namely by the compensatory handing over of the thing, price, or service that, in turn, will bind the initial contracting party" (Mauss 1990, 64). Unlike the receiver of a gift who is now in possession of a *res* imbued with the spirit of the giver, the beneficiary of a trust has no obligation to take the benefit nor any legal obligation to reciprocate. If Mauss held that the system of gift-giving constituted society because of its very incompleteness as there was always something left to be repaid, in a potentially endless cycle of credit and debt, then what might this imply about the kinds of social relations that the trust engenders?

The trust creates asymmetrical relations between its social categories that, however "complete," always hold one party (the trustee) under obligation. At the same time, the other may choose to accept or ignore this relationship. Within the Indian context, Heim describes *dāna* (the Hindu gift) as "unilateral and unreciprocated. As a one-way gesture, usually vertical and aimed upward to the religious elite, it gives rise to a relationship that cannot be defined according to the values of equality, mutuality, and balance cherished in modern perspectives" (Heim 2004, xx). The trust's asymmetry does not connote an upward hierarchy (nonelite to elite), as Heim shows in her discussion of *dāna*. While managing giving does endow the trustees with power, it also binds and burdens them with what they *should be* doing regarding the settlor's intentions. At the same time, the beneficiary carries no obligation to give back.

However, it is not just the practice of giving itself but the expectations and disappointments of future giving that frame relationships. Biruk (2018) shows how the expectations of reciprocity in data gathering (interviews for soap in Malawi) frame how research participants are recruited and retained to produce "clean data." For Parsi trustees and beneficiaries, receiving assets and services from the trust is entangled in a complex moral distribution. Many trustees I spoke with seemed frustrated that Parsis treated the trust as a never-ending giver without any compunction to reciprocate and that this had caused mass entitlement in the community and was a source of general laziness.[27] The beneficiary's lack of obligation to reciprocate—that is, they only take, never give—is understood by trustees, like Ardvan above, as a sign of ingratitude. Yet, it can also be read as a logical expression of their place in the tripartite structure of the trust. It is trustees who are obliged by the mechanism to continue to distribute the charity per the intention of the settlor. The logic of the trust reorganizes religious giving into an intergenerational relation of obligation and accountability held by the trustees, not the beneficiaries.

Jerbai's present then, was not just the giving in trust of her vast estates and funds but also ensuring accountability through time. Her gift to the Parsis was the obligation she attached to those properties. However, these obligations move through the chronotope of the city asymmetrically. Jerbai's descendants, as trustees, should adhere to her wishes, and the trust should provide for its beneficiaries, who legally do not have to reciprocate in kind or at all. In this way, the charitable presents of founders like Jerbai set the trust, the trustee, and the beneficiary into a perpetual asymmetrical relationship hinged together in perpetuity.

Besides large donations, which come only occasionally, the trust receives tenancy payments, small fees, and interest earned on its conservative investments. The trust and trustees see redevelopment as a way to receive and make good on the investment that the trust itself has made in the city by accruing so much real estate value over time. The change in pugree regulations shows once again how law and capital are so intimately tied together, as this shift has allowed for a once-dormant landscape of real estate circulation to be mobilized, awakening the potential for capital movement. The legal shift has allowed Jerbai's perpetual wish to now attach to an accelerating velocity of urban development.

The following chapters will examine some of the effects of these new attachments. They will focus squarely on the organizational form of trust, its ways of giving, and how these asymmetrical obligations form the contours of kinship and disputes within the community. The beneficiaries are in a relationship with Jerbai's wish, yet they may receive benefit only directly from the trustees' obligation to give. The trustees cannot give back to her, as she had a mortal life, but only be beneficiaries, which is why that designation (who is counted as a beneficiary) has such high importance. Hence, while the trustees must give to all Parsis, because of the structure of the trust, they also may get to define who is a Parsi. These shifting definitions over time are taken up in the following two chapters.

CHAPTER 3. **NO HOUSE, NO SPOUSE**

The Bombay Parsi Punchayet

The landscape of charitable offices in Mumbai today is large and very complex. There are scores of government welfare programs, nondenominational NGOs, and religious charities; all are denoted in the trust directory mentioned in the previous chapters, which runs over a thousand pages and is in the digitalization process. Again, in wanting to research an understudied topography of real estate betwixt and between private housing and informal settlements, I focused most of my research on real estate that was communally owned by charitable trusts, and within that, on Parsis; since the community is such a prominent land owner, to whom I had access. Even though there are multitudes of Parsi trusts in Mumbai that provide a variety of subsidized housing for Parsis, much of my fieldwork focused on the Bombay Parsi Punchayet (BPP), primarily due to its prominent presence in Mumbai, as well as its role in the governance of the community at large. As an amalgam of several smaller trusts and funds that were once personal and familial assets, the BPP today is an example of how the trust mechanism functions to professionalize and bureaucratize religious giving.

The BPP offices on D. N. Road are in a grand Indo-Saracenic building (see figure 3.1), which primarily houses a Parsi school. This is a bit of a misnomer these days, as although it was founded and run by a Parsi and is currently managed by a Parsi trust, the school has only a few Parsi students in it today. They are given admission and a tuition waiver to entice more Parsi parents to enroll their children, although most Parsis of means seem to prefer to send

FIGURE 3.1. Building of the Parsi Punchayet, D.N. Road, Fort. Photo by author.

their children to convent or international schools. The main hallway of the building is quite grand, with a huge and beautiful curved wooden staircase. There is also a small elevator cubicle, but its age and slack pace made me reconsider in favor of the stairs. As I ascended the staircase, with many of the steps worn down into a concave surface by years of use, the sound of children, and often the sight of many of them running about in their smart uniforms, slowly gave way to the sounds of a working bureaucracy, with phones ringing and office workers walking briskly.

At the top of the stairs, one immediately sees the insignia of the BPP with its image of two winged bulls, harkening back to the Achaemenid Empire of Persia. Next to the front entrance was a long bench with several people waiting in the center of the hall. One end leads into the main office hall, encased by cabins, enclosed offices belonging to the senior staff. On the other side is the BPP boardroom, where meetings are held, and the site of the library, the BPP's small archive of its own life story.

The main hall is vast, with its high ceilings, which make it appear even more prominent. Many rows of ceiling fans further cool down the big room. There were many desks in the middle section, each with stacks of papers in folders held closed by string. A few desks had large desktop computers, but almost none seemed to be turned on. The main staff of the BPP were primarily middle-aged, both men and women, with several clerks who walked at a quicker clip to either pick up or deliver something. The male support staff were primarily in slacks and shirts, while the women wore either *salvar kameez*, *kurta* tops, or sometimes frocks, which are particular to Parsi and Christian women in Mumbai. These dresses are usually cotton and fall below the knee. Most of the staff were Parsi, but not exclusively, especially the clerks.

While I was hoping to have sustained time at the BPP offices for fieldwork, the trustees and officers I spoke with, while interested and forthcoming during interviews, did not wish to have someone hanging around all the time, especially since there were so many squabbles between trustees. My time there was mostly by appointment, except when using the small archive, consisting of a few glass-fronted Godrej cabinets in the boardroom. Initially, my days there were spent alone, only interrupted when a clerk would politely ask me to leave if a meeting was to commence. After a few days in the archive, an older staff member, "Mr. Mehta," was appointed to assist me. I assured the staff that I needed no assistance with the few bookshelves of materials, but it was made clear that Mr. Mehta would remain seated behind me for the duration of my stay. As I began to understand that my presence had caused some worry, I agreed and continued to read through materials in the archive while Mr. Mehta sat behind me against the wall, more often than not, nodding to sleep in the heat of the late afternoon.

When the BPP CEO finally had a moment to meet with me, I was very eager, as he was the senior-most permanent administrator of this enormous institution. I was told by the clerk who usually waited at the front of the hall to announce myself to the clerk in the back for "Mr. Batliwala." I filled out a small note with my name and occupation and was asked to wait, which became awkward as there were no chairs available, and I was forced to hover beside a desk where a staff member was conversing with a beneficiary. A middle-aged woman in a simple dress stood before me and pleaded with the clerk to let her speak with Mr. Batliwala on an urgent matter. She looked quite desperate. The clerk obliged, while the woman behind the desk curtly assured the waiting woman that her request would not be possible that day, as that amount of money was not available without the approval of the chairman. Just then, Mr. Batliwala stepped out. I recognized him from the BPP publication I had been studying before I arrived. The clerk first directed him to the waiting woman and Mr. Batliwala confirmed the same amount quoted before; she looked disheartened and pleaded, making eye contact with me as I tried to signal some empathy with her. Mr. Batliwala then offered her less than the amount she wanted on the spot, or she could return after he received permission from the chairman for more. She pleaded again, this time more desperately, which caused me and the others nearby to look away to avoid embarrassing her further. Mr. Batliwala, now in a reassuring tone, asked her to wait while he ushered me into his office. As we were seated in his cabin, a small, windowed office with a desk and a few chairs, Mr. Batliwala let out a frustrated sigh. I asked if I should return another time, but he wearily shook his head and mentioned that pleas like the one we had just witnessed happened almost every day.

Mr. Batliwala had degrees in commerce and law and began accounting for trusts until he acceded to the CEO position. He joked that the trustees came and went every seven years, as is their term of office, but he had been there for many years and would also volunteer his accounting services at other trusts and charities. Upon his desk were several sheets of paper and notes covered by glass that he would often point to as he spoke, but otherwise, his cabin was empty of files. He described the various projects the BPP managed and publicized in its newest venture, a monthly newsletter of about thirty glossy pages, *The BPP Review*.[1] The newsletter was a way to let the community know about all the "multifarious" activities the BPP manages. Multifarious indeed. At that time in 2011, the BPP managed the Doongerwadi funerary grounds, about fifteen housing colonies spread all over the city, two temples, a rest home, an eldercare facility, a health clinic, an employment bureau, a matrimonial bureau, a Parsi museum, an IVF facility, and a student hostel. It administered the funds and operations of several educational scholarships, welfare payments to poor Parsis, and "housing and rent subsidies to the deserving."[2] Mr. Batliwala ended by proclaiming that the BPP would serve a Parsi "from the womb to the tomb."

In actuality, the BPP does even more than provide a lifetime of services for Parsis. The Indian state also recognizes it as the representative of Paris-Irani Zoroastrians to the government. It nominates delegates to the Parsi Matrimonial Court, which deals with Parsi family law (marriage, divorce, inheritance).[3] While it is empowered by the state, it is also checked by the Office of the Charity Commissioner, which annually overseas its budgets and expenditures and hears the complaints of any beneficiaries or feuding trustees. Furthermore, the Punchayet is recognized as the apex body of the Parsis for all of India and is the leader of the umbrella organization, the Federation of Parsi Zoroastrian Anjumans of India (FPZAI), which coordinates the participating regional community associations and trusts in India.[4] Other scholars have deftly shown its transitions from a council of elders to a formal trust through the centuries (Palsetia 2001; Desai 1977).

The focus of this chapter will be to analyze the BPP as a functioning religious bureaucracy, one obliged to manage a portion of the property and funds of an ethnoreligious minority. It will examine its role as the Parsis' largest landlord and the particular ways it wishes to promote Parsi family life and its reproduction through bureaucratic programs and procedures.[5] It will examine how demography becomes a kind of fact that needs to be acted upon (Poovey 1998). Unquestionably, the BPP's workings affect Parsis in Mumbai and beyond today, but how does the organizational form of this charity, as a large trust and bureaucracy, relate to these effects? Through methodologies from the emerging field of the anthropology of bureaucracy, the chapter will examine how the trust itself offers some interesting insights into the "confluence of materialities (physical structures, technologies), discourses (personal assurances, rules, laws), and the experience of time" within this bureaucracy (Hoag 2011, 86; 2014). It will show how the BPP spatially wields Parsi property to ensure particularly gendered forms of Parsi propriety.

Within work on religion, the anthropology of Christianity, for instance, tends to focus more on denominational structures and beliefs. In contrast, more needs to be analyzed about the extensive network of Christian bureaucracies and their internal practice. Interestingly, for Islam, the huge wealth of *waqf* studies and those on Islamic finance have looked very closely at governing boards, halal regulators, and the workings of Islamic banking (Maurer 2006; Rudnyckyj 2011), but these tend to juxtapose an "Islamic way" against the norms of Western finance and money management. While most scholarship on the anthropology of bureaucracy in South Asia focuses on the state or state institutions (Hull 2012b; A. Gupta 2012; N. Mathur 2016), little has been written explicitly on religious bureaucracies, with the exception of Appadurai (1981) and Presler (1987). Within South Asian studies, we receive glimpses of analyses on religious bureaucracies through scholarship on religious charities (Kozlowski 1985) and temple networks (Appadurai 1977, 1981; Appadurai and Breckenridge 1976; Breckenridge 1976), seen mainly through the frames of the religious and secular. This chapter attempts to look at a religious trust and focus on its own logics of bureaucracy and organization and how those logics affect its charitable mandates and obligations in the light of contemporary Parsi demography.

Direct Giving to Philanthropy

From the time Zoroastrians experienced minority status, first in Iran and then in India, charitable giving was a way to serve the poor and maintain religious boundaries. Several authors, like White (1991), have written very convincingly about the role of charity as a mode of communal identity preservation among the Parsis.[6] I wish to take this a step further. I show that not only the funds and services brought about by charity but also the very organizational form of charity, through the trust, has very particular effects on social relations within the community today because of the way the trust structures social relations and the temporality of those relations. As the Parsi community has transitioned over time, so has its modes of giving and its governing structure, the BPP.

Early Parsi charity in India after settlement in Gujarat was mainly employed in the service of the poor, enabling them to be initiated into the faith and for *ghambars* (communal feasts). Rustum Manock of Surat (1635–1721) became renowned for philanthropy after becoming one of the first brokers to early British merchants. He used his wealth to aid the poor and paid the jizya (the poll tax levied on non-Muslims) for the entire Parsi community in the area. His descendants were crucial figures in constructing much of the communal infrastructure necessary for Parsi settlement in Bombay. White shows, through the life of Rustum Manock, how his charitable giving corresponded to various moments of crisis that were obtained in Surat (White 1991, 314). Manock's giving was directly to the recipient without the aid of formal intermediaries.

In contrast, Manock's grandson established institutional giving through the Parsi Punchayet. His charitable works narrowed in on Parsis alone and aspired to circumscribe community boundaries rather than to respond to crises. Manock's heirs "helped to create the institutional structures within which Parsis conducted community affairs, while those very structures served to create a minimum set of religious and social criteria, adherence to which defined one as a Parsi in the more complex setting of Bombay" (White 1991, 318). Nineteenth-century Parsis were eager endowers of their assets through the instrument of the trust, and for a multitude of reasons. Mitra Sharafi has shown that in a larger sense, Parsis did not avoid interacting with the colonial state but pushed through it "protect[ing] community interests to a significant degree by embracing the methods of colonial law and infiltrating its institutions" (2015, 9). This was a time of significant wealth accumulation for many in the community. They migrated from Gujarat to Bombay and shifted from traditional occupations like farming and weaving to international commerce and trade. As will be further discussed in chapter 6, Bombay merchants of all communities made enormous fortunes in the China trade and invested in real estate, both private and for religious purposes.

If charitable in intent, trusts could avoid the reach of the Raj's tax regime. The selection of which assets the state allowed to be exempt from taxes remains a powerful indicator that these assets were viewed as being used for proper charitable purposes. While wealthy individuals like Rogay, Sassoon, and Shakershett endowed properties and funds for their respective communities (Ranganathan 2019; Weil 2019), settlors like the Petits, Jeejeebhoys, Camas, Wadias, Adenwalas, and Chinoys endowed lands, buildings, and funds to the Parsi community. Their largess allowed for the migration of their poorer coreligionists from Gujarat to Bombay and built hospitals, schools, and other public works. As urban land and real estate became popular and stable sources of investment, they also became targets of colonial revenue collectors who had formerly concentrated on rural revenue (Dossal 2010, Section I). These settlors accrued immediate social capital and prestige but also longevity as their legacies remain imprinted in the streets and buildings of the city.

The BPP, as an endowment, was established through the creation of a property trust in 1884 to preserve Zoroastrian funerary grounds in southern Mumbai (Desai 1977). However, the Punchayet as a governance structure has been traced to at least 1725, if not earlier. There is some disagreement about the origins of the BPP. In my view, this disagreement is based on the varying forms and functions of the Punchayet. As a committee overseeing aspects of communal life, the Punchayet could date back to the seventeenth century, and in its insignia, the BPP holds its origins to 1681. However, as a formal legal endowment, the trust as we know it today was settled in 1884 (Palsetia 2001, 66). Sapur F. Desai, in his internal account of the BPP as its Secretary, noted that by 1732 some funds were being dispersed, but "we do not have a clinching record to show how the money was collected and who kept it and dispensed it" (1977, 129). The Punchayet has known many iterations and has moved through phases of being a quasireligious and powerful body to a circumscribed administrative institution (Davar 1949; Desai 1977; Palsetia 2001; Hinnells 2005; Hinnells and Williams 2007).

Most see the BPP's transformation in four phases. The first dates from about 1630 to 1830, when it was officially the head of the community for social and moral issues under the Portuguese and early British colonial periods. The second phase from the 1830s saw the trusteeship becoming hereditary. Many saw this as delegitimizing its goals, causing Sir Jamshedji

Jeejeebhoy, a powerful China trader, industrialist, and trustee, to found a rival organization, the Parsi Benevolent Institution, in 1849. Then in 1851, the two bodies were merged with Sir Jeejeebhoy at the head, marking the third phase. This state later became the contentious basis of the famous suit *Petit v. Jeejeebhoy* in 1906–1908. After the *Petit* case, the fourth phase finds the BPP as the custodian of the funds and properties but perhaps continually spilling over its mandates.

"The Petit Case"

The case discussed in the following section is vital not only for its contribution to the legal definition of who might be a Parsi today but also because many of its details are known and repeated by most Parsis in India to either defend or attack its outcome in terms of conversion and intermarriage;[7] that is, the case is part of the Parsi repertoire of common knowledge, albeit with the facts understood in multiple ways. While the main issue before the court from 1906 to 1908 was the transmission of trusteeship through inheritance, the more inflammatory part of this case was religious conversion and the rights of converts to trust properties. Ratanji Dadabhoy Tata, a famous and wealthy Parsi businessman, married a French woman named Suzanne Briere in 1902. Very controversially, she had a *navjote* (Zoroastrian initiation ceremony) performed by a high priest. Tata claimed that she was granted the privileges of being a Parsi, including access to fire temples and placement in the towers of silence upon her death. Due to the unprecedented nature of such an initiation and the high profile of Tata himself, a very intense debate ensued, along with the formation of a committee to discuss *juddin* (non-Parsi) initiations.

The BPP and its secretary at the time, Dr. Jivanji J. Modi, sought legal counsel, which came to no resolution, and the case was brought to the Bombay High Court in 1906 as the *Parsi Panchayat Case, Suit no. 689*. The plaintiffs were members of the Tata family and included other Parsis of note who held that initiated persons should be recognized as Zoroastrians and therefore entitled to trust benefits. They also pointed to an electoral discrepancy that would nullify the authority of the current standing BPP trustees, who were vehemently against Briere's initiation. The BPP was represented by Jamsetji Jeejeebhoy, another titan of industry. The case involved many aspects of trust law and the authority structure of the BPP and was followed avidly by the Parsi press (Hinnells 1985). While deciding against the rights of non-Parsi spouses to Parsi spaces, the *Petit* judgment went beyond the case to establish a distinction between Parsi and Zoroastrian, and the rights of intermarried Parsi men to have their children counted as Parsi, but not the same for women, a custom taken up further in the next chapter. Ratanji and Sooni, as she was now called, had five children. They include J. R. D. Tata, who has served as the Tata Group's chairman, and were all recognized as Parsis, as their father was Parsi.[8]

After the turn of the century and this landmark civil case, the BPP's role was redefined to be the custodian of the funds and properties of the trust(s) under its purview and to represent the community before the government. In terms of its organizational form, this judgment constituted the fourth phase of the BPP as we encounter it today. It narrowed the focus of the BPP as a trust to be a manager of its endowed funds and properties. This case exemplified the intimate connection between issues of religious propriety and the organization of religious charity; as the definition of who could be recognized as a Parsi narrowed, so too did the mandate of the BPP. However, the number of people receiving aid from the Punchayet grew as its charitable mission narrowed after the *Petit* case, from around 75 people in 1871 to about 3,733 by the end of the 1930s.[9] Litigation has been crucial to defining the BPP as it is today. Such court cases dealing with the processes and issues of administration and bureaucracy have often been, at their core, about who is a Parsi and a worthy beneficiary.[10] This is a result of the specific entanglement of a religious community, bureaucracy, and the trust form.

"Crisis": Death by Numbers

From the mid-nineteenth century until the post-WWII period, Parsis were a small but highly successful community in their estimation and by the measure of colonials and other Indians. Several Parsis were heralded as captains of industry, especially in sea trade, shipbuilding, and textiles, some of colonial India's most profitable sectors. At its peak, the Parsi population of Bombay reached over 100,000, and the city was teeming with public works and settlements founded or managed by Parsis. Many of Bombay's schools, hospitals, and roads bore Parsi names, and the community was known for its philanthropy for both communal and cosmopolitan purposes. While Parsi identity and status were at one time marked by economic success and philanthropy, by the end of the Second World War, a new imaginary took hold. Tanya Luhrmann's (1996) ethnography addresses the transformation of the community's self-perception of being a contributor to Indian modernity to one saturated with the sentiment of decay and anxieties about community decline. Indeed, since the 1980s, this trope of decline has been evoked in all kinds of media relating to the ever-decreasing numbers of Parsis in Mumbai and the world: "The Parsi Crisis," "Dire Demographics of Parsi Zoroastrians," and "Why Is India's Wealthy Parsi Community Vanishing?"[11]

Several theories of the demographic decline of the Parsis circulate, including low fertility rates and the genetic consequences of endogamy, and Paul Axelrod notes that the Parsis of India have experienced one of the most dramatic population declines ever recorded outside of Europe (1990, 404). In his study, Axelrod found that Parsis have a history of late nuptiality and low nuptiality. Seeing a close correlation between marriage practices and levels of education, Axelrod found that 35 percent of those educated above high school never married, and the average age of marriage for women who had completed college was 27.1. This late age for marriage can be seen as early as the 1890s. In contrast to such local cultural factors, high levels of emigration and exogamy make demographic figures problematic. Younger community members are increasingly internationally mobile, creating relatively large diasporic communities in North America and Europe.[12] Furthermore, it is estimated that one in three Parsi women marry out of the community. The acceptance of exogamy for men, but not women, was one of the outcomes of the *Petit* judgment, albeit in a section that was *obiter dicta* (of no precedential value). Even though this section of the case has no formal legal standing, many conservative Parsis act as if it does. They often refer to the *Petit* judgment as legitimizing their narrower definition of who may count as a Parsi. In many cases, exogamy by Parsi women is equivalent to excommunication for all practical purposes. For instance, any children born to such unions are not counted by the Punchayet.[13]

A survey of young Parsis conducted by the Tata Institute of Social Sciences in 2008 found similar patterns to Axelrod's in that Parsis, mostly involuntarily, choose to live in extended families and more and more desire "love marriages" as opposed to those arranged by family members. Much energy goes into finding a suitable partner who, combined with one's income, can afford a flat separate from either set of parents. Many young Parsis, therefore, wait to marry until the criteria are fulfilled. This desire to avoid joint family housing may conflict with the urban social environment of Mumbai with its lack of affordable housing space, characterized by Appadurai as "the most public drama of disenfranchisement in Mumbai" (2000, 28). These studies and my research emphasize how constraints on living space provide a material context for Parsi demographic decline and a spatial imaginary where available space is seen as a possible solution to the declining numbers (Upton 1996).

However, as the following will show, a bureaucratic call to crisis about demography must be analyzed with care. It is also a discursive and epistemological practice involving varying definitions, subjective accounting, and statistics.

Parsiana, a very popular reform-leaning, Parsi-centered periodical with a global circulation, publishes the names of children born and the names of the deceased in every issue in the last pages of the magazine.[14] This might not be unusual for a community periodical, but the deaths are not only listed as obituaries but rather in the style of a ledger, with the deaths outnumbering the births almost three to one. This is accompanied by a table of statistics and marked by an asterisk: "These figures pertain to information provided to and collected by Parsiana. They do not represent the total number of births, marriages, and deaths in the Zoroastrian community in India and Abroad."[15] Here demography is "not a question of obscure statistical analysis, but a prominent element in Parsi consciousness and debate" (Hinnells 2005, 54). No matter the disagreement about the causes and extent of the decline, the overall sentiment of demographic crisis was ubiquitously expressed in my interviews and is a vivid part of Parsi self-perception in Mumbai. Older Parsis joke wistfully that one should touch a Parsi for good luck before they are extinct, like the white tiger. During my fieldwork, while I encountered sentiments that echoed Luhrmann's analysis, my interlocutors often spoke of crisis and decline in real terms: census figures and counts. Parsi life in India had become a numbers game.

Bill Maurer (2002) connects the work of accounting as audit, narration, and religio-cosmopolitical judgment in Islamic finance. He concludes that accounting is a "specific form of rhetoric that occludes its own rhetoricity," insisting on its own transparency when in fact, it is a form of argumentation at various scales (Maurer 2002, 662). In the previous chapter, we examined several forms of accounting and accountability, some inherited by descendants like Tanaz and Nusli Wadia, and others by elected trustees like Ardvan and Firdaus. The very particular self-understanding of a declining minority by Indian Parsis today has congealed around this condition of demographic decline, and many trusts have set themselves the task of ameliorating this predicament. The continuing discourse of demographic crisis brings forth specific kinds of productions of knowledge and, in turn, unique interventions. Janet Roitman reminds us that whether these anxieties are real or founded in evidence, to name something a crisis is a highly efficacious claim (2013, 17). If we see crisis as one kind of prognosis of time, these calls to crisis by the BPP and echoed by the media at once denote a history of better times and a present and future that are growing more uncertain.

From its inception, the BPP has managed sacred spaces and funds for medical and educational support for its beneficiaries—that is, Bombay Parsis, especially the care of widows, the disabled, and poor Parsis. They receive a kind of dole each month. In the 2000s, the ubiquitous discussion of community crisis was fueled by the results of the 2001 Census. The BPP shifted the focus of much of its giving away from welfare programs targeting poor and elderly Parsis toward increasing the population of Parsis, a new moral imperative and obligation that all Parsis now carry. Various initiatives were announced to reverse the trends of Parsis marrying late, having few children, or marrying out of the community altogether. To encourage young Parsis to marry each other early and have as many children as possible, the BPP had already instituted a three-child policy in 1993 wherein a family would receive monthly aid for their third and subsequent children. This policy was amended to reward families for even their second child in 2009. The Punchayet continued to increase efforts to promote positive demographic growth through forms of giving, particularly with housing, culminating in a controversial IVF scheme.

From Nomination to Election: Becoming a Trustee

In 2005, alarmed by demographic decline and the growing trends toward intermarriage, a group of conservative Parsis formed the World Alliance for Parsi Irani Zoroastrians (WAPIZ). The group was and continues to be funded by a Parsi soft-drink magnate from Gujarat. The group was founded in direct opposition to the World Zoroastrians Organization (WZO), which allowed memberships for non-Zoroastrian spouses. WAPIZ gained a considerable following and began to have more and more influence on issues managed by the Punchayet. Critically, it was the status of the trust's funerary ground, Doongerwadi (discussed further in chapter 5), that urged WAPIZ members to become more involved in the BPP organization, as many of the standing trustees were considered to be too liberal and a danger to this sacred site.

By 2006, the BPP trustees, split ideologically between conservatives and liberals, were in constant disagreement. The CEO at the time resigned after many years of service, recounting to me, "The situation had grown perverse. We [couldn't] be at war every day." Many sitting trustees pushed toward making the BPP more democratic by having elections for the trusteeship instead of closed nominations. Since 1908, the BPP trustees had been nominated and agreed upon by an electoral college called the Anjuman Committee. The committee was made up of only those who donated to the trust (who got a double vote) and other notable Parsis, around three thousand people. In past generations, trustees had been illustrious men and women from highly successful industrial and trade families such as the Jeejeebhoys and Petits, a who's who of the rich and famous in Bombay's merchant history.[16] Beginning in 2006, six of the seven sitting trustees petitioned the High Court to change the 1908 election scheme of the Punchayet. These trustees felt that WAPIZ was stacking the nominations from within the Anjuman Committee. The court decided that trustees would be elected by Universal Adult Franchise (UAF)—that is, by any adult Parsi registered with the BPP to vote in Mumbai.[17] There would now be about forty thousand voters, and many hoped this would "reduce the scope to purchase votes" within the Anjuman Committee.[18]

This was a dramatic shift in terms of the makeup of the institution, and it had almost immediate implications for the kinds of projects the BPP undertook as well as longer-term results. In the older system, the Anjuman Committee had the effect of many trustees providing part of the trust's corpus. Investments with those monies were made judiciously and conservatively as trustees saw the BPP as part of fulfilling their philanthropic legacies. The role of the trustee was honorary and taken to be a duty of the privileged philanthropist with a protective vision of the community; a noblesse oblige (Hanson 2015). The trusteeship was a moral post with only a secondary managerial focus.

Today, the UAF system has shifted many of the ways in which the BPP achieves its objects, charitable or not. Elections now require high levels of campaigning, either with many volunteers able to reach out to Parsis all over the city, or great deals of money for advertising, or both. During my fieldwork, two elected trustees were social workers who went door-to-door with their proposals. Another two were part of WAPIZ, which had its own newsletter as a mouthpiece. A further elected trustee was Dadrawala, who specializes in trusts and ironically is the only one who supported the UAF to begin with. The chairman at the time, Dinshaw Mehta, was the only incumbent with vast experience with the Brihanmumbai Municipal Corporation (BMC). The seventh trustee was a successful Parsi real estate developer who is said to have spent crores on his campaign.

I was able to attend at least thirty election and campaign events in Mumbai for the special election in 2011 initiated after a trustee's resignation. Each campaign meeting had senior citizens bussed in from various colonies and was often followed by lavish spreads of food to entice attendance. Most of the crowd within campaign events were seniors, while younger Parsis, returning home from work, milled about behind the rows of plastic chairs and sometimes watched along. As election day neared, the atmosphere of the meeting grew tenser as the two candidates seemed neck and neck. Many of the sitting trustees also made speeches during the campaigns, favoring one side over the other, which made their trustee work more antagonistic. At one of the last events, I was close by when I heard yelling, which quickly escalated into a fist fight, and a crowd swiftly formed around it. Clearly, the stakes were high both in terms of reputational and perhaps financial gains.

While the trustee position is still honorary, with no direct payment for service, it was no surprise to many that housing and real estate became a big focus of the current terms. Many in the community were unhappy with the 2008 board of trustees, who seemed to be in unending squabbles over personal and trust differences. During this tenure, enormous funds were also allocated to fighting legal cases discussed in the next chapter, one of which reached the Indian Supreme Court before being settled through mediation. Litigation costs discussed in chapter 4 pose an enormous strain on the BPP's liquidity, leaving trustees looking for new ways to encourage growth in their cash corpus.

In one sense, the UAF significantly elevates the status of the beneficiaries of the BPP, who overwhelmingly supported universal adult franchise for the trust. The UAF system further enforced the idea of a global community; wherein all Parsis could participate if they registered and appeared in Mumbai to vote, all Parsis were made beneficiaries. However, along with this status came many more lawsuits brought by individual beneficiaries of the trust as well as class suits pursued through self-titled "watchdog" groups (L. Vevaina 2021).

"No House, No Spouse"

Today's Parsis are not what they were even fifteen years back. We have lost ethics and morals and the respect of other communities. We always wash our "dirty linen" in public. Our forefathers had foresight; we all have a roof over our head. Our youngsters don't have ambition; they wait for flats to get married, and it may be that we are becoming ghettoized.
—Interview with housing trustee, 2011

The population statistics discussed above had legitimated the BPP's policies to turn to provide housing, the trust's most valuable and productive asset, as the cure for the present and future demographic crises. Fully embodying a spatial imagination (Upton 2016), the BPP trustees looked toward housing and real estate to manage the crisis of numbers. As a former BPP official put it to me, "no house; no spouse," relating the reluctance of many young Parsis to marry (and bear children) without the ability to live as a nuclear family in a separate flat from their respective parents. Constructing Parsi housing was seen as the first step toward increasing communal reproduction. Another former BPP official was insistent in an interview with me in his office in Fort that there was only a small window within which the BPP had to work. With a pencil and paper, he jotted something down on his large desk and pondered aloud: "We have late marriage because we educate our girls; they keep their careers so a child is possible only in their thirties; then early menopause too, much earlier than the Indian average. So, how many childbearing years?" He never finished the calculation but only held up his fist with his thumb raised and waved it back and forth with a glum expression, a sign that it was a "no-go," no hope. His depressing prognosis connected both production and reproduction, the social and biological, naturalizing and medicalizing a form of population management and biopolitics. In addition to this truncated reproductive window, he believed living within housing colonies was critical to the retention of everyday Parsi customs and the reproduction of community norms and codes. He had been key to establishing the payment programs for Parsis to have more children, a bureaucratic policy now vacated of its gendered politics.

A Parsi priest further encapsulated this sentiment best: "When we distribute ourselves thinly in cultureless, concrete structures, there is no life in that. Intermingling leads to dilution of cultures."[19] While Peshotan from the last chapter articulated the potential loss with redevelopment at the level of communal sociality, the priest expresses this spatial imaginary in more charged terms: that Parsis would, as a culture, be diluted.[20]

Hence, the population growth sought by the Punchayet for the community was not about sheer numbers but also about the quality of the community. At the time, about one in three Parsi women married out of the community, and their children were not counted as Parsis by trusts like the Punchayet. Retaining within the fold intermarried Parsi women and their children would be a simple and fast measure to increase the population numbers. Still, the BPP remained within the frame of endogamy, at least for Parsi women, and a preference for Parsis living among one another. By 2009, the discourse around demographic decline among the Parsis in India had reached a fever pitch, and in a significant media announcement, the Punchayet proposed to build 3,125 new flats for Parsis in the city.[21]

Therefore, while it may seem questionable that a trust with dwindling beneficiaries should spend millions on constructing more housing only for Parsis, many Parsis and charity officials I interviewed took the new housing projects as a logical organizational response to demographic decline. They wished to concretize their spatial logic through their bureaucratic and organizational processes.

Colin Hoag reminds us that bureaucracies "fundamentally prescribe or proscribe behavior of an ideal, universal, and abstract sort . . . ideals which are always in deferral, and they can operate as depoliticizing technologies, masking the exercise of power in the guise of an always emergent—but never attained—perfect order" (2011, 82). Here the calls to demographic crisis broke this bureaucratic deferral and called the ideal (Parsis living with Parsis and having Parsi children) into being in the present. The demographic crisis narrative allowed a reshuffling of who was prioritized as worthy of the trust's beneficence. It entailed two critical shifts in the workings of the BPP and who precisely the trust was mandated to benefit.

The first was a shift in who could claim priority to receive trust housing. To rent a flat, a Parsi might either inherit the rent certificate from a parent, child, or sibling or make a new application to the Punchayet. Shifting away from the poor and needy Parsi that used to receive priority for housing, the BPP now gives priority to young couples of childbearing age, whom it may have brought together through the matrimonial services on its website. To allot its flats, the BPP has employed a "Merit Rating Scheme" for types (1) and (2) below, whereby each applicant for housing is rated by the board of trustees along several criteria. This scheme has caused much controversy and even litigation as the criteria and point system remain opaque, and flats are allotted out of application order. In 2006, in an interview with the then housing manager of the BPP, he related how he was constantly accused of "giving flats out of line," or widespread nepotism. The flats were always allotted at the trustees' discretion, but this new scheme made the process more occluded.

The second shift was to turn toward redeveloping buildings within their existing *baugs*, as discussed in the previous chapters with Nowroze Baug. Not surprisingly, this concentration of effort also coincides with Mumbai's enormous building and real estate boom since the 1990s. Since then, this relatively small community has had a flurry of building activity to augment their various housing benefits. The BPP has three housing typologies:

1 *Charity Flats*: These flats are rented out with little or no fees or rents attached. They are usually smaller and less maintained than

the other types and are in much older buildings. Since many of the families have lived there for generations, these flats are under Rent Act agreements, allowing no rent increase since 1947 levels. Other residents of charity flats are deemed tenants under the law; that is, they have, over time and through precedent, acquired the same rights as those under rent control.

2   *Leave & License/Tenancy Flats:* This is the majority of BPP housing stock. Most residents (some are legal tenants, some are not) pay heavily subsidized rents to the BPP. Residents who predate 1947 are legal tenants and fall under Mumbai's rent control laws. Some pay very low rent that has been unchanged for decades, but the BPP does levies and increases fees to make up for some of the loss. As people vacate these flats, the BPP is slowly trying to introduce the Leave & License scheme to all new residents. Rents and fees can range from Rs. 50 to 7,500 per month ($1–$150), and the license is on an eleven-month renewable cycle but does allow the BPP to evict someone who breaks the terms. One criterion for eviction is being a Parsi woman married out of the community.

3   *Ownership Flats:* This scheme was introduced in the 1980s but has had much more use since 1991. Under these agreements, newer flats are sold to Parsis only. The income to the trust is registered as a refundable security deposit, which does not count as income. Because of the BPP's fear that the new residents could resell to non-Parsis and hence revoke the Parsi-only character of the property, the new owners sign away or agree to limit their rights of resale. Also key to this typology, the owners only own the flat itself but no portion of the land that the building is built upon. Due to the restricted quality of the sale, these flats are usually priced significantly below the potential market value. Still, they are only affordable to upper-middle-class Parsis or Parsis from abroad. Ownership flats tend to be large, with separated bedrooms and living rooms (see figure 3.2).

Shifts in housing styles and the new schemes have shown the transitions and potential for more changes in how Parsi families are structured. Rural Parsis in the mid-nineteenth century were known to live within large joint-family arrangements, which remain the Indian norm. The earliest colonies, like Gilder Lane, somewhat replicated these structures in apartment settings by having much shared space, including shared bathroom and kitchen

FIGURE 3.2. Ownership buildings in Rustom Baug, Byculla. Photo by author.

facilities. Since the 1920s, these configurations began to be considered old-fashioned and inconvenient by many Parsis. The later baugs like Cusrow and Rustom Baug are constructed as a series of 4–6-story buildings with private entrances and 2–3-bedroom flats with private bathrooms and kitchens. Like Hilla Towers, discussed in chapter 2, the new leave and license flats being proposed instead look skyward to the "hi-finance" buildings that dot Mumbai's landscape, complete with rooftop swimming pools, doormen, and underground parking.[22] The new ownership flats are proposed to be even bigger, with the bedrooms larger than the common spaces and "modern amenities that will attract the rich Parsi investor," as one trustee told me. They are far from the older charity model, which privileged outdoor green space, meeting and prayer halls. While the profits are promised or earmarked for the poor of the community, the BPP's move into cash-rich high-stakes redevelopment can be seen as a giant leap away from its older charity model. The allotment of flats and, indeed, the entire workings of the BPP are subject to oversight by the courts via the office of the Charity Commissioner, making housing a core issue of individual and communal disputes that, in good Parsi tradition, take place in courts.

A Clash of Temporalities

The merit-rating scheme has awarded many a coveted flat. I met Behram at a colony fair, where several residents were selling their homemade crafts to earn money for some sporting equipment for the colony youth. The fair was in the open *maidan* of Rustom Baug and was dappled in the light from the setting sun before strings of overhead twinkle lights blinked on after sunset. Families walked about buying tickets to the very small, rented carnival rides. Many bought small snacks from established Parsi caterers and men and women selling home-cooked Parsi delicacies like *batasas* and *nan khatai* biscuits. Having never grown up around many Parsis, I found that the fair was a real testament to the kinds of communal sociality that Peshotan, from Nowroze Baug, had described of colony life.

At the fair, Behram, an office clerk in his forties, recounted how he had successfully applied for and received housing from the BPP through the merit-rating scheme. "You see, my brothers and I lived in a 'red-light' area," he exclaimed, "and we all applied in our twenties after becoming engaged. They [the Punchayet] met with us and checked all our documents and letters to make sure we were serious about marriage." Once a flat was granted, a notice was published in several Parsi periodicals as to the name of the proposed resident, asking for any evidence in objection to the application. It is not uncommon that there are objections that the applicant already has a good housing situation. Behram and each of his brothers received a charity flat within a few years. They have since married their respective betrothed and had children. "Many people try to trick, you see, but our case was real," he assured me. However, this type of success story was often overshadowed by the multiple rumors and cases of malfeasance in flat allotments by the Punchayet housing unit.

I visited the BPP housing manager in his office cabin one evening in 2011, and he motioned for me to sit down and ask him questions quickly. The trustees were in a meeting in the boardroom, and he had to wait around in case he was called in on a specific issue. "So, how does one apply for a flat?" I inquired. "Why, are you interested?" He worriedly asked. "No," I replied with a chuckle, "I just want to understand the process." He explained that a new applicant must pick up a form and submit it between 2:30 p.m. and 4:30 p.m. any day the office is open. They must submit all their details and provide an income certificate. Then they are issued a card with the application/case number, and it is up to them to renew the form every three years. Unlike other trusts I visited, the BPP keeps a running waitlist, not a list per available flat. Since the onus is on the applicant to renew the form, it could be possible that the applicants currently on the waitlist were not all good candidates for a flat by the time of availability. This seemingly benign bureaucratic application procedure is ripe for deferrals and uncertainty for the applicants. The BPP's new scheme had caused much controversy and even litigation, as the criteria and point system remained opaque. Cries of corruption continue to erupt when it is perceived that flats are allotted out of application order.[23]

The scheme prioritizes Parsi couples engaged to be married; the housing manager estimated that about 20 percent of applicants were in this category. They do jump the queue but must produce a marriage certificate before they may take possession of the flat. In the past, many men would pretend to be engaged to get the flat, "but now we investigate every case," he said, as he wagged his finger warningly. When a flat becomes vacant or the turn arrives, he inquires, "Is the form alive?" An investigation is then conducted in which a BPP official personally visits the current residence of each party, conducts interviews, and checks up on financials. Once a flat is granted, a notice is published in several Parsi periodicals as to the new residents' names, asking for any evidence in objection to the application. This allotment scheme of prioritizing those of child-bearing age over the more general category of the poor and needy caused many to bring the Punchayet before the charity commissioner.

In L. Vevaina (2018a), I analyzed the following case of the 104 through the story of my interlocutor, Niloufer. The analysis showed how the crisis narratives shifted the trust's framing of the "the good" and hence, its proper mandate. I showed that as the trust focused more and more on offering housing to young married couples, it moved away from prioritizing the poor and the needy. In the analysis here, I will show how the crisis narrative exposed a clash between a bureaucratic temporality and a reproductive one.

I met Niloufer in 2011 at her place of business and agreed not to use her real name in my research as she was part of an ongoing case against the Punchayet and feared backlash from her Parsi employers in the small shop where she worked. As we sat together, she almost cowered through the conversation. She winced even as I noted her initials in my notebook, which I immediately scratched out, noticing her discomfort. She told how, in 1991, she was married and with her husband was forced to move within the circuit of Parsi sanatoria housing every four months. As described in chapter 1, Parsi sanatoria were originally built in the city to temporarily house sick and recovering patients. To the dismay of their trustees, they have evolved to being rundown, permanent housing options for poorer Parsis. The various residents of Parsi sanatoria were required to move rooms or leave the residences every four months so that they would not have any case to claim tenancy and, therefore, legal permanence under the Rent Act.

In 1992, when her daughter was born, she filed her first application with the BPP for charity housing. As of 2007–2008, she and other Parsi families had not moved off the waiting list for housing that had stretched to three thousand applicants. Eventually, they banded together and became the 104 families who sued the BPP with the help of community advocates who assisted them legally and financially through the process. According to the trust's selection guidelines, Niloufer should have had first preference, having a low income and being newly married with a child on the way. But "other people with money got the flats first," she claimed, referring to alleged bribes being paid along with the application. "That's how some applications rise to the top of the pile."

In 2008, Niloufer and a block of applicants on the waitlist filed a court case to force the BPP to reveal how and why they had allotted certain flats. The case was finally resolved when the Bombay High Court appointed a former supreme court justice to carefully review all 104 cases and determine who deserved flats under the scheme. From the vantage of the current trustees, the case stemmed from a dispute in the scheme of allotting flats between the old (pre-2008) trustees and the new. Officially, the BPP claimed it prioritized marrying couples, priests, and those who needed to be relocated from "red light areas,"[24] like Behram. The 104 applicants, however, claimed that other applications were put at the top of the stack—given flats out of turn by bribing or currying favor with the BPP administration or trustees.

After the 104 cases were settled in 2010 by the retired judge reviewing every case individually, many families like Niloufer's were no longer viable candidates for charity housing. No wonder. After almost twenty years, Niloufer was no longer newly married nor expecting more children and was subsequently denied a charity flat. Saddened and deflated by the whole experience, Niloufer related, "Imagine what it's like having to shift flats every four months. My children could not even stay in the same schools because of the distances. We did it because people like us [the 104] have no choice in these things." Of the 104, one trustee told me that about 64 were still good candidates for flats, but the other 40 were not. One of the most significant issues in this case, as exemplified by Niloufer's story, was that because of the temporal delay from application to decision, many who were eligible and would have had priority at the time of application were now no longer eligible. The reproductive time window of Parsis, like Niloufer, had closed; it was a no-go. By shifting the priority of the housing applications, the BPP had put the 104 out of time.

Meeting Niloufer and other lower-income Parsis, who relied on trusts like the BPP for their residence, income, or medical care during my field-work, kept me wondering: in a community so well-endowed in land and real estate and so renowned for its philanthropy, how did so many people fall through the cracks? After all, the BPP is one of Mumbai's largest private landowners, with real estate for housing, schools, and hospitals all reserved for Parsis. Yet, as I found, by redefining the notion of good charity to address the demographic crisis, the BPP's policies privilege certain forms of giving and transfers that are slowly having dire effects on the more underprivileged segments of the community—ironically, the very segments that were to be the beneficiaries of charitable trusts in the first place (L. Vevaina 2018a). Was this a bureaucratic failure? Was the trust derelict in its mandate?

Colin Hoag describes dereliction as "a liminal state between the policy and the practice of that policy. The concept describes those moments when hopeful observers (e.g., clients, anthropologists, bureaucrats) of bureau-cratic processes become skeptical: when their prospective perspective on the paperwork not yet arrived slips into a retrospective perspective on bu-reaucratic failure" (2014, 411–12). The trust, however, unlike other types of bureaucracies, did have redress to this failure. A trust's objects are not rules; they have a different valence and legal standing, and with a charity com-missioner, an additional enforcement mechanism. Living thoroughly in the subjunctive mode after settlement, the trust, as an obligation attached to property, is more like a promise of what one should do with assets at the moment of endowment. This promise then becomes a legal obligation once the trust is endowed and registered with the charity commission. The trust bureaucracy's self-perpetuation is both from within (the ambition of its trustees and office managers) and from without. As discussed earlier, the law does not allow charitable trusts to fail, only perhaps shift their ob-jects. Niloufer was able to file a complaint as a beneficiary, and the court did hear her case, but the temporality preferred by the merit-rating scheme was contracted in contrast to the longer time window of the application and decision process of the trust bureaucracy and the courts.

Niloufer's story showed how the trust's shifting mandate of addressing the demographic crisis with housing gave preference to the bureaucratic and material temporality of building new flats over the more politically charged temporality of appropriate marriage age. In the final section of this chapter, I will continue to show how the very particular relationship of the trust as religious bureaucracy further entangles the property of Parsis with its propriety. While the work on the anthropology of property is indeed extensive (C. M. Hann 1998; Verdery 2003; Verdery and Humphrey 2004; von Benda-Beckmann, von Benda-Beckmann, and Wiber 2006), much less has explicitly been written about propriety. For the political theorist J. G. A. Pocock, these two terms were interchangeable in the past. They both referred to what was properly one's own to use and what was proper use in a moral sense (Pocock 1981). We can think of it as what one should do in relation to material things. The commodity understanding of property seems to overshadow this secondary usage, the latter holding that even privately owned property was meant to serve the public good (Alexander 2008). With Alexander, Carol Rose (1994) goes further to analyze "property as propriety," that is, as the material foundation for maintaining the social order, especially social hierarchies. This strand of scholarship points to how the management of property (by the Crown, the state, etc.) relates to particular forms of social and power relations. By managing Parsi property, the trust also deeply engages with Parsi propriety. The following will show how the trust has turned toward a controversial fertility scheme to further address declining demography and how in doing so, masks a sociopolitical problem as a technical one with a "rational" solution that can be free of an ethical stance (Scherz 2013). Through bureaucracy, the trust is able to occlude its rhetoricity and the deeply gendered stance it has on Parsi reproduction.

Babies for *Bawas*

Community leaders decried the fact of greater loss of numbers and the community's dwindling presence in this megacity at every census result. While matrimonial bureaus, a second-child, and third-child support fund already existed, the BPP and other Parsi groups have pushed for a more productive intervention in recent years. Funded by the UNESCO ParZor program and the Indian government, and managed by the BPP, the Jiyo Parsi "live Parsi" scheme aims to ameliorate this demographic crisis through IVF treatments for infertile Parsi married couples.[25] The scheme was borne out of the government of India's Minority Commission, which has a Parsi delegate. The plan was first proposed in the 2010 Union Budget but was turned down by the Planning Commission, as it feared it would set a bad precedent and encourage other communities to ask for the same.[26] Studies conducted by the above groups state that late and nonmarriages, fertility decline, emigration, out-marriages, and separation and divorces are important factors in the Parsi population decline.[27] The scheme's aim was amended in 2017 "from being an infertility treatment project to a project that addresses concerns of attitudinal change regarding the health of the community." The scheme's target had shifted from reproductive biology directly to Parsi propriety.

The second half of the Jiyo Parsi scheme, running from 2017 to 2020, was funded by the Indian government with Rs. 12 crores ($1.6 million). The scheme offered 100% assistance for in vitro fertilization (IVF) and accompanying costs to those Parsis with annual income below Rs. 15 lakhs ($25,000). In addition, "Parsi boys and girls of marriageable age (adolescent to the 30s)" are also offered screening and treatment of clinical problems resulting in infertility (Jijo Parsi, 11). Further assistance is also provided to those with elderly dependents who put off having children due to the care required by parents. Requirements to enjoy the benefits of the scheme are as follows: 1) the married couple fits the income eligibility; 2) the male or female "belongs to the Parsi community"; and 3) the married woman undergoing treatment is of childbearing age (Jiyo Parsi, 12). The Parzor Foundation, along with the local *anjuman*, or punchayet, is responsible for evaluating these criteria for benefit through an application process.

The Jiyo Parsi scheme itself and its vociferous support from the government of India clearly exhibits the sentiment that Parsis are a minority worth saving. This is a great contrast, for example, to the rhetoric about Muslims and stereotypes of them having (too) many children and aggressively converting others through "love-jihad" marriages (Strohl 2019). The scheme also clearly goes against the decades of campaigning from the Indian government promoting birth control and family planning (Visaria and Ved 2016). But for most of my Parsi interlocutors, the scheme's marketing and the actual selection criteria earned the most vociferous critiques.

The scheme approved a good amount of money for advertising and approached a well-renowned Parsi advertising firm, which agreed to work pro bono. I met with advertiser Sam Balsara at his offices in Andheri in 2018, a few years after the first ads were released to the Parsi media. He explained that he was approached by the Jiyo Parsi team and was asked to "increase sensitivity to the [demographic] problem" without resorting to older unsuccessful approaches like encouraging having children for the sake of the community or being too serious about the demographic decline. He insisted that he wanted couples "to do it for their own sake" and took the approach of making the campaign "a bit cheeky." He and a team, including his daughter, worked on the print campaign directly.

FIGURE 3.3. Jiyo Parsi campaign advertisement, "Be Responsible." Madison Advertising.

Indeed, some of the ads in Phase I, released in 2014, did raise a few eyebrows.[28] One print ad (see figure 3.3) depicts a couple with their arms around each other and the caption, "Be responsible. Don't use a condom tonight." In smaller print, "So make a wise decision after dark. Let there be nothing between your togetherness" (Jiyo Parsi ad, Madison World). Another features a Parsi man sitting in front of a vintage car; the caption reads, "Your grandfather's 1955 Fiat . . . Your dad's 1982 Gold Rolex Oyster. Who is going to inherit all of it?" and below this, "A family heirloom presupposes a family. Regrettably, our dwindling numbers have meant things passing into collectors' hands rather than the next generations." Another directly addresses the Parsis' place in India, featuring a group of elderly Parsis chatting; it reads, "The milk is in grave danger of running out of sugar" because "Indian milk is going to taste rather bitter, and it'll be all our fault." Another that targets a stereotype of young Parsi women being "too picky" and status-conscious to pick a Parsi mate and subsequently to marry out of the community reads, "Will your boyfriend ever be as successful as Ratan Tata? Who are you to judge, Nicole Kidman?" with the sub-caption, "If you think his success is a pre-condition to getting hitched, think again. Because maybe it's only with you by his side, that he'll attain the heights of glory" (Jiyo Parsi ad, Madison World). In phase I, the ad that conjured the most controversy (see figure 3.4) from within the community and from the general public depicts a woman looking confused or concerned while standing in front of a well-known Parsi fire temple in Dadar Parsi colony, with a sign in front that reads "Hindu colony." The ad reads: "If you don't get married and have kids, this area will have a new name in your lifetime. Our institutions were gifts from our ancestors. They've shielded us, nurtured us and been the backdrop to our way of life. But if we don't all marry early and have plenty of babies, these colonies are going to be empty. Till other people move in. Think about it . . . Keep our Parsi colonies, Parsi" (Jiyo Parsi ad, Madison World). Simin Patel, a Parsi historian and blogger, stated in an interview:

> What we're seeing—insular, regressive programmes of breeding, state-sponsored at that—is an absolute reversal of the way Parsis were a century ago. The contrast is stark and heartbreaking. Throughout history, we've had mixed blood through the male line. When I saw the ads, I was upset, ashamed. Is this all we can produce, to wreak paranoia, to take us back to Stone Age? How about addressing issues of tolerance instead, opening up our temples to all communities? How about talking about homosexuality within the Parsi community? How is marrying late a Parsi-specific issue? It's happening in all communities, across the world. (Quoted in Neha Bhatt, "That Inward-Looking Mirror," *Outlook*, December 8, 2014)

The Balsara team, as well as the Parzor director, have called these criticisms unfounded. In my interview with Balsara, he even mentioned that the negative news in the press gave the campaign an even broader platform: "Every Parsi in the world has seen or heard about the campaign! As a professional communicator, it couldn't have been better achieved. It is a

HINDU COLONY

If you don't get married and have kids, this area will have a new name in your lifetime.

Our institutions were gifts from our ancestors. They've shielded us, nurtured us and been the backdrop to our way of life. But if we don't all marry early and have plenty of babies, these colonies are going to be empty. Till other people move in. Think about it. Then, address the issue. Should you face any fertility obstacles, JiyoParsi is a 100 million rupee initiative to increase the numbers of the community, by the Ministry of Minority Affairs in association with Parzor. Keep our Parsi colonies, Parsi.

Get IVF assistance up to 5 lakhs*
*Conditions Apply

JIYO PARSI

www.jiyoparsi.org | parzor.com

FIGURE 3.4. Jiyo Parsi campaign advertisement, "Hindu Colony." Madison Advertising.

household name." Balsara is correct in that the ads were only published in three Parsi periodicals, on Facebook, and sent to twenty-five of his friends. The backlash made the campaign national news, and indeed, every Parsi I spoke with at that time had heard about the campaign.

In my discussion with Balsara, he seemed genuinely invested in the cause and not just in the success of his advertising. Of his opposition, he noted that they were "misdirected." According to him, the campaign was not targeted against intermarriage, the practice of which was never mentioned in the ads. In reply to those who say that focusing on reproduction puts an undue burden on Parsi girls and women, he responded that the ads actually feature more men than women; he acknowledged the stereotype of Parsi men being "mama's boys" and that perhaps many of the [female] opposition were "bitter" because they had intermarried.

The ads are more somber in the second phase of the campaign, which Balsara acknowledged was meant to be more aggressive.[29] They focus on what life without children would be like. The print copies are in black-and-white in contrast to the color images of Phase I. One ad depicts a young woman sitting at a café with a coffee and soberly pondering a checklist: "Honda sedan. 1 lakh salary per month. 2 bhk in Napean Sea Road.[30] Wait to check all boxes and you may check into an old-age home. Alone." Many Parsi women have responded that the ads and scheme put an undue burden on Parsi women to "breed like pandas" and demeaned the high education and career success that many Parsi women enjoy. "I'm appalled by these ads; they are in such poor taste. It's like telling us, if you don't marry a Parsi boy and quickly have kids, you are nothing" (Divya Cowasji, quoted in Neha Bhatt, "That Inward-Looking Mirror," *Outlook*, December 8, 2014).

Others critique the advertising campaign as a kind of Parsi chauvinism with its negative depictions of other religious groups in Parsi spaces. One ad depicts an upper-middle-class Parsi man sitting in an armchair in a high-end residence. "After your parents, you'll inherit the family home. After you, your servant will." Below the image, it states, "But it's never too late. Even 60-year-olds today are looking for partners." When I pointed to this ad and its rhetoric, Balsara retorted with a chuckle, "We knew that one was controversial," but he claimed he was vindicated a few months later when, he claimed, a Parsi flat was inherited by a domestic worker.

Balsara insisted that part of the problem was conflicting marriage ideals. Young people, especially young, educated women, had too much westernization and a liberal outlook. "They think, *te game, te kare*" (whatever you like, you do). In parallel condemnation of the expectations of young Parsi men, he exclaimed, "They are evaluating their worth through the flats they inherit; they don't achieve anything." Therefore, in Balsara's view, both young Parsi men and women were not behaving properly, as the women were too willful and the men too complacent and entitled, and "this has put [Parsis] in a mess."

The tone of the ads can be read in many directions, from tongue-in-cheek to provocative, to chauvinistic in terms of gender as well as exclusionary toward other communities. However, it is clear that the ad makers believe young Parsi women and men had failed in their propriety. They had not acted in the best interests of their community but only in their own. The spatial imagination is more than active here as individual marriage age and choice of partner (propriety) become entangled with housing (property) and the physical Parsi presence as a group in Mumbai. The ads also deftly conjure the Parsi historical origin myth of the sugar in the milk to its souring and the concomitant downfall in India in the future.

A further aspect of the Jiyo Parsi scheme with important consequences is the requirement that the prospective father be Parsi and the assistance be given to Parsi couples. Although one person managing the scheme claimed it was open to a non-Parsi mother, he demurred when I asked if any non-Parsi woman had been supported by the scheme financially or otherwise.[31]

One scathing commentary in the media from a woman with a Parsi mother and non-Parsi father exclaimed, "Instead of preserving the Zoroastrian faith and culture, the Jiyo Parsi campaign aims at preserving an ethnic community, one that believes that it is a separate blue-blooded race, whose race purity will be lost if Parsis marry outside the community" (Mukherji 2017). The author then compares the scheme to Nazi Germany and apartheid South Africa. Others retorted that this critique missed the whole point of the campaign, which was to preserve an ethnic group; otherwise, it would have been called "Jiyo Zarathushti" (Wadia 2017). This was the response of several of my interlocutors, who insisted on the validity and necessity of preserving Parsis as an ethnic group. The director of the scheme said, "Every community in danger of dying out is protected in India. . . . We are not Neo-Nazis, as is being portrayed on the social media. We are only serving a community need. Nobody is holding a gun to anybody's head to get married and have kids. . . . The issues the Parsis face, however, are morbid and serious" (Shernaz Cama quoted in Bhatt 2014). As Balsara firmly stated in my interview, "We have a right to survive!" The perpetuation of the community through biological reproduction had to be supported through the perpetual instrument of the trust, with its primary means, housing and now the IVF support.

Indeed, the trust form mirrors this sentiment of exclusivity and distinction. The minority religious trust is an inherently discriminatory legal mechanism, as it can discriminate and share assets only with whom it deems its beneficiaries. Trusts like the BPP are able to appeal to the government as a demographic but not an economic minority in need of government assistance. The Jiyo Parsi scheme and campaign exemplify the process of a bureaucracy addressing sociopolitical and highly gendered issues like marriage choice and the desire for children, in purely technical terms, like providing flats and IVF.

In its own perception, the BPP trust's obligations to distribute its assets to its beneficiaries can only be maintained perpetually if beneficiaries exist. Therefore, reproducing its beneficiaries becomes the object itself. Its structure has become its purpose (Friedman 2009, 199), one that has increasingly been conditioned by the crisis narrative, a present call to save the "better" past and imagined future. The crisis narrative circulating among Parsis has allowed for the bureaucratic definition of the beneficiary to define a certain kind of gendered Parsi identity. This property definition is evacuated of any kind of political value. By so deeply entangling its bureaucratic mandates with its reproductive mandate, managing its allotment of flats and reproductive services becomes a way to manage Parsi propriety and grow its beneficiaries in perpetuity. But while matters of propriety are dealt with within the community, these have effects outside the community as well, where housing and IVF treatments for a microminority are given disproportionate value in a city overburdened by housing scarcity and poverty. But far from just managing real estate, the trusts reveal a much more capacious understanding of property, intermingling kinship practices with real estate. The next chapter will delve into the legal history of how Parsi trusts have defined their beneficiaries and have made distinctions between Parsis as an ethnic group and Zoroastrians as a religious community. It will further explore how being a Parsi itself comes to be seen as property.

CHAPTER 4. THE BENEFICIARY, THE LAW, AND SACRED SPACE

During fieldwork, I often kicked myself for not having gone to law school nor having the ease and legal prowess that some legal anthropologists with both a JD and PhD in anthropology have. I did my best with legal textbooks that I bought in small shops in the Fort District near the High Court to learn about trusts. These shops were packed to the ceiling with books stacked in every which way and were the go-to destinations for young law students and sometimes even a legal professional, recognizable by their black-and-white clothes. The voluminous and heavy books therein had a very particular smell of printing and still had flat pages, as they had never been opened and exposed to Mumbai's humidity. Mr. Vakil, the senior advocate, had given me some names of books. As I leafed through them at home, I was understandably perplexed and frustrated at my lack of technical knowledge, which perhaps would have made my reading more manageable. At times, this frustration became an asset during fieldwork, as I could honestly tell an interlocutor that I did not understand something, and they were eager to explain it to me more often than not. After I seemed perplexed by an explanation of trust regulations, Mr. Vakil pointed to an entire wall in his office cabin lined with legal texts and said to me, "The law is far from common sense."

This chapter will begin by exploring how the ubiquity of trusts within the landscape of Parsi life in Mumbai has created particular forms of legal knowledge. One can assume that Parsis' frequency of dealing with the law is due to their relatively high economic status and levels of education, but I argue that it is also a consequence of the extent to which Parsi life in Mumbai is entrusted. This legal and temporal form constitutes a ubiquitous scape of property relations in their everyday lives. Trusts are their landlords, the keepers of their sacred spaces, the funders of their education or medical expenses, the grantors of their divorces, the timekeepers of their fertility, and sometimes even the hands that feed them. This has led to a very high degree of legal literacy; that is, working knowledge of the law and the processes of the legal system, a legal ease, if you will. The more Parsi tenants and other beneficiaries know of the law and trust matters, the better they can advocate for themselves. Even someone as financially burdened as Niloufer from the last chapter was able to come together with the help of a Parsi legal advocacy group to sue the Parsi Punchayet.[1]

Katharina Pistor (2019) writes of legal expertise as a critical vector in the process of coding capital. Those able to harness this legal expertise, usually the wealthy, are at a considerable advantage within capitalism as they can utilize this knowledge for their benefit, particularly for tax advantage. Their wealth allows them to employ multitudes of lawyers and accountants and to utilize techniques of legal arbitrage for their own benefit. Reading Pistor reminded me of Parsis, who have a long and exalted history of taking community matters to courts (Sharafi 2010) and are stereotyped as especially litigious and argumentative. Apart from being a disproportionate number of litigants in India, Parsis also have an overrepresentation within the Indian judiciary as lawyers and justices, especially in Mumbai. Thinking through Parsis as experts in the legal code of capital in terms of consolidating wealth and challenging power structures, this chapter will present some courtroom ethnography that allows a different focus than simply an analysis of finalized legal judgments. This method shows how legal knowledge (and capital) is produced, refuted, and coded into the law. Courtroom ethnography can offer us a view of the meantime of law making.

Eager to find out more about the 104 case detailed in chapter 3, from the perspective of the eminent retired justice who was asked to review the petitions by the Charity Commission, I met with former judge, "Justice Desai," in his small office in Nariman Point in south Mumbai. The office was part of a former military barracks and unadorned. He explained that he had seen many Parsi litigants in court during his tenure at the Bombay High Court and repeated a joke to me that even when alone, a Parsi would argue with themself in the mirror. I heard this aphorism several times from Parsis, often told with a tone of incredulousness but often also with a tinge of despair. Many seemingly private or intracommunal disputes between Parsis are fought through the Indian legal system, and as a consequence, in the public sphere of the press rather than mediated through communal bodies. The trope of the feisty Parsi abounds, but this chapter will explore some of the contemporary moments that capture what is at stake for Parsis in the disputes and conflicts they bring before the law today. During our meeting, Justice Desai at first seemed at ease, leaning back in his chair, with the demeanor of a relaxed older man happily retired. However, this changed after I introduced my interest in the 104 case, which made him sit at attention and breathe more heavily with exasperation. He then dismally recounted the infighting, the accusations, and the disappointments associated with the case.

Sharafi sees a shift in Parsi use of the courts from religious legislation to litigation, especially litigating trust matters from the nineteenth into the twentieth century (2010, 21). One apparent reason for this is the greater use of trusts over this period and the fact that when trustees go to court, the trust pays the legal fees. Hence, trustees have no personal liability or financial risk if they go to court and lose. While Sharafi's research focuses on the colonial period, the issue of liability and legal costs still holds today and is a significant cause of disagreement in the community, especially with high-profile cases. Legal costs have become a substantial portion of the Bombay Parsi Punchayet's (BPP) operating budget, not just for the suits they initiate (evictions, etc.) but mostly for being sued by beneficiaries. After the Universal Adult Franchise (UAF) system, many trustees even make promises of lawsuits as part of their campaigns to wage legal battles against opposing ideologies.

Another reason disputes are often waged within courtroom walls is the expanded role of trusts like the BPP. If they manage property for Parsis "from the womb to the tomb," then any dispute within a beneficiary's lifetime becomes a matter of trust, relating to the legal rights and obligations of beneficiaries and trustees. Again, the trust deed is a constitutional document, as it inaugurates and structures social, legal, and fiduciary relations among its settlor, trustees, and beneficiaries. Legal texts refer to a trust document as the first material instantiation of the "obligation attached to the ownership of property" (Rajaratnam, Natarajan, and Thangaraj 2010). The written deed then, is a unique document as it not only serves as a "script for the collaboration between two parties" (Riles 2011, 50) but also constructs these parties as subjects. Hence, "law is not merely an instrument or tool working on social relations but is also a set of conceptual categories and schema that help construct, compose, communicate, and interpret social relations" (Silbey 2005, 327). Most Parsis in Mumbai are deeply entangled in these relations.

While we can think of the trust and the dead hand as stopping property, a more helpful analysis is understanding the trust as hinging together new social relationships. This legal technique inaugurates the trustee–beneficiary relationship, a binding of persons and things. Critically, this inauguration initiates a particular temporality that continually is future-oriented to maintain its obligations while accruing new ones in time and space. On the other side, disputes settled by law look toward the past to solve them in the present. As discussed earlier, the trust form intimately entangles Parsi property and propriety with its own chronotope and future-focused temporality. The following disputes addressed in this chapter reflect differing views of correct religious practice and the ongoing tug-of-war between lay Parsis, the Punchayet, and the priesthood. They exemplify struggles over religious propriety through the mediation of property over time.

After a court judgment for the *Petit* case in 1908, introduced in chapter 3, it was established that as a traditionally patrilineal religion, Zoroastrianism, and Parsi identity, may be passed from a Parsi-Zoroastrian father to his children whether or not his wife is a Zoroastrian as well. From this decision, the children of a Zoroastrian father may be given a *navjote* (Zoroastrian initiation), be accepted into the religion, and enjoy rights of access as a beneficiary of any Parsi trust. Furthermore, the nonbinding (*obiter dicta*) section of the judgment emphasized the distinction between Parsis as an ethnicity and Zoroastrianism as a religion. While Suzanne Briere, the French wife of Ratanji Tata, might have been initiated into Zoroastrianism, she was still denied the right to become a Parsi. This judgment implied that to be Parsi, one must have a Parsi father, if not Parsi parents. Women marrying out of the community could not have their children counted as Parsis. Members who consider themselves orthodox religionists in Mumbai tend to be the strictest about disallowing intermarried Parsi women to participate in any Parsi rituals outside of the home, especially entering the agiary or accessing Doongerwadi, the tower of silence funerary complex.

Historically, the Bombay Parsi Punchayet has also reserved the right to bar entry to Doongerwadi and manage the practice of *dokhmenashini* (the excarnation of the corpse by vultures) as a tool to discipline the community, as its control of sacred spaces is a crucial aspect of its authority (Palsetia 2001, 82; Desai 1977). Critical to proper Zoroastrian funerary practice are vultures who excarnate, or remove the flesh from, the corpse within the Towers of Silence. Since the 1980s, there has been a dramatic decline in Indian vulture populations due to urbanization and the birds' consumption of an anti-inflammatory commonly used in dairy farming and given to humans (L. Vevaina 2013). As the next chapter will show in further detail, decisions about consignment to the funerary grounds were usually made ad hoc. They were related to the political and social leanings of the trustees. Since the 1990s, fears of growing cases of intermarriage were amplified by concerns about the community dying out through demographic decline. Furthermore, more Parsis were growing dissatisfied with the state of traditional funerals and were moving to other avenues like cremation. These trends caught the Parsi Punchayet somewhere in the middle of the debate of who may access the site for mourning prayers (in case of cremation) or consignment. More attention in the press and ongoing litigation have put pressure on the Punchayet to make authoritative, definitive decisions about the rights of intermarried females and the priests who perform rituals for them.

Through an ethnographic analysis of a court case, *Kanga v. BPP*, attended during fieldwork, this chapter will show how access to sacred spaces by socalled renegade priests is furiously debated and negotiated by the community through the Indian judiciary. Critical to this case are the rights and duties afforded to the beneficiaries of religious trusts, which manage sacred spaces for Parsis. This case and other related suits also reveal how critical beneficiary status has become to defining who exactly is a Parsi and may claim rights as such. These cases express the new cleavages over not only proper funerary practices in the face of a perceived crisis in demography and ecological possibility, but also the various authority structures and negotiations among the trustees, the courts, lay Parsis, and priests. The legal configuration of trusts creates multiple and overlapping authority structures for sacred space jurisdictions, wherein priests, trustees, beneficiaries, and courts have legitimate mandates and claims within Indian personal and civil laws. This chapter will show how the trust structures legal obligations among trusts, trustees, and beneficiaries through property. It will show how the trust hinges together the intimate relation between managing Parsi religious propriety through access to property.

A Good Deed Never Goes Unlitigated: *Kanga v. BPP*

As intermarriage and cremation cases grew, a few high priests and orthodox community members began to push back through several initiatives.[2] In 2009, a group of high priests, part of the Athornan Mandal, an association for priests, castigated two other priests for performing obsequial ceremonies for cremated Parsis and initiating the children of Parsi mothers who had married out of the community. The high priests maintained that priests who perform such rituals for those "that have wrongly chosen the cremation route where dokhmenashini is available, are by their very actions . . . weakening the faith."[3] The newly elected BPP board at the time, led by its two prominent orthodox trustees, members of the World Alliance of Parsi Irani Zarthoshtis (WAPIZ), then issued a resolution banning the two "renegade priests" from performing ceremonies at the Towers of Silence complex, the only working dokhmas in Mumbai, and at the two temples under BPP management. While the BPP oversees only two of the city's 49 temples, many other temple trustees also supported the ban for the sacred spaces under their management. One of the priests, Framroze Mirza, accepted the ban, desisted from performing these ceremonies, and took no part in the following legal case. The other, Khusroo Madon, while also not being a party to the case, did not accept the ban and continued to practice at venues that would have him.

In 2010, two lay Parsis, Jamsheed Kanga and Homi Khushrokhan, took up the matter. They challenged the legitimacy of the priest ban in the Bombay High Court, claiming that it overstepped the BPP's purview as a public charitable trust. Kanga and Khushrokhan were champions of the liberal cause and have sued the BPP over several instances of litigation. Khushrokhan is a well-respected and connected business executive. Kanga was an expert in housing and city matters as he was formerly at the Brihanmumbai Municipal Corporation (BMC), the governing body of the city of Mumbai, and a former trustee at the BPP. After the priest ban, they petitioned the court, in an Originating Summons, to interpret the Trust Deed of 1884, the primary deed of the Punchayet and ascertain whether the BPP had a right to bar priests from its premises. They claimed that the ban interfered with their rights as beneficiaries of the trust, that the BPP was not vested with the right to decide on religious issues and should restrict its power to the financial and administrative—that is, the secular functioning of the trust. From the beginning of the suit, the boundary between the sacred and secular spheres of a religious charitable trust was in question.

Talal Asad (1993) argues that instead of understanding secularism as an inevitable process that delineates the movement of religion from the public to the private realm, secularism should be considered as the very management of this delineation in historically and contextually bounded locations. More specifically, Bhargava (2007) insists that one should view Indian secularism as a project of values intended to make Indian society more egalitarian and not as a finished process of privatizing religion. I argue further that we must understand secularism as a process of the conceptual and spatial management of religious life—as the process by which religious space is ordered in public and private and not the separation of those spheres themselves. From defining the religious and secular aspects of communal trusts, to examining the right of access by beneficiaries, the following cases are deeply entangled with the promises and constraints of Indian pluralism and the rights of communities.

Trusts structure communal membership in unique ways. While they discriminately give access to their properties to beneficiaries, this principle often conflicts with trusts' status as charitable entities under the gaze of the Indian state and reaches further back to the colonial period. To various extents, this brings the religious sphere clearly within the purview of civil law, a reach that the policies of Indian legal pluralism aimed to keep separate (Derrett 1968; Agnes 1999; Bhargava 1998). Colonial law was itself split on the private–public divide, as after the administration of India was transferred to the British Crown, the distinction was made between the laws of the personal and public spheres, with the former left to be managed by native laws (Agnes 1999, 58). The British had already concluded that family law was religious, so with this proclamation, family law came under the purview of personal law, and all personal matters (marriage, divorce, inheritance, custody) were deemed religious (Agnes 1999, 61). In contrast, the Indian Penal Code and the Indian Contract Act, both uniformly applicable to all citizens, regulated the public domain. The Parsi trust straddles these two realms, being at once for a religious or charitable purpose, and at the same time for a subset of the public, an ethnoreligious group. It further entangles these issues as beneficiary status overlaps with the ethnoreligious recognition that one is a Parsi.

Kanga v. BPP moved relatively quickly through the High Court system. Both sides provided stacks upon stacks of evidence in their favor, but the main piece of evidence was the text of the 1884 deed of the Bombay Parsi Punchayet. When I arrived in Mumbai, this deed seemed like the Holy Grail; I assumed it would be challenging to see a copy after my other requests to see deeds over previous summers were met with much hesitation and suspicion. The opposite was true. Perhaps because of the case's high profile, I was handed a copy of the deed in my first week of fieldwork. Stunned by its sudden arrival and importance as a document to Mumbai Parsis and myself as a researcher, I kept it in a locked drawer for a few days before delving into its faded photocopied pages.

The deed is about three hundred pages and is an amalgam of earlier deeds, for example, the gifting of the Wadia baugs and later addendums. It is written in quite oblique British-style legalese, and the lay reader is only rescued by the short comments typed along the side summarizing each section. Like other deeds, the document first lays out the various settlors' original wishes to entrust lands and funds to beneficiaries. It goes on to name the trustees who are to manage and ensure the execution of those wishes. The first endowment discussed is Doongerwadi, the tower of silence complex. Then within the schedules, the deed enumerates all the properties, moveable and immovable, that are entrusted. Hull (2003) reminds us that an official file contains at least two histories: "a chronicle of its own production" and "signs of its own history [that] are continuously and deliberately inscribed upon the artifact itself" (296). A deed for such a large working trust, like the BPP, is a living document that continuously grows. Still, since the case only dealt with the matters surrounding the tower of silence, all the other properties and funds of the BPP were not included in the widely circulated copy. The circulating copy, bound by spiral and enclosed within plastic covers, is a historical document of the life of the trust in just one moment of its being. In contrast, the larger deed kept in the BPP offices shows signs of constant accumulation, with addendums and notes. The trust as a file in the Charity Commissioner's sliding shelves is more accurate to portray the vivacity of this legal entity, as it is in an open file, unbound.

Days in Court, March 2011

Homi Khushrokhan, whom I had previously met on a few occasions, phoned and told me about the court date that week in March. I had missed some days due to other fieldwork and kicked myself for the lost opportunities but made firm plans to attend the court. I had some trepidation visiting the court since I was not quite sure if a person not attached to a case would be allowed to simply walk in. The Bombay High Court is located in the Fort area, which is resplendent with many of the city's neo-Gothic structures. I was relieved that my taxi driver knew the correct entrance for visitors, as only justices are allowed to enter from the grand main entrance. I went much earlier than the case time, and after going through the security check, I urgently searched for court No. 40. After walking the long stone corridor in the impressive neo-Gothic building, I finally found the courtroom and entered hesitantly during the proceedings for another case. At first, I sat at the back since the parties to the case seemed to take their places toward the front, along with a few journalists I recognized. After a few moments, I asked if anyone was allowed to sit in front of the bench since the acoustics were terrible and I could not hear the advocates, who faced the justices as they spoke. As the hour approached, the court filled up with many black-robed bodies and others who appeared to be clerks and petitioners. The courtroom was quite spectacular, with high ceilings, a gallery space now used for the air conditioning, wooden benches, and huge portraits on the walls. I was told that this used to be Justice Davar's court, the same one in which the landmark *Petit* case of 1908 was decided, and that seemed fitting for what could be another monumental judgment for the Parsi community. As it was admissions day, when new cases are proposed, the court was packed for a few moments, and then people left after they had been granted a forthcoming date.

As the room settled, I glanced around and saw several of the BPP trustees, the petitioners, and a few other people I recognized. The respondents (the BPP) began with their senior advocate, Rafique Dada, who continued his arguments from the previous session. The BPP's main argument throughout the proceedings was that the court should not interfere with the management of sacred spaces like Doongerwadi. Dada stated that Doongerwadi, the tower of silence grounds in Mumbai, had a degree of sanctity and significance to Parsis, who believe there is divine energy, making the place itself sacred and insinuating the court's lack of jurisdiction in such a place. Dada continued while one of the justices, Dr. D. Y. Chandrachud seemed to listen distractedly, nodding his head and shuffling through papers in front of him.[4] Almost throughout the proceedings I witnessed, he appeared bemused and sometimes bit his lip as if he were about to laugh, reflecting the attitude of many onlookers and the mainstream media that this case was a "storm in a teacup," another case brought by this "eccentric" minority that should have stayed behind communal gates. The justice's tone throughout the proceedings was consistent with his statements of regret that this case even came to court and could have and should have been resolved within the community itself. Justice Mohta, who remained silent through most of the proceedings I witnessed, joined Chandrachud on the bench.

My initial impression of the grandeur of the room and the moment dissipated fast as all my energy began to concentrate on hearing and taking notes on the proceedings. Many lawyers I spoke with agreed that the acoustics of the High Court are terrible, and even though microphones are available, they are seldom used. It struck me that these kinds of proceedings are not meant to be for public consumption but rather are debates between legal professionals on fine points of law, even though they have enormous impacts that reverberate far outside these grand halls. Presenting this material in ethnographic form allows us to see a glimpse into the "making of the law" with all its fits and starts, its contingencies, and entanglements (Latour 2010).

When Dada finally came to discuss the "renegade" priests, the justice interrupted and asked, "Even your side [the BPP] states that the priests have been ordained into Zoroastrianism, so does the trust have a right to exclude them?" Dada replied that the two had been declared unfit by the Athornan Mandal of high priests and had not challenged this status. He stressed again that becoming a priest was not a civil right but a sacred oath. Again, Dada, the BPP's advocate, emphasized that the role of the priest was part of the sacred realm and not a civil right, the latter being under the purview of the court and the former belonging to the authority of a sacred community.

Clearly trying to ascertain the connection between the Athornan Mandal, the committee of high priests and its authority, and the BPP, the justice kept pursuing this line. Since lawyers may not relate evidence in the High Courts, the Justices are left with the "paperbooks," the documents submitted by both parties as the evidence in the cases.[5] These were the papers that the justices were ostensibly shuffling through as the lawyers moved through arguments. On the BPP side, several letters and resolutions from the Athornan Mandal were presented alongside the Punchayet's documents, but the Mandal and the high priests associated with it were not parties to the case since it was brought by the petitioners, Kanga and Khushrokhan, to clarify the deed in terms of the BPP's authority.

Switching tacks, the justice continued down another avenue: "Why are some for cremation? There must be a perception that the traditional method is not working." He continued that the community must work these things out, and the two factions, orthodox and "modern," must come to reconcile. He stressed that the BPP needed to show more leadership or the community would "disintegrate." Dada's response to each query was that this matter was very sensitive as it dealt with religious belief. The justice kept nodding and re-asserting that the solution to the problem of the dokhma needed to come from the BPP trustees. His statements seemed to reinforce the court's ambivalent stance on getting involved in this matter.

As the court day was approaching an end, Dada continued to read some affidavits supporting the ban from a few high priests. Justices Chandrachud and Mohta listened quietly as the sun shone brightly through the windows. Most of the audience began to resign themselves to listen until suddenly Chandrachud looked up and asked for clarification: "So how many high priests are there?" At this point, Dada, Iqbal Chagla, the petitioner's advocate, and several onlookers rose and animatedly shouted out, "Six!" "Nine!," "Eight." The audience was shaken out of their reveries in the gallery and began to discuss with each other. This was clearly not straightforward. Seeing this simple line of inquiry also as controversial, the justice then shook his head in dismay and asked Dada to move on. These moments in court crystallized to all present not only how contentious each aspect of the role of the priests was but also how brittle forms of authority in the community were.

Dada then asked, "Why should Mr. Kanga object to the ban if Mr. Madon [one of the banned priests] does not object?" Good question and one that had come to mind when I first heard about the case. Why hadn't the two most affected by the ban, the priests, brought the case themselves? I learned later that Mirza was not interested, and Madon did not have the wherewithal for such a costly case. Kanga and Khushrokhan had taken the approach that the ban interfered with their rights as beneficiaries; that is, their right as Parsis to choose any priest to perform ceremonies for them. As previously mentioned, Madon and Mirza, the two so-called renegade priests, had no part in the case. Mirza accepted the ban and did not perform the controversial ceremonies for a time.[6] At the same time, Madon chose to avoid the BPP properties but continued to perform cremation ceremonies and prayers for the intermarried at other venues. As the case was a petition against a public charitable trust and not an employer, any beneficiary had legal standing to appeal its practices.

Justice Chandrachud then turned to the copy of the deed in front of him and the stack of other papers in the various volumes of the paperbooks. He recounted that before 1873, the BPP was the manager and custodian of several smaller properties, which were all amalgamated into this one deed. Leafing through it, he asked, "Is dokhmenashini referred to in the deed specifically? I understand that this is not a secular place." He then trailed off, perhaps finding his answer in the text. This line of questioning occasioned one of the more conservative trustees, Khojeste Mistree, a vociferous champion of the traditional rite of dokhmenashini, to stand up nervously.[7] His concerned demeanor shifted the tone in the room as many people began to sit upright and pay more attention. The Justice Chandrachud, quoting from the trust deed, asked, "Every Zoroastrian is entitled to use the property, so where is the power to exclude?" Dada retorted that Parsis did not necessarily have the choice of a priest but that the trust should decide who was allowed on the premises. He attempted to guide the argument into one of jurisdiction rather than beneficiary rights.

The justice then paused and seemed to ask the whole room to contemplate the following thought experiment: "What if a priest committed pedophilia? Then could the trust exclude?" This provocative query set the room abuzz again. People in the gallery turned and murmured with one another. Dada answered that yes, the trust had the right to exclude, to which the justice responded and asked whether the trustees had a right to excommunicate people. Dada quickly retorted that religion was "a serious issue" and the BPP should have the right to choose who performs within its properties. Chandrachud nodded in understanding and replied that the court would only decide about the deed. Its concern remained with what the deed allowed regarding both the rights of trustees and those of beneficiaries.

The justice then motioned that the session was all but over, at which point both sides' advocates stood up. The BPP vigorously pushed the strategy that the court had no place to adjudicate on this matter, which seemed to irritate the justice, who repeatedly made clear that the court had only been asked to interpret the deed, a legal document, and nothing more. The High Court was the designated venue to settle disputes because the trust was registered with the Charity Commission. When the session was over, we all stood up as the justices rose from the bench and were formally escorted out of the courtroom. Almost immediately, the present BPP trustees huddled together and nervously looked around to ensure they were not being overheard. The petitioners spoke a few words with their lawyers, and since there was no case following, everyone slowly exited the room into the hallway. I quickly inquired of one of the journalists I had met as to when the next court day would be, and with this next appointment in mind, slowly descended through to the central courtyard and left the High Court into the hot and bustling streets of Fort, outside the gates of the court.

On the next date, the petitioner's side was to present before the court on March 4 but the BPP lawyers asked for a brief time to continue from the previous session. I sat toward the back again, and the audience was again full of people, some trustees of the BPP, a Parsi journalist, and a few others interested in the case. Dada continued to stress that the *Petit* judgment of 1908 settled the issue and that the courts had no place in these matters—a curious juxtaposition of arguments since he was at once confirming the authority of the court with the precedent of the *Petit* case while insisting on the limits of the court to adjudicate over this matter. He emphasized that the rights and ceremonies of a trust are sacred, even if monies are spent on them. The justice interrupted to remind him that Articles 25 and 26 of the Constitution of India reserve the right to rule on the secular aspects of the trust. Dada replied that the ban was a religious ban by the high priests and continued.

After over an hour of repeating everything that was said in the previous session, the opposing counsel, Iqbal Chagla, one of the senior-most advocates on the bar and also from an eminent legal family, began to speak on behalf of the petitioners. Chagla had taken on the case pro bono and was assumed to be personally interested in the proceedings, as his wife is Parsi, while he is a Muslim.

Chagla's strategy was to immediately bring the focus back to the deed, what Kanga and Khusrokhan's Originating Summons had asked the court to interpret: can the trust restrict Parsis from choosing certain priests? Justice Chandrachud responded that the BPP was vested with the powers to preserve the tower of silence, and did this not include the right to exclude? He asked further whether the trustees were bound to the decisions of the high priests. Chagla then interrupted and stated firmly, "The duty of the court is to the beneficiary." This last comment was interesting in that it brought to mind that the Charity Commissioner and the High Court, overseers of public charitable trusts, must hold trusts obligated to their deeds, and the objects made within to their beneficiaries.

The justice began once more to rifle through the pages of his copy of the trust deed and seized upon another issue that caused the audience to perk up and pay attention. "The term 'exposure' in the trust refers to the dokhmenashini system." Chandrachud and Chagla briefly went back and forth about the petitioners and their position on dokhmenashini, the traditional rite of excarnation. Chagla insisted that the petitioners had no issue with the system, that even Khushrokhan's father was placed at the Towers. Still, the two petitioners were certain that the system was not functioning and maintained that lay Parsis should have a choice for cremation. In a curious tone, Chandrachud replied, "Cremation is allowed in other areas, like Delhi . . . but only because there are no towers." Chagla retorted, if this was a religious issue, then how is it logical that it is allowed in Delhi? The justice replied, "In matters of religion, logic is not an issue." With so many entangled issues on the table, the justice nodded, not necessarily in agreement, but just to signify that he was finished with this line of inquiry. He shuffled some papers and decided to break for lunch.

As the court quickly emptied as everyone rushed to have a break before the next session began, I was asked if I would like to join a group going to the Ripon Club just down the street by the journalist of a liberal-leaning Parsi periodical. The club, named after a Viceroy of India, is a Parsi-only club that used to be even further limited to Parsis in the legal profession. It was founded in 1884 by Pherozeshah Mehta, Jamshedji Tata, and Sir Dinshaw

Petit. As we made our way out of the court building, we saw BPP trustees and their supporters slowly making their way along the street. It seemed like we were all heading in the same direction.

As we arrived at the club, my party made our way up the three flights of stairs only to enter the club at the same time as the other group, who took the lift. The waiter looked confused and asked, "All together?" at which point both sides yelled a vehement "No!" The groups took to their corners, so to speak, and stole suspicious glances at the other's table. I admit I was quite uncomfortable as the two groups seemed to have so much animosity toward one another, and it was perhaps assumed that I had picked a side. The large room that spans almost the floorspace of the building was empty except for row upon row of tables and chairs set for lunch. The atmosphere was complete by the many windows with sunlight streaming through the room. Even though this was only the third floor, it gave it a very airy aspect. Dark wooden tables and other furniture against the white marble tile gave the place a stately atmosphere. One could almost imagine early twentieth-century barristers seated under the myriad ceiling fans in their crisp collars, sipping whiskey and eating the daily offering between court appointments, perhaps delayed by the several grandfather clocks that all told different times. Portraits of distinguished Parsis, most likely club secretaries and eminent jurists, adorned the walls with their name plates so worn that one could barely make them out. The club had an old colonial charm, as it seemed pregnant with the possibility of a bustling lunch crowd. Yet if one noticed how few of the tables were set by noon, this had probably not been true for many years.

After quite a rushed meal, we all walked quickly back to the courthouse, following the steady stream of black robes now being fastened in preparation for the following sessions. As the post-lunch session began, Rafique Dada, the BPP's advocate, pointed out the many places that dokhmenashini is referred to in the deed. Chagla, the petitioners' advocate, responded, "Yes, we know the property is dedicated as such; the petitioners and interveners are not opposed to the property being used in this manner. This is about freedom of thought and belief. Can we prevent a priest for a belief? What prevents the trustees from saying that someone holds contrary beliefs and can't come in? You can't say no to a belief. What prevents them from excluding others? This will set a bad precedent and will bring more civil suits. The administration of a trust is a secular matter. Trustees stand on no higher authority." Chagla framed the argument to emphasize the actual conservative nature of the petitioners' stance. Neither Khushrokhan nor Kanga, in this instance, had advocated for any change to the tower of silence property nor the process and practice of dokhmenashini. Chagla pointed to the ban of priests from BPP properties due to prayers for cremations and *navjotes* at other venues managed by other trusts. Hence, he surmised that the ban from BPP properties was due to the "contrary beliefs" of these priests. He reminded the court that the administration of a trust was part of the secular sphere and hence within the court's purview. Chagla then cited that the *Jaganath Temple* case [of 1964] definitively split the trust into its religious and secular aspects.[8] Justice Chandrachud then quickly retorted, "The person who performs ceremonies is religious. The Supreme Court makes this distinction clear."

Justice Chandrachud then changed his tone with the following provocative question pushing against the limits of propriety: "Can a priest who is convicted of rape be kept out? Implicit in management is control of who has access, not just custodial duties." However, did this give the trustees too much power? Chandrachud mentioned that the trustees were following the authority of the high priests, to which Chagla responded that the high priests were not mentioned in the deed. Shifting into a more frustrated tone, the justice replied, "This issue is splitting the community. There is a deeply felt urge of small religions to hold onto their identity," to which Chagla loudly retorted, "This is the Taliban!" At this point, the audience murmured loudly, some in agreement with Chagla and some in shock over his comparison of the BPP to the Taliban.

In a firm and measured tone, Justice Chandrachud responded, "A certain degree of fundamentalism is seen in all [religions]. Birth, marriage, and death are the most important aspects of any [religion]. It matters whether the high priests have the authority to bind. . . ." Again, Chagla pulled the court back to the deed: "Shouldn't the trustees just be bound to the deed and not a third party? The BPP are now [after the amendments of 1884] only custodians. Otherwise, they have too much power. He [a trustee] cannot look outside of the deed, or he commits a breach of trust."

While the justice seemed to be deliberating over the fine line between the religious and secular aspects of the trust, Chagla's point was to remind the court that although the BPP was more than just an endowment, its functioning has shifted since it became a trust from a larger role as adjudicator of community affairs (see chapter 3 on historical shifts of the BPP), to a more limited one after 1884. He reminded the court that the trustee, just like the court, must remain within the deed; these were both obligations of the trust and the court.

The two Justices, Mohta and Chandrachud, leaned toward each other and quietly discussed between themselves. When they returned to facing the advocates, Chagla continued that the high priests did not invest the trustees with power. He asked if someone was misconducting themself on the property. No. They were being punished for something done outside. Chagla's narrative insisted on a spatial understanding of ritual practice in a few ways. Firstly, he highlighted several times that Madon and Mirza's ritual performances for intermarried people or those who chose to be cremated were never performed within the boundaries of BPP properties. Hence, to ban them from these properties was an overstepping of the BPP's limited authority, as it retaliated against the priests' contrary beliefs. Most importantly, he reminded the court of its own spatial jurisdiction over at least the administrative, hence secular affairs of the trust.

He finished by restating that the administration of a religion in the end was secular, to which Chandrachud asked, "Is appointing a priest religious or secular?" Chagla responded by stating, "A Parsi Zoroastrian engages a priest—all are beneficiaries; this doesn't impinge on the rights of anyone else [if they choose someone controversial]. We must remain with the deed. The BPP did have a dual position before the current deed. Now it is the trustee of the funds and immovable properties that are under the management of the deed. In Schedule II, the permit of the towers belongs to 'every member of the Parsi Zoroastrian community only.'"

Finally, judgment day arrived on March 11. The court filled with BPP trustees, representatives of the Parsi press, and many others, some even standing since there were no longer any seats. Justice Chandrachud began with what I recognized as his usual grin and almost gleeful face. Before beginning to read out directly from the text of the judgment, he prefaced:

I hope we are correct in this judgment, which is divided into several parts. We have also seen to the scope of an Originating Summons and have deemed it sufficient in this case. The BPP trust has changed over time. Previously it was endowed with the authority over social life. But, the trust deed of Sept 25, 1884, changed this to just the funds, and the role was then divorced from religious disputes. It became secular. The tower of silence is to be used as a matter of right for all Zoroastrians. The deed states that the trustees must permit and suffer every member of the Zoroastrian community, and this does not give them the power to exclude. Different towers were given for different purposes. The judgments of 1908 (*Petit*) and 1925 (*Bella*) were in the context of their times;[9] before the Indian Constitution and Article 25, which allows for the free exercise of religion.[10] The service of the priest is secular—he must be ordained according to the tenets of the religion. A beneficiary is entitled to engage any priest. The trustees have no right to exclude any ordained priest; if not, the trust is likely to be subject to grave abuse. The judgment must return to the trust deed. The trust does not have the power to divest a priest. The ban then constitutes a veiled threat. Its power of exclusion becomes a betrayal of human rights.

Justice Chandrachud paused and then began to read aloud directly from the judgment, quoting the deed: "The property shall be held upon trust at all times forever, and the trustees shall permit and suffer the land, towers, and structures to be used by every member of the Parsi community professing the Zoroastrian religion as a place for the exposure of the dead and for the performance of religious rites and ceremonies." The justice declared that the deed confined the trustee's functions to the trust's administration alone, even if the trust had a religious purpose. As such, the trust had no right to ban anyone from the premises if they fit the description of a beneficiary. Further, the trustees had no right to disallow a Parsi from choosing any "duly ordained Priest" to perform ceremonies at the site. The justice commented that since burial, cremation, and obsequial prayers are allowed in places where a *dokhma* is unavailable, the practices themselves could not be said to be irreligious.[11] Since it was established in the court that although some viewed the performance of cremation prayers as being misconduct by the priests, those ceremonies were never actually conducted on the properties of the BPP; therefore, the ban was not due to misconduct on the premises and was an overreach of the Punchayet's authority.

During the reading of the judgment, the tension was very high in the courtroom, held utterly silent by the justice's voice. I found myself leaning forward in my seat and straining to hear the justice even though I knew I could read the judgment in a few days. The elation of the petitioners' side greatly contrasted with the slumped shoulders of the BPP trustees in the courtroom. One trustee left the courtroom saying that he had expected this. As the proceedings ended, the remaining BPP group began immediately strategizing about the appeal as others filed out of the room. I felt at once that this moment was a historical one, in the same chamber as the *Petit* case over one hundred years ago, but at the same time, it felt banal as the participants of this case filed out and others strode in as the court day moved forward with the next case.

Although this suit was specific to the BPP, it seemed like the judgment could be used as a precedent for many other kinds of religious trusts. And indeed, the newspapers and blogs in the following days asked what this might mean for various other communal charities. The judgment firmly emphasized that the administration of a religious trust is a secular activity and hence under the purview of specific constitutional guarantees. The case and the judgment further solidified the multiplicity of Parsi authority in Mumbai, giving weight and power to lay Parsis, priests, and the Punchayet, the latter of whom solidified its claim that Doongerwadi was exclusively for dokhmenashini. The BPP trust here was caught out of time, at once seen as a relic from a colonial past that needed reform while simultaneously being justified in continuing its mandates. Above all, at the center of the case remained the questions of access to space and the importance of the location of religious practice, which I claim constitutes a topography of sacred space and its role in structuring legal obligations. The judgment effectively laid out a particular topography of proper practice wherein certain religious rituals are spatially sanctioned or disallowed (L. Vevaina 2022b). It was evident in emphasizing the sacred nature of the tower of silence complex and the importance of maintaining religious rituals, but at the same time, did acknowledge that for various reasons, many Parsis were moving away from the traditional practice of dokhmenashini.

The justice frequently commented that the opposing sides and, indeed, the community at large should refrain from taking these kinds of matters to court. These matters should be resolved through nonlegal means. Nonetheless, the BPP, spearheaded by its two orthodox trustees and funded by WAPIZ, an orthodox advocacy group, filed an appeal to the Supreme Court of India, and both parties agreed to mediation procedures. While the mediation proceedings in 2015 were not publicly available, bound by a confidentiality clause, my recent communiqués with the involved parties revealed that the meetings had been very contentious. After mediation, it was agreed that while the ban on Madon and Mirza would remain except for rituals for their own families (they too are beneficiaries, after all), the BPP could not ban other priests from its sacred spaces. The judgment and the appeal made the Mumbai papers, and there was a flurry of discussion about the implications for other religious communities with trust matters.

Any legal judgment reveals details of the case at hand and builds itself into a complex chain or genealogy of legal argument, becoming part of a series of legal precedents. Another case that *Kanga v. BPP* had direct reference with and to is the second high-profile case heavily discussed during my fieldwork. It involved a Parsi intermarried woman, Goolrukh Gupta née Contractor, who was suing her local punchayet in Gujarat after it imposed a ban on entry to all intermarried women to its sacred spaces, including the local tower of silence.[12] Gupta's claim rested on her contention that although she married out of the community, she remained a beneficiary of the trust as she was born a Parsi and has continued to follow the Zoroastrian religion even after her marriage—and therefore has a right to enjoy privileges as a Parsi Zoroastrian including the right to offer prayers in Zoroastrian sacred space. Gupta's petition claimed that she and other intermarried women were being discriminated against, violating Articles 14 and 25, equality before the law and freedom of religion, respectively, of the Indian Constitution. In contrast to women, male Parsis who intermarry are allowed access to these spaces after marriage, a custom set by the *Petit* case of 1908. Furthermore, Gupta contended that this current view favoring males over females is held by the orthodox, "ignoring the law of the land," having no basis in scripture, and is a contested notion even amongst the high priests of the religion.[13] Thus, she was fighting for her "fundamental right to have free access for the purpose of worship and other ceremonies as available to all Parsi Zoroastrians."[14]

While Gupta sued as a beneficiary of her local trust, in contrast to the *Kanga* case, it was her very status as a Parsi that was challenged by the respondents, who argued that her intermarriage was deemed a conversion away from Zoroastrianism. The 2012 judgment in the Gujarat High Court agreed with the *Anjuman* that Gupta was no longer a Parsi after marrying a Hindu man in a civil marriage following the Special Marriages Act. Hence, the judgment shifted the terrain of the case away from her alleging discrimination as a beneficiary but actually removed her from her beneficiary status and her religious identity through her intermarriage.

Just as in *Kanga v. BPP*, the Gupta case revolved around whether certain duties were an essential part of religion, which could be ascertained from religious doctrine, or whether they fell under secular management. Referencing several Supreme Court cases, the justices in the Gupta case carefully carved out the position that while much reverence must be given to religious institutions to regulate themselves, the courts would step in and regulate if the religious provision conflicts with the Constitution: "No usage, which is found to be pernicious and considered to be in derogation of the law of the land or opposed to public policy or social decency can be accepted or upheld by Courts in the country (*Gupta v. Anjuman Trustees, Section 3, Paragraph 18*)." The following paragraph referenced *Kanga v. BPP*, *Petit v. Jeejeebhoy*, and *Saklat v. Bella* as precedents. These cases were now entangled as links in a chain. The justices referenced these suits on issues of conversion and court interference with religion as well as the conclusion that the administration of a religious endowment is still a secular activity.

During both cases I attended, the justices frequently inquired with the parties about where they may find an expert or where they may look for textual authority.[15] In the *Kanga* case, Justice Chandrachud asked the court how many high priests there were in an effort to inquire about priestly authority. As several people in the gallery yelled out different numbers, the justice was bemused and realized that this would not be a productive line of establishing expert knowledge. If the group of high priests at the Athornan Mandal in Mumbai agreed, this did not exhaust the possibility of a disagreement with another high priest, and there is no uncontested structure or hierarchy among them.

Perhaps a return to the sacred texts? This was another lost avenue as there are few who can actually read them in the original, and translations vary. Furthermore, a rush to the text is perhaps not appropriate in the first place as the Parsi Zoroastrian tradition is not composed in a parallel fashion of an uncontested set of texts containing regulations and proper custom as with some other religious traditions. The more authorial texts of the community seem to be trust deeds and court judgments. Hence, to answer the justice's prompt—"Is there an expressed prohibition of intermarriage" and concomitant ban from sacred space in the texts?—even the respondents had to answer no, or that they had no evidence as such. This continuing oscillation between gaining legitimacy from text or from custom is further complicated by adding the courts into play. If one did return to a text, one would have to return to a trust deed. While the Punchayet's deed of 1884 was at the center of the *Kanga* case, and indeed the case was decided upon its interpretation, interestingly, in the *Gupta* case, the Valsad Anjuman's trust deed was not even entered into evidence. The question was whether Gupta was a beneficiary in the first place and not a matter of her rights once she was recognized as a beneficiary.

This rush to a textual tradition to find legitimacy within is further paralleled in legal argument as well (Suresh 2019). Any legal judgment reveals details of the case at hand and builds itself into a complex chain or genealogy of legal argument itself, becoming part of a series of legal precedents. Several cases are referenced and rereferenced in each case, building a chain of argument that becomes authorized by the ability of that same case to be built into another chain (Latour 2010). For instance, justices judge the case as well as the law. Clearly, in the *Gupta* case, Chayya and Patel adjudicated the Special Marriage Act, which allows for civil marriage between two parties, just as much as the merits of her case. Their questioning of this law will further open the act of inquiry for all related cases in the future. Legal precedents are time-keeping protocols: "Reasoning by analogy to precedent creates a *false* historicity in that it perpetually reclaims the past for the present. . . . 'The law' thus accumulates, but it never passes; at any instant, it represents a totality" (Greenhouse 1989, 1640). Like trusts, precedents, offering another chronotope of law, oblige faithfulness to the past within a common law system (Valverde 2015a, 2015b).

Another rush to text is perhaps the obvious rush to read and analyze new legal judgments, as legal scholars and legal anthropologists are wont to do. What anthropology, especially fieldwork from within the court setting, offers is a view of the meantime, the making of the law (Latour 2010; Das Acevedo 2016; Suresh 2019). For instance, in the *Kanga* case, it was clear to the justices and those in the courtroom that while the mandate of the Originating Summons was to interpret the deed of a charity, the trustees had an outsized role in the religious affairs of Parsis that could not be ignored. Courtroom ethnography offers a different kind of view into the polyvocality of how legal judgments and hence precedents come to be as accretions of narratives, documents, and arguments. It can elucidate which kinds of these win out over others and what some of the motivating arguments of the justices might have been as they came to their final decision.

The Locations of Practice

What is so striking about these cases is that they go beyond what constitutes or should constitute the boundaries of proper Parsi Zoroastrian practice. These cases are critically about the very location of practice. Gupta's case is specific to the agiary and tower of silence in Valsad even though she lives in Mumbai and has the right of entry in some Mumbai temples, and has the right at Doongerwadi, the tower of silence in Mumbai, to be laid to rest. As we might imagine, her own case might have undermined this right as it gives a precedent for the BPP to revoke any rights for intermarried women henceforth, since the Valsad trustees have not been forced by the court to rescind the barring of intermarried women from their trust spaces. Not surprisingly, Gupta has deployed her legal ease and appealed her case to the Indian Supreme Court.

In the *Kanga* case, Justice Chandrachud repeatedly asked the respondents (the BPP) whether the priests had ever conducted these "heretical" ceremonies on the very property of their trusts; that is, in the two agiaries they manage and the Doongerwadi complex itself. Since they had not, the judgment was clear that the priests' conduct or misconduct, as it were, did not misuse or abuse those locations, and as such, the ban was an overstretch of the BPP's jurisdiction. The BPP could have censured the priests had they performed ceremonies for intermarried women or cremation prayers on the site of Doongerwadi, but not otherwise.

These cases show varied instances of the legal concept of jurisdiction and the law's spatial obligations. This speaking of law can imply the power and authority to apply the law and, secondly, the limits or locations at which authority may be exercised. The idea of jurisdiction is fundamentally about the concept of authority in space. Where can certain activities occur, and who has the right to comment on, censure, or encourage such practices? Jurisdiction is the conceptual nexus of property and propriety. We think of jurisdiction in terms of state bodies, the courts, the police, etc., but religious bodies have their own landscapes of authority. Religious bodies as trusts engender a very particular kind of topography of practice. They enable us to think about secularism beyond just the state's management of religious life but, critically, how the state might manage the very locations of religious practice in India. Hence, while the cases themselves are about the jurisdiction of trusts and how far they may exercise authority, they also crucially point to the spaces within which the assumed "short arm" of the Indian judiciary can reach into the lives of religious groups.[16]

In its logics, legal recognition is a parallel spatial practice to secularism. The latter does not entail the removal of all aspects of religion from the public to the private realm, as secularization theory would have it, but rather delineates its capacities and efficacies within those realms (Asad 1993). So too, with recognition, the law does not strive to provide further legal (public) recognition to, in this case, communal claims but to enable or limit those claims within the public sphere. Thus, legal recognition is fundamentally a jurisdictional practice critical to the potential of communal groups to make claims on the state or manage their own affairs away from the gaze of the state. I have shown how the communal trust further complicates the negotiation of this jurisdictional practice both for those like Gupta who appeal to the law to secure their religious rights and for the courts, which must decide where and in which cases the law and the logics, aspirations, and obligations of the Indian Constitution apply.

The relative legal ease of Parsis has historically had some profound advantages, as they were able to formulate and codify their own personal laws, albeit sometimes disadvantaging Parsi women. But as this chapter shows, their legal ease is deeply entangled with the various topographies where trusts speak the law. The concomitant chronotope forces many disputes to require decades-long, arduous, costly, and emotionally draining litigation even among family members, stretching between a small village in Gujarat to the Indian Supreme Court. These trust matters are not just about property but people and property.

Anaita, a travel agent in her forties, recounted that she received the call on her mobile after eating *dosas* one Sunday afternoon in 2011. "Oh no! How did it happen? When?" Learning of her great-aunt's passing was definitely sad, but the woman was in her nineties, ninety-six to be exact, and had lived alone for decades after being widowed and having no children. When asked if she ever wanted to have children, Siloo Aunty used to say that she married late, at twenty-nine, and had always been "sickly." Plus, being the eldest of six children, she felt like she had already taken care of her share. Siloo was looked in on by her nieces and nephews, but even those visits had grown sporadic as those who still lived in Mumbai were often busy with their own lives and children, and the others lived in Canada and the UK and only traveled to Mumbai to see their aging parents. Anaita inquired with one of her uncles about the funeral arrangements. "She never wanted to go to Doongerwadi"; she thought it too gruesome, exclaimed he exclaimed. "She just wanted the prayers at home and then to be cremated." Living near the Doongerwadi tower of silence complex off Napean Sea Road, Siloo had never taken a liking to visiting there for funerals and had heard and read so much about the system not working. Like many aging Parsis, she had made provisions in her will detailing her desire to be cremated after the necessary prayers were conducted at her home.

Anaita's grandfather had wanted a traditional funeral, and the procedures seemed clear. Anaita had received instructions from Parsi General Hospital to call the office at Doongerwadi first and make arrangements for the body to be transported to the small morgue within the complex. As the body lay in the morgue, prayer ceremonies were conducted in one of the bigger *bunglis*, or cottages, on the complex, as the family had expected many mourners to attend. The next task delegated to Anaita was to write a short obituary and announcement of the *uthamna* ceremony open to mourners for the *Times of India*, Mumbai edition; the *Jam-e-Jamshed*; and for *Parsiana*, the most read periodicals among Parsis in the city. Unsure about the effectiveness of this approach, Anaita inquired with her grandmother, also in her nineties, whether this was enough to alert those who potentially would attend the services. "Of course," said her grandmother. "I read that section of the paper every day!" Indeed, with around three Parsis passing away daily and the community being as small as it is, obituaries had become critical markers of community news.[1]

This time around, too, Anaita offered to help. "I can help with any of the arrangements," she said to her aunt, the daughter of Siloo's younger sister, who was unofficially in charge. Anaita was instructed to write the obituary mentioning that Siloo had passed at ninety-six, had led a long and happy life, and that her *uthamna* prayers would be conducted at home. "Yes, that's how it's done now," said her aunt. But would they find a priest to perform the ceremony? "Yes, we can call Ervad Madon, the one they call the renegade priest; he does the prayers for cremation. He also did the *navjote* (Zoroastrian initiation) for Freny and Rajiv's kids.[2] Just make sure to put the home address in the announcement." This was the first of many adaptations that Anaita had to make quickly without knowing what was proper to do. At least if the body were to go to the towers at Doongerwadi, there would be an established protocol, but with cremation, Anaita learned, everything had to be done a bit differently.

Although it remains uncommon for someone as devout as Siloo to opt for cremation, she, like many others, had grown dissatisfied with the current conditions at the tower of silence. They must weigh their discomfort with *dokhmenashini* against the possibilities that their last rites are improper or irreligious, which many contend that cremation is. The placing of the corpse, the ultimate impure matter (*naso*), into the purity of fire is beyond the boundaries of proper Parsi Zoroastrian practice, which for centuries has preferred dokhmenashini (Lueddeckens and Karanjia 2011; Stausberg 2004b; Stausberg and Vevaina 2015).

From excarnation to ashes, this chapter will examine the entanglement of ritual infrastructure, created and managed by the trust, and what is considered proper religious practice. It will explore how the BPP trust deed, established in 1884, was both a preserver and a constraint of Zoroastrian funerary practice until ecological conditions and a legal judgment encouraged a new trust to form to support ritual innovation. For mortuary rituals, the crisis of the trust was not declining beneficiaries but the growing impossibility of proper rituals that forced the trust to shift its obligations. As shown, the history of Parsis in India is a history of migration that intimately connects political and economic factors with the construction and availability of sacred infrastructures and spaces. These connections have placed much authority over religious matters with trustees and the spaces they manage rather than with priests and texts. This chapter will explore possibilities for ritual change when placed within the constraints of the trust's chronotope, temporality, and spatial ordering.

Death in the Infant City

While Parsis historically had permanently settled in western India, especially around Sanjan in southern Gujarat, they did not break ties with the small communities of Zoroastrians still living in Iran, particularly in Yazd and Kerman (Palsetia 2001). Over time, further migrations from Iran ebbed and flowed with the shifting relations between this tiny minority and the Safavid rulers. Zoroastrian priests from India and Iran exchanged religious inquiries, known as *rivayats*, between one another from about 1478 to 1773 (Ringer 2011). These dialogues led to the solidification of religious authority of the priests in the small town of Navsari in Gujarat. Navsari came to prominence as a religious center when the sacred fire was shifted there after the sacking of neighboring Sanjan. The Navsari priests formed an *anjuman*, or organized body, and were at the apex of communal authority among Parsis until another critical migration shifted the balance of power in the community (Dobbin 1970).

In contrast to their initial arrival in India to seek refuge from Iran, the second phase of Parsi migration from Gujarat to Bombay was spurred on by economic opportunities coupled with the availability of ritual spaces like *dokhmas* in the early colonial city. Newer settlers to the city tended to settle near older migrants to enjoy proximity to temples and access to communal living spaces. In the late 1670s, wealthier Parsis had received permission to build the first Towers of Silence and fire temples in Mumbai. They began establishing robust support networks for the increasing numbers of Parsi migrants from Gujarat. The large migration from Gujarat to

Bombay took place in the middle of the nineteenth century, aided by the existence of support networks and employment with public works projects that were established by the Bombay Parsis. This historical development of Parsi settlement, which grew to maturity within the urban landscape of Mumbai and within the legal structures of colonial India, is critical to the contemporary importance of the dokhmenashini practice (Palsetia 2001; Desai 1977; Dossal 2010). As the following section will show, the construction of the first towers in early Bombay encouraged later migration to south Bombay. The towers were also fundamental in establishing the trust as the legal mechanism for managing Parsi sacred spaces in the city.

In terms of governance, the Parsis, like other communities, formed panchayats, or committees, to adjudicate more minor claims and intracommunity disputes. The Bombay Parsi Punchayet (BPP) in Bombay slowly took on the role of formulating binding regulations regarding religious or cultural issues. In 1787, the British colonial government recognized the leadership of the Parsi Punchayet in Bombay, providing the first step in consolidating authority over the rest of the community.[3] The Parsi case is unique even in the Indian context as the BPP, their apex body, is composed of lay individuals, not priests nor legal scholars. As shown in earlier chapters, this historical composition of the Punchayet and its power as a legitimate authority over community matters has continually been challenged by lay Parsis on the one hand and the priesthood on the other (Dobbin 1970; Palsetia 2001; Desai 1977).

A pattern was soon established of Parsi traders and businessmen acquiring masses of wealth, securing large land estates in Bombay from the British, and then donating them to the Parsi Punchayet to be used only in specific capacities such as housing, hospitals, sanatoria, etc. Due to this unique pattern of the organization of the built environment, Parsi immigration to Bombay followed the geography of sacred spaces instead of the spatial structures themselves being constructed for the needs of the community (Palsetia 2001). Proper Parsi practice was then dependent on nearness to Parsi sacred properties. Far from the center of priestly power in Navsari, authority within the community began to shift toward secular leaders like industrialists and philanthropists entrusted with managing temples and other sacred spaces.

Wherever Parsis moved and settled, they built sacred spaces to maintain Zoroastrian laws of purity and pollution in their new environment. The first dokhma in India was built around 1300 in rural Gujarat to service the burgeoning community. Dokhmenashini is one consistent ritual that has marked the Parsis in India since their arrival. This traditional Zoroastrian practice involves the excarnation of the dead by leaving the corpse in large towers, or dokhmas, to be eaten by vultures or other carrion birds or left to desiccate in the sun.[4] To transport the impure corpse, or *nasa*, are a special occupational class of Zoroastrians called *nasasalars*, who alone are allowed to touch and move the bodies after the four traditional days of funeral service.[5] The services are officiated by at least two priests before the body is placed in the dokhma. The proper practice of dokhmenashini thus requires towers, priests, nasasalars, and vultures to devour the body. The practice goes back to medieval times in Iran. It reflects the Zoroastrian observance of not defiling natural elements (fire, water, earth) with dead bodies, considered the ultimate impure material.

Dokhmenashini and the infrastructure of excarnation have oriented Parsi settlement in Mumbai, the home of the largest concentration of Parsis in the world, but have also inaugurated one of the first and most critical trust agreements for Parsis in the city (L. Vevaina 2013). In 1669, an application was made to the British colonial Governor Aungier of Bombay to construct the city's first tower of silence (Palsetia 2001, 37). The petition was initiated by a wealthy Parsi, who had lands on Malabar Hill, "a jungle then infested with jackals and hyenas" in south Bombay (Desai 1977, 44). The space was deemed appropriate because it was somewhat out of the way, with limited access to the hilltop, yet was close to the Fort area where Parsis had settled. The tower was functioning by 1675, and later other benefactors constructed more towers along with nearby bungalows for prayer services. These benefactors dedicated the towers for use "by every member of the Parsee community professing the Zoroastrian religion as a place for the exposure of the dead and the performance of other religious rites and ceremonies" (The General Trust Deed of 1884, 9). The dedication was first informal and then thusly inscribed into a trust deed only in the late nineteenth century, which formed the early BPP, the apex trust and authority for Parsis in India. This agreement established early Parsi governance and formalized older customary practices of giving.

While housing was seized upon as the most critical intervention in the current demographic crisis, as discussed in chapter 3, most BPP trustees have vowed to protect the Doongerwadi complex and the practice of dokhmenashini against any and all threats. This was an essential pillar of most campaigns for those running for election to the BPP in 2011. This obligation was further cemented by the judgment in *Kanga v. BPP*, which stipulated that the towers and land were dedicated for excarnation only. Yet these sacred towers remain a critical battleground for orthodox and liberal Parsis to fight over what constitutes proper practice and even who is allowed to be a Parsi at all.

The Doongerwadi complex in Mumbai is a hotly contested space today but has sustained the practice of excarnation for Parsis in the city for centuries. In 2004, it was surveyed that up to 98 percent of Parsis in the city chose to have their funerary rites at the towers. But in recent decades, the hilly terrain of Doongerwadi, in Malabar Hill, has also become a troubled topography. The site marks the demographic, ecological, and ritual crises of the Parsi community. Historically, the Punchayet had reserved the right to bar entry to the tower of silence and manage the practice of dokhmenashini as a tool to discipline the community; employing its control of sacred spaces is a crucial aspect of its authority (Palsetia 2001, 82; Desai 1977). Decisions were usually ad hoc and related to the trustees' political and social leanings. As detailed in the last chapter, beginning at the turn of the twentieth century and until recently, access to the Doongerwadi complex has been bitterly fought over in the courts and the Parsi press.[6] If one takes a historical glance at the controversies surrounding the Doongerwadi complex and who has been able to access the site, we come upon many critical moments like the *Petit* case, *Kanga v. BPP*, and the *Gupta* case, wherein the definition of who is a Parsi is at stake.

Doongerwadi and the Infrastructure of Excarnation

Doongerwadi remains on the highest part of Malabar Hill in the southern section of the peninsula, but what was a dense jungle now is one of the city's most expensive areas for real estate. This tower of silence complex encompasses approximately sixty acres of land in what is now one of Mumbai's most exclusive neighborhoods. From the busy intersection at Kemp's corner, one can walk or drive up several steep roads to the first level, where the prayer halls, office, and small morgue are located. One can see lush trees and flowers along the road, and the first level is well landscaped and maintained. The prayer halls, or bunglis, must be rented, and there are a few different sizes and levels of ostentation to accommodate all economic levels of the community.

After the initial days of prayers with the body, the corpse is carried on an iron bier to the towers on the highest level by corpse bearers, nasasalars, dressed in head-to-toe white with white gloves. They are then followed by the presiding priest and a procession of mourners, who walk in twos with a white handkerchief held between them. The dokhmas (towers) are massive, open, circular stone-walled structures with a well in the middle. In the past, only male Zoroastrian mourners were allowed to walk up to the towers, but today, female Zoroastrians may follow as well. After the procession walks further up the hill to the towers, the body is placed on a stone slab about knee-high from the ground for the mourners to say their final prayers and is then taken through a gate to the designated tower by corpse bearers. After about one hundred feet, it is impossible to see the set of towers themselves due to the thick vegetation and landscaping. The mourners can then return to the prayer hall or the fire temple on the upper level of the premises.

Non-Zoroastrians are not allowed in the prayer hall, near the towers, or even to see the face of the corpse after the prayers. They are allowed to pay their respects in a separate hall. This issue has generated much debate in recent years, with more and more cases of intermarriage. In 1990 a young intermarried Parsi woman, Roxan Shah, died in a car accident, and there was much controversy within the community about having her remains accepted at Doongerwadi. After this episode, it became established that intermarried women could only be placed in the towers if the family of the deceased provided an affidavit attesting to the woman's continued practice of the Zoroastrian religion until her death.[7] These restrictions and further crucial concerns about the viability and functioning of Doongerwadi as a mortuary site have set many Parsis in search of an alternative location for their funerals. These concerns are directly related to the urban environment and ecology of Doongerwadi—more precisely, the disappearance of the vultures in the megacity.

Excarnation and Exposure

Researching the Doongerwadi complex at Malabar hill has grown increasingly difficult recently as the debate about its functioning has intensified. Photography has been strictly prohibited and security tightened by the Punchayet. As I am Parsi, I have attended funerals outside my research capacity. I have also been given a guided tour of the grounds with a notebook while repeatedly assuring my guide that I was not carrying a camera. While constantly wary of non-Parsis on the premises, site officials have become increasingly concerned about community members themselves exposing the area with photographs. This fear escalated after a case in which a Parsi woman leaked photographs of the tower interiors to the press as evidence to support her contention that the process of dokhmenashini was not properly working.

Dhun Bharia, a middle-aged Parsi woman, made news in 2005 when she sent pictures of the rotting corpses at Doongerwadi to the broader Indian press. In 2011, Bharia asked me to meet her at the charity office she set up in her mother's name, which is within a municipal school near what used to be a Parsi neighborhood near the Marine Lines neighborhood. I walked up the wide half-broken steps to the third floor and followed a simple printed sign to the office. Her office was quite cluttered with papers and rows of files. On the walls were generic posters of babies and horses, and her office was otherwise very modest. In my interview with her, she related the following: In 2005, her mother, and only close relation, died. "Mummy was all I had," she related, and even after the initial four days of prayers, Bharia went to Doongerwadi daily to pray at the temple there and began to chat with the corpse bearers. She asked the bearers, "*Iyan* bodies *thai chaich*?" (are there bodies still here?) She related how she was told that the bodies were all naked, and some had their eyes eaten out by crows that would also "snatch out their private parts." She spoke to me mainly in Gujarati, but some phrases were then emphatically repeated in English.

Horrified by the images, her first thought was to consult with the BPP since it is the manager of the space. She spoke to the trustees about the conditions and even complained about the smell from the towers. She said the BPP simply shrugged it off, dismissing her, saying it was in the hands of the priests whether the rite should continue. She then contacted a few of the high priests. It was explained to her by one of them that the "body is our house for our soul"; when we die, the vultures eat the body so that the soul may leave. They said that nothing could or should be done. She claimed she warned them of her intention to go to the press with evidence if nothing changed. Bharia emphasized that she thought she had no legal recourse, power, or willingness to go to court, so her only option was the press.

She then showed me a set of photos, which I admit I did not want to see. They depicted almost bloated yet mostly intact corpses. "How did you get to take this photo?" I asked. It was a Parsi photographer, she said quickly, immediately trying to assure me that she was trying to be respectful by not breaking the code of non-Parsis viewing the faces of the corpses. But, she admitted, she had to bribe many people, making their "*hath garam*," their hands warm. "There are so many watchmen now, but at that time, there were fewer," she said. One hundred ten photos were taken, and she made a CD. In her desperation and concern to spread information about the disturbing circumstances at Doongerwadi, she went from house to house in every Parsi housing colony. She showed the pictures to whoever was interested to see them.

After the pictures went to the press, she got many phone calls and visits. She showed me newspaper clipping after clipping as the story was reprinted several times in Mumbai and national papers. She said she only submitted distance shots and no close-ups out of respect. The few photos I saw depicted corpses arranged neatly around the circular inner well. Most were bloated, but none seemed to have been devoured in any way. Bharia was forthright with me that she had embarrassed the community but only out of desperation, mixing in English words for emphasis. She kept repeating over and over that I had to understand that the bodies were "*naga,*" naked, and left for all to see, not picked clean as they should have been. Her dear mother had not been properly consigned.

Bharia's exposé to the press was incredibly controversial. While many were deeply shocked by the conditions, they were also quite humiliated that this internal, private, and sacred matter was revealed to the public. Others were inspired to push for alternative methods like cremation. A measure currently in place was a proposal put forward by community activist Homi Dhalla, who wished to retain the practice of dokhmenashini in some form and installed solar panels to dry and decay the bodies faster. This solution is rejected by those who claim that the bodies are then literally "fried" in the summer and left to rot during the cloudy monsoon season. One high priest even likened the practice to solar cremation (Hinnells 2005, 117). After Bharia's actions, the BPP was forced to explain why the system was not functioning as it should have been, and all evidence pointed to the lack of vultures critically required to devour the bodies. Therefore, the Punchayet was then entrusted with dealing with what had happened to the vultures.[8] There were several proposals to build an aviary and even a model initiated by British "starchitect" Thomas Heatherwick in 2010, which has not been pursued due to cost and other issues.[9]

One elderly Parsi remarked in an interview that in the 1970s, when he was younger, one could see a multitude of vultures lining up on the walls of the dokhmas as soon as the body began to be carried toward it. He explained animatedly about how walking up the hill to the towers and being accompanied by these enormous birds overhead used to have him in awe. Today, one only sees clear skies dotted by a few kites and crows, none too interested in the towers. Punchayet officials agreed that there had been a significant decline in the carrion birds. Many vultures are naturally steered away by the city's congestion and high-rise buildings. It was hypothesized that the construction noise of a new Parsi colony abutting the complex in the 1980s also discouraged the birds from flying near the site.[10]

Recently, a more definitive cause has been uncovered that ties Parsi ritual practice and vultures to the treatment of other animals in the local ecology. Diclofenac, a drug used on cattle farms, is found to produce gout, renal failure, and death in the birds when ingested. Although the declining population of three species of South Asian vultures was noted in the 1980s, it was not until 2003 that microbiologists working with the Peregrine Fund and Washington State University isolated the cause of the decline. The three species were dying after ingesting the carcasses of livestock treated with diclofenac, an anti-inflammatory used on cattle to diminish the pain of constant milk production, and a painkiller given to humans. Further studies show that vultures cannot survive even if less than 1 percent of the drug is in the carcass upon which they feed (Swan et al. 2006). While the government of India banned the drug in 2006, it is estimated that about five million animals were treated annually before the ban, and humans continue to take the medicine. Apart from their role in Zoroastrian funerary practices, vultures are also an integral part of other religious groups' ecologies as they help consume the millions of other livestock untouched by many Hindus because they are cattle and untouched by Muslims if they are not ritually made *halal*. The decline in the vulture population, while not limited to the city of Mumbai, has contributed to the declining viability of the dokhmenashini practice in the city.

Even before Bharia's photos, a former BPP trustee founded the Disposal of the Dead with Dignity Action Group (DDDAG) in the early 2000s to press the trust to construct a crematorium within the complex at Doongerwadi. Conservatives in the community lashed back that cremation was an irreligious practice and that the uproar over the photos was misguided. Another former BPP trustee, Burjor Antia, from a priestly family, remarked in the press, "Naturally you will find dead bodies there and not a valley of flowers. . . . If you open a grave, will you not find worms and a half-eaten body?"[11] Furthermore, the trustees of the BPP insisted that there was nowhere in the trust deed that allowed for a crematorium on-site at Doongerwadi. The DDDAG then amended its mission to just having one of the bunglis on the property reserved for prayers for those who chose cremation. This too was heavily contested and never established. Bharia's photos and the DDDAG group's advocacy not only aggravated conservative religious sentiment but also revealed to many that while the trust had protected the space and ritual over centuries, the trust, as a mechanism undergirding ritual infrastructure, was also a constraint to any possible ritual change. As per the trust deed and further reinforced by the judgment in *Kanga v. BPP*, the site could only be used for excarnation. The case narrowed the scope of what trustees could do, as the dokhmenashini ritual was what should be performed on premises at Doongerwadi as per the deed. Therefore, at the tower of silence complex in Mumbai, continuing the practice of dokhmenashini, *as if* it was functioning, was the only way forward. The trust's objects of 1884 prevailed in 2011.

An Alternate Topography

For generations of Parsis who have lived in smaller cities or less densely settled areas, dokhmenashini was never an option. Their bodies have been buried in cemeteries, or *aramgahs*, for centuries (Desai 1977, Hinnells 2005).[12] In Mumbai today, inaugurating a new cemetery is somewhat out of the question because of the exorbitant cost of city real estate. Although more and more Parsis in Mumbai were moving toward alternatives to dokhmenashini, the actual practice of cremation required alternative protocols and, even more critically, a site of practice that would be seen by at least some in the community as a viable alternative. It is important to note that, even for the reformists, who wish to move away from the practice of dokhmenashini due to its unviability, the tradition of prayer rituals and the location of those prayers remained highly critical. Until recently, the place of Doongerwadi in the Parsi imaginary was still vital to their self-understanding of how funerals should be performed and to reaffirm their space as a minority in the city (Walthert 2010).

Even until 2014, the BPP insisted that the traditional system of excarnation at Doongerwadi was still viable: "The system is working perfectly with the help of sun rays. The vultures are a secondary option. The BPP does not encourage or discourage the community from opting for cremation. But we believe fire is sacred and the dead body is impure and thus cremation is not allowed in our religion. Those who opt for it can perform the prayers in the halls outside and we do not have any objection to it."[13] Before a new prayer hall for cremation was inaugurated in August 2015, prayers had to be conducted in a private residence. Coming back to Anaita's story, I was present at her great aunt Siloo's *uthamna*. The funerary ritual was performed in her small drawing room, as she had few kin and had already seen the passing of most of her peers. Those who could, gathered in the tight space while the priest, Ervad Madon, and his assistant spread out white cotton sheets on the floor and had the body placed upon them in the correct manner. At that time, Madon was one of the few priests willing to perform the rituals for a Parsi who chose cremation. He moved quickly around the space, arranging vessels and the other ritual implements. More and more people arrived, and some had to stand in the doorways and pray through the sweltering September heat and humidity, through the clouds of smoke from the *afarganu* (silver chalice that holds fire) that quickly choked the room. Anaita and I stayed through the ritual ceremony, and then we followed the hearse in a private car to the municipal crematorium in Worli.

The crematorium was right on the sea, and in that sense, the area was scenic with a cool breeze, but inside, the building was a vast, empty warehouse. The walls were chipped from the salty sea breeze and stained with *paan* (chewed betel leaves and spices) in some places. There were about ten broken plastic chairs in the middle and then on a higher platform, the ovens themselves. Siloo's body was placed on a rolling platform. The steel door was briefly opened, and the body was rolled inside. The attendant slammed the door shut using a rag to cover the iron handle and said quickly that we could pick up the ashes in a few days, giving her relatives a tiny slip of paper with a serial number. The small group of close relatives initially stood there and then slowly wandered back to the parking lot. Anaita's aunt remarked that she was going out of town for a few days, and then an uncle mentioned that he, too, had commitments. Seeing that nobody was stepping forward, Anaita again offered to help by picking up the ashes. Everyone seemed relieved.

"But wait, what should I do with them?" she asked. In the parking lot, the consensus was reached that she should not bring them to anyone's house, as the ashes were impure. Her aunt recalled that for her mother's funeral, she had thrown them at her mother's birthplace in southern Gujarat, where Siloo was also born. "So, is anyone going there soon?" Anaita asked. "No, not until after the monsoon," they replied. Anaita proposed that she scatter the ashes in Siloo's tiny garden, where her great-aunt had spent many an hour on her beloved flowers. "No, that won't work" because the *mali*, Siloo's gardener, was very superstitious and would stop coming if he thought the garden had spirits. "Just go throw them in the sea," was the final request.

When Anaita returned to the municipal crematorium a few days later and exchanged the slip of paper for Siloo's ashes, she recalled that they were in a terracotta pot that was still warm. She decided to walk out to the small stretch of beach just beside the crematorium and throw the ashes there, with a view of the new Sea Link bridge connecting Worli to Bandra. Anaita recounted, "I didn't know whether to say anything, some prayers or some kind words about her, so I just said an *Ashem Vohu* and threw the pot.[14] The ashes flew everywhere and then the surf brought the pot back, and I had to throw it again." Anaita described feeling distraught that she could not properly honor her great aunt. "I just didn't know what I was supposed to do. At least at Doongerwadi, it's so beautiful, and people help you." Anaita remembered that at previous funerals she had attended at Doongerwadi, although it was somber, walking behind the bier being carried up to the tower, holding a white handkerchief between her and a relative made one feel like a community of mourners. This just felt empty.

Excarnation to Ashes, Trust to Trust

Before the new prayer hall for cremation prayers was built, many Parsis like Anaita and Siloo had hoped that one of the Doongerwadi bunglis could be used for prayers for those cremated. However, while the infamous "renegade priest" high court judgment in *Kanga v. BPP* did reject the Punchayet's ban on priests like Ervad Madon, it affirmed that the trust deed for Doongerwadi was specific for its use for dokhmenashini only. Hence, while the case initially decided in 2011 was in favor of beneficiaries and their rights to engage any priest they wanted for rituals at the tower of silence, it did foreclose the option to hold prayers for cremation or even a crematorium itself within the Doongerwadi complex (chapter 4). Any other kind of funerary practice at Doongerwadi could constitute a breach of trust. The obligation attached to the property of the 1884 trust deed did not allow for ritual innovation on site at Doongerwadi.

Ironically, while the *Kanga* case was taken up to protect the rights of beneficiaries regarding funerals within the tower of silence complex, its judgment actually forced the hand of reformers to abandon the space at Doongerwadi. It furthered and severely constrained the obligation, as Doongerwadi could not be used for another purpose. Yet the existing ritual process was becoming increasingly unviable. As the orthodox members of the community were affirmed in their protection of dokhmenashini, the reformists continued to search for other options.

Only the birth of a new trust in 2015 could create new conditions of possibility with their own perpetuity. The Prayer Hall Trust was endowed by many familiar characters involved with the Death with Dignity movement and the two petitioners in the "renegade priest" case, Kanga and Kushrokhan. The new endowment was funded by the A. H. Wadia Trust, one of Mumbai's wealthiest Parsi trusts, and private donors after an appeal was posted in the Parsi press. The new trust made a proposal to the Municipal Corporation, the city's governing body and where Kanga was a former commissioner, to build and donate a bungli; it would have two halls to the municipality to be used by all faiths with preferences given to Zoroastrians at certain times of the day and could be used even if the body had been cremated elsewhere. A "sister trust" was endowed to collect and dispense funds for the maintenance and security of the hall. Since August 2015, the Prayer Hall Trust has been functioning, and the space has been given over to the Municipal Corporation.

I was briefly able to visit the Prayer Hall in 2018. It is brightly lit and modern in style. The Hall is quite large and can be split to accommodate small or large groups of mourners. The content of the prayers and rituals is said to be the same as before. Family members can even stay in guest rooms to perform early morning prayers, like the arrangements at Doongerwadi. After the first six months of use, the Hall had served fifty Parsi funerals and, at its peak, ninety-seven in 2016. It now offers mourners the sale of sandalwood and *divos* on site.[15] Flowers can be arranged easily, and they even have some facilities for Skype so those who cannot attend in person can participate in the ceremonies. The trust's website also updates daily with notices on *paid-ast* ceremonies and short obituaries, similar to what the Punchayet offers with Doongerwadi on its website. Hence, while the death ritual for some Zoroastrians has dramatically altered from excarnation to ashes, the mode of perpetuating ritual infrastructure has continued; that is, through philanthropic giving and the trust. The trust is the mechanism to manage funds and property communally. It also promises to maintain and nurture the new relationships of space, time, and people it inaugurates, into the future.

Priests and Power

Since the construction of the Prayer Hall, the high priests and the Punchayet have lost one of their most effective punishments for those they deem irreligious, and over the long term, perhaps even a revenue stream, since the considerable upkeep of Doongerwadi was partially supported by the many donations and fees at funerals. Currently, in Mumbai, the two funerary systems are running concurrently.[16] While dokhmenashini is still preferred, the innovation in mortuary ritual will destabilize the already fragmented constellation of Parsi authority (priests, trustees, lay Parsis). Furthermore, it has the potential to shift some of the hierarchies within the priesthood.

For years since the ban, priests like Ervad Madon and others were effectively blacklisted from the tower of silence and performing rituals at several more conservative temples. I was eager to meet Ervad Madon, one of the "renegade priests," in a more official capacity in 2011, while the ban on his services at Doongerwadi was still in effect. He asked me to his home at Godrej Baug, a Parsi colony that abuts the tower of silence complex. While the BPP reserves flats for priests, he does not live in the building that provides housing for priest families but in another of the blocks. The room we sat in was tiny and cluttered with a trophy case, motorcycle helmets, and other bike paraphernalia, as he was an avid motorcyclist. In general, full-time priests live humbly as they are only paid per service and rarely receive any kind of salary since their work is irregular. I had expected that the ban had certainly affected Madon's livelihood and reputation.[17]

Madon rushed between me and the kitchen as he fixed us some tea, a strange reversal since, in public, he would typically have been the one being attended to. When we finally sat together, he explained that there were about 40 percent outmarriages in the community, so there was a growing demand for his services. "Lots of rich people get away with it," he said, implying that richer Parsis have much less trouble hiring priests to perform cremation ceremonies or prayers for those who intermarry and their children. He continues to point out the double standard that he is being punished for, what many appreciate and others get away with. With resignation, he commented, "Some call me Mr. Madon now," instead of the honorable title of Ervad.[18] There was also a petition to evict him from the baug at one point that did collect some signatures but was later abandoned. While the ban personally burdened Madon, he continued performing ceremonies at other venues and did not challenge the BPP in court. As soon as the Prayer Hall was opened, however, Madon has been in high demand. He was one of the first four priests to conduct the opening *jashan*, blessing ritual, and now finds regular work.

One of the chief supporters and organizers of the ban against Madon and a fervent defender of dokhmenashini has been High Priest Peshotan Mirza.[19] A reporter from *Open Magazine* spoke with Dastur Mirza by phone about his reaction to the new Prayer Hall. He responded, "These people, the priests who work with them, they are all renegades.... Have they studied Zoroastrianism? Who are they to start a prayer hall?" He reportedly hung up the phone and then called back to urge the reporter not to "malign the community in the press."[20] While many conservative priests have written articles and given speeches decrying the new cremation practice and Hall, there is little they can now do to enforce their authority or religious views. Both legally as well as ritually, the new Prayer Hall Trust has inaugurated a viable alternative funeral.

Some embrace this new ritual infrastructure as a way to balance their sentiments, religious and scientific. A retired Parsi engineer wrote in an op-ed:

> Cremation is regarded as contaminating fire with dead matter. It is a moot point whether fire can ever be contaminated. As an environmental scientist myself, I have always understood that fire can destroy even the most toxic chemicals in the world. Fire purifies everything. When the time comes, I would like to be cremated after geh sarna prayers are recited. The ashes should be taken to Poona where an aramgah [Parsi cemetery] reserved for Parsis exists near Koregaon Park. I have paid to reserve three places for my family in this aramgah where our ashes will be deposited.
>
> Why ashes? Why not direct burial? I could have chosen direct burial if I was living in Poona, but as I live in Bombay it would require the body to be taken to Poona after securing police clearances which might be time consuming. I wish there was an aramgah in Bombay! By burying ashes, I cannot be accused of polluting the soil (although, as I have said earlier, no pollution occurs).
>
> A marble tablet will be fixed over each grave with a suitable inscription. The traditional dakhmenashini system leaves no trace of the individual consigned to the dakhma, whilst cremation followed by burial of the ashes would provide an everlasting spot which my family can, hopefully, visit once in a while—and lay flowers![21]

His public statement is quite interesting on many points. As an environmental engineer, he wields his scientific expertise to counter the religious injunction of separating the pure from the impure. Burial does not stand as a viable alternative due to issues of geography and convenience. He also expresses his desire for a style of burial wherein his loved ones may be able to visit his grave. Opinions like Arceivala's buttress support for reformers who believe that electric cremation is the only viable alternative left to them in Mumbai. For conservatives, such scientific rationalization runs completely counter to the authority and teachings of the high priests.

The actual endowment of the new Prayer Hall Trust points again to the strength of the Parsi laity. In the mid-nineteenth century, "industrious" lay Parsis left southern Gujarat with its concentration of priestly power to move to Bombay and settle new ritual infrastructure. Once again, we see lay Parsis who have collected funds, garnered community support, and endowed a trust to support the ritual innovation of cremation. If this leads to a reinvigoration of the priesthood, currently also declining in numbers, it remains to be seen.

For many orthodox Parsis, the Prayer Hall remains illegitimate, irreligious, and perhaps irrelevant, but for more liberal Parsis I interviewed, the Hall offers them a way to reconcile their beliefs—to have a "proper" funeral in their own estimation. The Prayer Hall has received donations from many Parsis abroad. I reason that supporting this alternative in Mumbai offers them an acceptance of their funerary adaptations in the diaspora, which do not and cannot include excarnation.

Up until the construction of the Prayer Hall, the endurance of the trust at Doongerwadi had been one of the critical constraints on forms and alternatives of Parsi mortuary practices in the city. Through its bans on intermarried women from entering sacred spaces or on priests who perform ceremonies for interfaith couples or their children, the BPP and other trusts were able to enforce certain forms of what they deemed proper religious practice. They were able to maintain proper subjects by managing their proprietary objects. The 2011 judgment in the *Kanga* case denied the BPP's rights to manage both the trust's property and the beneficiary's propriety, affirming only the former. In fact, by the end of the legal arguments, the BPP's reach into the proper religious practice of Parsis was curtailed. The custom of not allowing non-Parsis into the bunglis at Doongerwadi to sit for prayers for their Parsi spouse, parent, or grandparent pushed many beyond the fold. While always having the backing of most of the high priests, trusts like the BPP gave further evidence that their trust deeds did not allow them to include non-Parsis, as the deeds specifically gave access to Parsis or those practicing the Zoroastrian faith. The establishment of the Prayer Hall Trust did not simply broaden the availability of prayers for those who wished to be cremated but served to enlarge and diversify the topography of practice, which I describe elsewhere as the spatial arrangement of religious infrastructure that enables ritual practice (L. Vevaina 2022b). This expansion further widens the potentialities of Parsi propriety through the property that religious trusts establish and maintain in perpetuity. This new ritual infrastructure was then able to offer a practical alternative to what some saw as an unviable practice and ultimately might legitimize a more expansive definition of who counts as a Parsi, retaining in the fold those who chose cremation.

This story of changing mortuary practices further shows the critical way that urban space and ecology become a constraint to ritual innovation.

Parsi migration and the endowment form show how powerful the trust remains as ritual infrastructure, hinging together property and propriety through time, even if faced with ecological unviability and ritual adaptation. The law, faithfully did not allow the 1884 trust deed to fail. The structure of the trust at Doongerwadi had now perhaps exceeded its purpose. The trust would endure, even if the rituals it supported could no longer. Furthermore, even while battling the tenacity of a trust like the BPP, petitioners like Kanga and Kushrokhan saw the solution to a failing trust was to birth another trust with alternate objects. Shifting from a jungled plot at the top of Malabar Hill to a municipal crematorium in central Mumbai, the new Prayer Hall Trust has rearranged the constellation of Parsi funerary space. As this new trust is added to the directory of trusts, it can allow for a new horoscope of Parsi funerals in the city. This renewed cycle of perpetuation creates a demand for new funds and, again, charitable giving. The next chapter will travel from Mumbai to Hong Kong and detail how the needs of propriety are being addressed with global trust properties and all the obligations they entail.

CHAPTER 6. **AWAKENING THE "DEAD HAND"**

Liquid and Solid Properties

Mr. Sodawala, a large housing trust manager, was an invaluable interlocutor for this research. As we sat in his office one afternoon, he told me the story of his baug, a Parsi colony in the northern suburbs of Mumbai run by a trust. He gave me an anniversary souvenir of the colony, a short booklet with the history and achievements of the colony. The original land of the baug was gifted to the settlor by a governor of Bombay, who came for hunting on the grounds. In 1909, the trust was formed, and in 1922 the plot title was transferred and endowed to the community. Like the Bombay Parsi Punchayet (BPP), this trust funds religious sites, ceremonies, medical bills, charity funds, education, and even the protection of animals. Mr. Sodawala estimated that 75 to 80 percent of the beneficiaries are not Parsis, except when involving the fire temples and housing, where the deed was specific that these were only for Parsis. He related the beneficence of the trust's settlor on several occasions. Mr. Sodawala then described the forms and uses of all the assets and properties he managed most reverently. It was clear from his descriptions that he felt entrusted with the significant legacy of the settlor and often looked upon his large portrait behind his desk as he spoke. While the trust decisions were governed by five trustees, all men and women of renown in the community who met once a month, the day-to-day complaints and problems were all handled by Mr. Sodawala, and these seemed to weigh on him. He grudgingly described the lawsuits, failed evictions, and municipal headaches he faced, exclaiming, *"Maru bheja khaech!"*

literally, "[they] are eating my brains." Then Mr. Sodawala switched his tone again and related how Parsis from Hong Kong had saved his trust.

While the center of Parsi communal life remains in Mumbai, the community, through its ties to shipbuilding and the opium and tea trade, has for centuries had a quiet presence in the city of Hong Kong (Hinnells 2005).[1] In the mid-eighteenth century, trade brought the Parsis to Hong Kong and a small group remained and settled after the British took over the island in 1841. Like in Bombay, the Parsis in Hong Kong built up multiple sectors in the colonial city, including banks, hospitals, the ferry system, and the university. In return, profits from the China trade made millionaires out of several of Bombay's illustrious philanthropists and helped to build some of this city's founding infrastructure. Names like Jeejeebhoy, Cama, Ruttonjee, and Mody are inscribed in the very cityscape of Mumbai and Hong Kong on streets, hospitals, colleges, and schools. These are the material traces of trade, industry, and religious beneficence etched onto properties all over the city.

As the previous chapters have moved through the Parsi topography of Bombay-Mumbai, we must remember that many of these endowments were initiated by the vast individual profits earned first with opium and then the cotton trade with China in the nineteenth century. Critical to this mode of accumulation and giving for the Parsis of Bombay was the role of investment in urban real estate, which moved from serving as personal equity into its fundamental role in communal investment and city life. I do not wish to claim that Parsis were the only Indians who became wealthy through trade and gave generously in philanthropy; for example, there were many others like the Baghdadi Jewish Sassoons, the Shankarshetts, and Rogays (Chopra 2011a; Ranganathan 2019) just to name a few who were prominent and influential givers in Bombay. However, Parsis also had the distinct advantage of being a colonial elite in both cities, giving them early access to land and favors denied to other natives. As we move between Bombay and Hong Kong, the following will tell a story of competing logics and temporalities: the risk and contingency of overseas trade versus the stability of land, and the perpetual nature of the endowment versus the varying velocity of the urban real estate market. The chapter will show how liquid and solid properties enable and constrain the trust mechanism within particular legal and municipal environments.

As this book has progressed, we have seen how trust objects, like funds and real estate, take on aspects of being subjects themselves, as maintaining the trust's structure becomes its purpose, key to its endurance over time. But there is a critical material difference between liquid funds and solid housing and other real estate that the latter glacially circulate, as trustees have a diminished form of ownership over assets, perpetually beholden to beneficiaries, and held to account by the Charity Commission. A trust engenders social relations, but in a particular form. With public trusts, the settlor relinquishes some rights of ownership, use, and alienation in regard to the asset at a future date. Rights of possession and perhaps ownership are held by both the trustees and the beneficiaries. The trustee takes on a kind of guardianship role over the asset. He or she does not have the right to alienate but has the duty to maintain and even enhance the asset's value through investments. Destroying or alienating value would be a breach. The beneficiaries are given the right to use the asset but cannot sell the asset. With legalized pugree, these use rights swing back into the right to conditionally alienate and generate more value. But regulatory changes and new financial practices can wake up this dormant scape. This final chapter will focus on this movement of wealth as a process of capital accumulation and property creation and the slow process of the financialization of religious giving.

The process or condition of financialization is commonly discussed as a twentieth-century mode of Euro-American capital accumulation, which privileges gains from financial transactions over those from trade or commodity production (Van der Zwan 2014; Riles 2010). But in my view, this understanding is too narrow. It ignores the long history of particular forms of accumulation that rely on rents and investments, speculation and risk, in techniques of formalized giving found worldwide. As the process of financialization refers to changing regimes of accumulation and a renegotiation of state–society relations, where risk and financial logic are brought to everyday life, it is very apt to describe the ways forms of giving shift over time. It is assumed that an endowment hinges together productive and unproductive capital in pursuit of an obligation—for instance, agricultural yields to support a temple or investment dividends to fund a school. The settled property is considered unproductive because it is stopped and tied up by the trust. It must be supported by some circulating property if it is to attain perpetuity. Hence many scholars refer to the trust as the "dead hand" (Maitland, Runciman, and Ryan 2003; Friedman 2009; Birla 2009).[2] This stems from the Roman law term of mortmain, *manus mortus*, the dead hand, a concept which Birla rightly notes has a "spectral life" alongside "its cousin, the invisible hand" (Birla 2009, 68–69). But the book has shown that what are being hinged together are forms of liquid, finance capital with solid, immovable assets like land and material infrastructure in pursuit of the objects of the trust. What is being fixed is the obligation that now becomes attached to property in the Parsi context. Critical to this analysis of financialization, of stopping and starting property with obligations, is its relation to social life, the history, and the itineracy of a community.

Novelist Amitav Ghosh, in his Ibis trilogy (2019), weaves the intersecting stories of nineteenth-century Indians involved in the opium trade and how this brings them across the Indian Ocean and the South China Sea to Canton. These novels are remarkable for their beautifully developed characters and for Ghosh's impeccable research into the details leading up to the Opium Wars in the 1840s. The second book chronicles the life of Bahram Moddie, a Parsi merchant from Bombay, who, through family business ties, lives his life on the sea trade between Bombay and Canton. This character is loosely based on Jamsetjee Jeejeebhoy and is a fictional example of the kinds of ties and obligations made between these two places. Before embarking on a short period of field research in Hong Kong during my postdoctoral fellowship, I was fortunate to have started reading the trilogy. The reader is immediately brought into the world of these deep inter-Asian connections across the Indian Ocean. Inter-Asia as a method (Ho 2014) as well as the burgeoning field of Indian Ocean studies in anthropology (Ho 2006; Srinivas, Ng'weno, and Jeychandran 2020; Gilsenan 2011; Mahajan 2021) has pushed scholarship to not only delve into themes of mobility, itinerancy, trading, and religious networks but also to add historical breadth to multisited ethnography.

Moving chronologically, the chapter will first briefly describe how individual trade fortunes in the China trade came to align and incentivize the slow migration of Parsis from Gujarat to Bombay at the end of the nineteenth century. It will then show how these fortunes came to build and mark the city through sustained communal philanthropy. I will move quickly to the twentieth century when the endurance of the trust in Mumbai comes up against municipal laws, aging buildings, and an aging community in one city. At the same time, another endowment in Hong Kong has much more mobility. The chapter will end with my own itinerary and how incorporated charity and its liquidity from the East contrasts with the burdens of concrete wealth in Mumbai and perhaps prophesizes a shift in the horoscope of this community in this city.

Opium's Traces (1750–1840)

As mentioned before, from about the sixteenth to the eighteenth century, Parsis who had settled in Gujarat transitioned from mainly agricultural vocations to shipping and trading with local communities and colonials. We can reframe this story of transition in India if we look at it from an inter-Asian lens. Rustum Manock, a Parsi in Surat, was a key broker, first with the Dutch and Portuguese trading companies. He amassed a considerable fortune and gave generously to his community and beyond. Charitable giving was marked by immediate giving from donor to recipient. It mostly was deployed in response to disasters. Many Parsis like Manock became highly involved in the "country trade" of tea, cotton, and opium between Europe and China. Trade at this point was in the private hands of merchants as large portions of western India were still not firmly under the rule of the East India Company (Farooqui 2006, 12).

As the political and economic fortunes of the more northern port of Surat were declining, the British began to move into Bombay and incentivized natives to do so as well. In 1728, Manock's son Naoroji set up the Bombay Parsi Punchayet (BPP) as a council for self-governance (not yet a trust) and a temple, which aided the arrival and settlement of Parsis in the city (Karaka 2000). Again, these early temples oriented a geography of settlement for Parsis in the city. This early period marks a shift in the history of Bombay as it grew from a set of small islands of fishermen to a colonial entrepôt.

To expedite the country trade, the British needed large ships. To incentivize his move to the burgeoning city of Bombay in 1783, Parsi master ship-builder Lowji Wadia was granted Lal Baug in the Parel section of Bombay as a completely tax-free grant. This was the original land grant that would later host the Wadia colonies discussed in earlier chapters. Further incentives like these were granted to industrious natives to settle by allowing construction wherever they chose "as long as the houses they built did not interfere with the defense of the island or adversely affect the commercial interests of the Company" (Dossal 2010, 34). In this way, large tracts of the emerging city were parceled off to colonial elites. Other than merchants, Parsi migrants to the city were weavers, carpenters, and other artisans working to service the East India Company (Guha 1984, 122). Over this period, "there was an intra-community structural change, an *embourgeoisement*—however immature—of more or less the entire Parsi community" (Guha 1984, 118). One of the primary reasons for this was the sustained nature of community philanthropy practiced by many of the Parsi merchants and others who made their fortunes in the China trade.

Ghosh claims that Parsis left few narratives of their experience in the China trade. (Ghosh 2013). However, I argue that their trade fortunes had more concrete residues in the built landscape of Bombay itself. Many traders like Framji Cowasji Banaji, who once owned forty ships, endowed Parsi temples and other sacred spaces for his community, orienting future endowments and settlements. In this early settlement period in Bombay, inter-Asian trade brought great fortunes to the city. These fortunes began to be invested in lucrative urban real estate for lavish private residences and communal sacred spaces. With the advent of charitable trust in the 1890s these personal fortunes moved into endowments and city improvements, and "the traces of opium further disappeared into the fabric and stone of the city" (L. Vevaina 2023).

Building Bombay (1840–1900)

The 1840s marked a shift in the trade fortunes of many of Bombay's trading elite as trade was opened up from the monopoly of the East India Company to other British traders who had access to better credit. Many Parsi and other Indian traders had huge losses during the Anglo-Chinese War of 1839 and were also losing profitability as the advent of steam shipping outpaced their older ships. Many others had already diversified their fortunes into banking and other profitable sectors like real estate.

For example, Hormusji and Pestonji Wadia earned so much in trade that they invested in land, and by 1809, their individual rental income was about fifteen thousand pounds annually (Guha 1984, 125). Pestonji's adopted son, Dadabhai Pestonji Wadia (1802–1885), owned about a quarter of Bombay Island and, at one time, three-eighths of the share capital of the Bank of Western India. Framji Cowasji held most of the Powai estate in the north, earned huge rental incomes, and performed agricultural experiments in the area. High-end real estate was bought and sold between Parsis and the British in exclusive neighborhoods such as Malabar Hill. It was noted in 1812 that almost all European-occupied houses were Parsi-owned property.[3] Guha (1984, 128) writes, "Parsi capital was considerably involved in land and real estates, sometimes even to the extent of wild speculation and wasteful expenditure on country houses and mansions. In 1864, one-fifth of all those enumerated as house and real estate owners in Bombay Island were Parsis." While the idea of wealthy individuals buying real estate in a growing city is rather unremarkable, what becomes essential about this history is how inter-Asian trade fortunes became a way to earn monetary capital through real estate investment and social capital. These merchants were not just regarded as wealthy but also as community and civic leaders who worked closely with their British patrons. Their wealth and power were put to use by British governors who were eager to see the city grow but who were already taking loans from businessmen for city projects to make up for civic revenue shortages (Thampi and Saksena 2009, 83). Bombay Governor Bartle Frere is quoted as saying, "When I consider the example set us by Mr. Cowasji Jehanghier . . . by the Jamsetjis, the Sankersetts and Sassoons, the Premchands, and so many others of our great merchants, I cannot but feel that come what will, History will write of the generation who built this pile."[4] Jamsetjee Jeejeebhoy (1783–1859), discussed earlier, is an example par excellence of the spaces in which traces of the opium trade mark the cityscape through civic institutions like the hospitals, colleges, and libraries he endowed (Palsetia 2005; 2008). Jeejeebhoy became a member of the Parsi Punchayet in 1823 and was considered by the British as one of the leaders of all native communities in Bombay after the 1830s. His partnership with Jardine Matheson and opium consignment made him one of the wealthiest men in the city. His proposal to build a hospital in 1838 brought forth a unique level of negotiation with the colonial government.[5] Palsetia (2005, 204) notes, "Jeejeebhoy exploited an opportunity for British-Indian collaboration based on co-opting British humanitarian charitable standards." His knighthood and baronet title were awarded for his charitable largess, which included several institutions of medical care, education, and aid to the poor. Homi Bhabha (2013, 13) claims that through philanthropic action like this, the Parsis were able to wield "soft power" and manufacture consent among urban Indians for the project of modernity by showing that essential institutions of native civil society could exist and thrive in India.[6] In her account of Arab legal history in the Straits, Yahaya (2020) shows how charitable giving within colonial settings was also able to tie the community to the public. Charitable giving on this scale served philanthropic purposes and reputational gains for the individual donor and the community.

A man of many firsts, Jeejeebhoy was the first Indian to be knighted (1842), the first to be named baronet (1858), and one of the foremost Parsi philanthropists to work together with the British colonial government in building several public works in the city of Bombay. Overall, he gave about 2.5 million rupees to charity, to both Parsis and non-Parsis, and even sent money to victims of the Irish famine in 1846, exhibiting his largess not only as a native entrepreneur but as a benefactor on par with the British. Jeejeebhoy's investments in the city's public works paid great reputational dividends, as his name continues to mark all kinds of spaces of the city.

In the mid-nineteenth century, the colonial government in Bombay, through land surveys, effectively transformed the island's multiple property regimes into one system of saleable plots of land, which "made possible the transition from a nascent to a full-fledged capitalist land market," according to urban historian Mariam Dossal (2010, 133). As Parsis already owned so much land in the city, they had vast stores of capital to invest in new industries. Stimulated by the closure of American Confederate ports, Bombay's cotton boom financed city-building and investment in centers of art, hospitals, road construction, and grand buildings. This period also saw the rise of many Parsi business houses once involved in trade and shipyards to shift into cotton mills and other industrial production. This speculative boom burst after the end of the American Civil War, which sunk cotton prices dramatically, causing much volatility in Bombay's land market, and many shifted their investments away from real estate and into endowments. Bombay's booms and busts and the concomitant effects on the real estate market and charitable giving have always been stimulated or contracted by global processes through this colonial port city.

A Continuing Tale of Two Cities

Many mark the mid-twentieth century as the beginning of a general period of decline for Parsis in terms of fame, fortune, and demography. As much as Parsi identity and status were at one time marked by economic success and philanthropy, by the end of the Second World War, a new imaginary took hold that we may now reframe through inter-Asian trade. As discussed in chapter 3, Tanya Luhrmann's (1996) ethnography addresses the transformation of the Parsi self-perception from a contributor to Indian modernity to one saturated with the sentiment of decay and anxieties about community decline. While Luhrmann attributes this to the loss of status as a colonial elite, economist Thirankar Roy argues that the Parsi sentiment of decline is intimately tied to Bombay and its place in the world economy: "For 200 years, they had been a vanguard in India's tryst with globalization," (2013, 74), but lost out after 1950 when the economy became more insular under Nehruvian policies. A mercantile community, made wealthy from international trade and emerging industries, was then constrained by Nehruvian socialist policies.[7]

As discussed in chapter 2, the very local trusts that kept Parsis in prosperity in Bombay-Mumbai have become financially strained over the years by the high maintenance costs of their properties and the lack of revenue from frozen rents at 1940s levels. Along with a decline of local donations, high maintenance costs and welfare projects have strained the corpus funds of many trusts holding property in real estate. Their solid, immovable assets, which had once stood as material evidence of their great fortunes and largess, now weighed down their prospects and projects.

During my field research, as I visited and attempted to document the different kinds of housing typologies of Parsi trusts all over Mumbai, I always paid attention to the small plaques adorning the front entrances of colonies. These were material traces of giving, a donor's name and wishes, often erected upon an anniversary of the inauguration of the building. For many big donors, like Jeejeebhoy, their names are garlanded atop gates, but for those who give generously but on a smaller scale, many just have a small plaque. In several places, including at trust properties run by big trusts like the BPP, I noticed that certain buildings' funds were donated from Hong Kong. Mr. Sodawala brought this inter-Asian giving up explicitly in our meeting, while other trusts mentioned Hong Kong donors within a list of others. The ties between the two colonial ports were never severed, and recent years have seen a resurgence of funds transferred from Parsi charitable trusts in Hong Kong back to Mumbai and other smaller Parsi settlements in India. Unlike the profits from individuals, these funds are funneled through charitable trusts, from one trust to another. For many Parsi trusts in Mumbai, funds from overseas have become vital to projects, as along with a dearth of local donations, the high maintenance costs of real estate and welfare projects have drained their corpus funds. As described earlier, many Parsi trusts view communal housing as a way to address declining demography and the high rates of marriage outside the community. As such, Hong Kong funds are often put toward building flats. By utilizing charitable trusts as the legal instruments of their religious giving, Parsi capital, once gained from global trade, has now been channeled into local institutions with religious and communal obligations.

One former Punchayet trustee explained, "The BPP has properties, not funds; housing requires funds, so we must sell flats." This liquidity or lack of liquidity seems to be a fundamental problem of older trusts that manage housing. As their building stock ages, they cannot generate enough income through frozen rents. Many then try to institute "monthly fees," which are only sometimes successful. In one housing colony, they have tried to institute parking fees as many residents have one or even two cars, but many residents shrug these payments off. Many trusts are forced to dip into their corpus funds for maintenance and upkeep, a short-term solution that threatens to thwart their activities in the future.

As argued in chapter 1, the legalization of pugree in 1999 and market liberalization caused a dramatic shift in potential Mumbai property values.[8] This regulatory intervention and skyrocketing real estate prices sped up the velocity of real estate sales all over the city and offered a solution to the liquidity crisis. For trusts with large estates, like the Punchayet, new redevelopment projects on trust lands suddenly had great potential to increase their liquidity, better maintain their current housing stock, and attract the wealth of richer Parsis in Mumbai and abroad with new developments.[9] Yet, because most redevelopments remained Parsi only, the BPP and many other trusts in Mumbai, in need of initial investments, turned eastward to their more liquid coreligionists in Hong Kong.

Hong Kong

Transnational trade and finance have historically connected colonial port cities like Hong Kong and Bombay-Mumbai. So too, has sustained transnational philanthropy. By 1841, the British had taken over Hong Kong, "a barren island with hardly a house upon it,"[10] and slowly populated by migrants from China. Parsis were principal buyers in the first land auction held in Hong Kong in 1841. The first Parsis settled upriver in Canton. As is the common pattern with Zoroastrian diaspora groups, they first invested in sacred space, a cemetery, in 1845 with collected funds from the Canton Zoroastrian Anjuman.[11] To give thanks for their fortune, this small group pledged a considerable donation to their poorer coreligionists in Udwada and Surat in Gujarat (Hinnells 2005, 162). As non-Chinese were only allowed to remain in Canton during the trading season, the community also bought real estate in Macau.

Historian John Hinnells remarks that some of the only clues to the demography of the early community in East Asia are the recorded donations and pledges. This was especially true of the small group of Parsis that settled in Shanghai, who kept extensive documents on their finances and donations. These associations initiated schemes of monies loaned to each other to set up their *anjumans*, or communal organizations and spaces. Once financially independent, they would repay or buy out the supporting association. Most of these anjumans had written into their deeds that they would give to charity any excess of income over expenditure. In 1934, $10,496 (roughly $200,000 today) was sent back mostly to Parsis in India and some funds to local Chinese charities.

While the small Zoroastrian settlements in East Asia remained close-knit and endogamous, they could not shield themselves from the significant and often violent geopolitical situations around them and sometimes even profited from them. Most had family businesses in trade and invested their profits into real estate, an incredibly profitable venture in growing Chinese cities. For example, when the Republic of China named Nanjing its capital in 1912, Parsis in Shanghai saw their investments increase by 350 percent (Hinnells 2005, 168–169). In 1932, the Parsis in Hong Kong fled to Shanghai and sent their funds to Canton, as they were targets for imprisonment under the Japanese occupation for being collaborators with the British. When the Chinese expelled all foreigners from its mainland in 1949, many Parsis (and other Indians) returned to India while others went to Hong Kong, with any moveable property they had, and endowed a trust of their own, the Incorporated Zoroastrian Charity Funds of Hong Kong, Canton and Macau, which is today the wealthiest Parsi trust in the world.[12]

Numbering less than two hundred today, Parsi residents in Hong Kong remain a wealthy minority. One of the most prominent members, Shapoorji Jokhi, was born in Navsari, a small town in Gujarat that was once the center of Parsi religious and communal life before migrations brought the community to colonial Bombay. At seventeen, Jokhi left for a job in Hong Kong, rose in the ranks, and founded his own firm, Jokhi, Parekh and Co., in 1937, trading in silks, oil and ivory, and eventually cotton between China, India, East Africa, and the Middle East. In 1944, Jokhi was held prisoner by the Japanese occupying Hong Kong. After being released, he married but never had any children. With much wealth and without direct heirs, Jokhi endowed his own charitable trust and was determined to help his coreligionists in his hometown, Navsari, and helped build Avan Baug in 1973, a housing colony he named after his mother. After he died in 1990, funds from Jokhi's estate, now run by his nephew from Hong Kong, have been utilized for several new buildings in housing colonies, a Zoroastrian temple in one of the BPP colonies in Mumbai, and a large donation to Parsi General Hospital. A spokesman for the funds has stated that although the family has given funds to Zoroastrian communities worldwide, they prefer to donate to Parsis in India.[13]

I made two short research trips to Hong Kong in 2017. Upon arriving in Hong Kong in the middle of March, it was remarkable how familiar the city felt to me, although it was my first visit, and I spoke no Cantonese. As I walked through Victoria Park on my way from my rented apartment toward Causeway Bay, the rising humidity, trees, and even bird song were so reminiscent of Mumbai, although the building stock and infrastructure are much more developed. The city also has similar traces of a former British colony, with parallel syncretisms in food, drink, and slang. In Hong Kong, one pays the "Shroff" for parking, a common Parsi surname, which means a trader or one who deals in money. I visited a few places and streets named after Parsis, the most conspicuous being the Ruttonjee Hospital, built by Jehangir H. Ruttonjee (1880–1960), and Hong Kong University, whose founding donation was given by a Parsi, Hormusjee Mody (1838–1911), both born in Bombay and migrants to Hong Kong. These Parsi connections remain unknown to most locals.

I was warmly welcomed by the managing trustees of "the Fund," as they called it, at the Parsi Club on Hong Kong Island. Parsi life in Hong Kong since 1931 has centered around the Zoroastrian Hall at Leighton Road, in the Causeway Bay area of the Island. "We are very fortunate here in Hong Kong," said the managing trustee of the Amalgamated Trust Funds of Hong Kong, Canton, and Macau. Indeed, the fund is the most prosperous Parsi charity organization in the world, giving about $1.6 million in 2010 alone to various causes. Beyond being early shareholders in "the bank," HSBC, it was real estate investment from traders such as Hormusjee Mody and Jehangir Ruttonjee that enriched the community. In the late 1990s, the Hong Kong Anjuman voted to tear down the three-story hall and build a tower, renting out all but three floors to commercial renters. "Much of our current ability to give so much is this," said the trustee, pointing around him on the fifth floor of the Zoroastrian building. The new building quickly gained 100 percent rental occupancy and raised an annual income of about HK$8 million (US$1.02 million). The fund was able to pay back the loan for development within a few years, and now all the rental income is invested, through the fund, for the community. Since then, they have been able to employ a full-time priest from India for their two-hundred-person community, a luxury that many Mumbai temple trusts cannot afford. Along with endowments from individuals, the trust in Hong Kong was able to donate the initial investments for many new developments in Mumbai, including Mr. Sodawala's baug.[14] This trust-to-trust transfer is one way to finance any medium- to large-scale charitable property projects in Mumbai, which require substantial initial liquid investments.

Mr. Sodawala remarked that his baug is an outlier in many ways for Mumbai. Located in the northern part of the city, it is far from other Parsi settlements. Unlike other colonies, it has a few multiresident buildings but is otherwise dotted with bungalows, some modest and some renovated on large plots of land. The residents built the bungalows to varying levels of ostentation and architectural style, the only rule being that they could only make one-fourth of the plot to keep the baug "a garden colony." It is also entirely forested and quiet compared to the main road in front of it, whose traffic belies the everyday bustle of Mumbai's northern suburbs.

Mr. Sodawala related how the colony's expenses were once greater than the rents frozen of Rs. 60–80/month ($1–$1.50). "We were deep in the red," and there was a proposal of making the colony cosmopolitan— that is, open to non-Parsis. The bungalow plots are leased for ninety-nine years, with the maximum ground rent set at Rs. 140/year (approximately $2)! The tenants of the baug are mostly older, and there is never a vacancy because upon death, "some relative shows up." There is much litigation here as well. "No one has ever moved out just with a[n] [eviction] notice," and in his younger years, Mr. Sodawala was often running back and forth for court dates. Then the Hong Kong trust funds gave Rs. 4 crores ($730,000) to his trust in Mumbai, and it built thirty new tenements on lease in its new construction named after the donors, a medium-rise building. This significant donation saved the trust and allowed it to maintain its original mandate (remaining Parsi exclusive) while accommodating new and "deserving" tenants. The injection of liquid funds from Hong Kong aided the solid properties in Mumbai.

Godrej Baug

One of the more recent baugs built by the Bombay Parsi Punchayet is Godrej Baug, which utilizes some of the fallow land that was available adjacent to the Doongerwadi property in Malabar Hill. The baug consists of sixteen buildings plus one constructed for the residence of Parsi priests and a temple. The trust first approached the Godrej family through their foundation, the Pirojsha Godrej Foundation, to develop about thirty thousand square meters of hilly terrain.[15] The Godrej Trust agreed to donate toward the new baug as long as the construction department of Godrej & Boyce Manufacturing Company Limited would perform the construction at cost. Significant funds were also provided through selling ownership flats to Parsis in the Spenta building on Malabar Hill. Critical to the smooth negotiation of the land parcel with the Municipal Corporation and the construction was that both the Godrej Trust and the BPP shared several trustees, including Naoroji Godrej.[16] They then approached the Charity Commissioner in a joint front to get necessary permits and clearances. A further delay in clearance was mitigated through the personal connections with then Prime Minister of India Indira Gandhi, whose husband, Feroze, was a Parsi and well known to the Godrej family. The colony was built over fifteen years with many engineering issues due to the uneven terrain. This project was indeed a result of communal and charitable ties.

During the slow construction process, the BPP appealed for funds from Hong Kong to build a fire temple within Godrej Baug. Religious opinion was sought from Dastur Firoze Kotwal, and additional funds were granted from the Jokhi family from Hong Kong. This project and others mentioned above were funded by the Shapoor F. Jokhi Charitable Foundation, founded by Keki Jokhi, Shapoorji's brother and copartner in the S. F. Jokhi Company of Hong Kong. The family provided finishing funds for the agiary and residential quarters for the two full-time priests, who would tend the fire there. The fire was brought over from a near defunct agiary in Navsari, the small town in southern Gujarat where the Jokhis were born before migrating to Hong Kong. Once brought south to Mumbai, the fire was led through the city with a contingent of about three hundred Parsis, beginning at dawn on December 21, 1999 (Hinnells 2005, 93–95), making for quite a spectacular scene in the city.

My first visit to Godrej Baug was to interview a priest residing in a building reserved for Parsi priests and then several times for meetings for the BPP trustee elections. He warned me that if I were coming by car to expect much traffic on the way as the main entrance for vehicles is from Napean Sea Road, notorious for its traffic. As one ascends the hill, passing by luxury residential buildings on the rear side of Malabar Hill, the scene becomes familiar again with the pale pastel yellow that marks the BPP baugs. Like other baugs, the buildings are low-rise structures each with multiple flats. Each building is adorned with a plaque of its primary donor. The baug has a large meeting pavilion and an agiary of its own. But walking along, I noticed a tall grey building (see figure 6.1) that I assumed to be currently under construction.

Since the 1990s, Mumbai has seen a building boom, often with older small-scale structures or informal settlements demolished for the construction of high-rise buildings. In a massive boon for real estate speculation, many development companies began the construction of the concrete foundations of a new and promising residential building. They then presell flats to continue the work. Many such projects successfully managed the construction time and costs with the buyers. Yet, some projects were speculative scams from the outset, with the developer having no intention of ever completing the building. Under such conditions, investors in flats had little recourse and

FIGURE 6.1. Unfinished
building at Godrej Baug.
Photo by author.

suffered huge losses on their never-to-be-built dream flats (Nijman 2000, 2007). What were once buzzing spaces dotted with cranes and workers hauling sand to make cement amid the whirring of cement mixers, became emptied of life, quiet and often thereafter, squatted upon. At different moments, the skeletal remains of these concrete giants could be seen all over the city.

Darius was a young Parsi professional in the real estate business. I met him at his office within a ritzy corporate park in lower Parel, quite close to the Phoenix Mills, a massive redevelopment project that turned defunct mill and chawl space into a luxury shopping center and residences. Like much of the new development in the area, the outside of the park was in stark contrast to the inside. The street had the usual blaring traffic of cars, taxis, and the "whomp whomp" of municipal bus horns, while street peddlers and many pavement dwellers mainly occupied the footpaths. The security guard at the corporate park seemed confused that I entered the gate on foot rather than in a chauffeured car or taxi and slowly sauntered over to me and waited for me to speak. Being unsure about the way in and which building, I said I had an appointment at the office and he pointed and told me the way. Like many newly built corporate parks in Mumbai, this one had the same generic office architecture of mixed glass and steel, with some architectural elements that do not contribute to any style, let alone purpose. A corner jutting out on one side of the building created a strange and empty triangular space inside or an area outside for a fountain or small reflecting pool left empty to avoid becoming a vector for dengue or malarial mosquitos. Inside these buildings, one cannot help but notice how these structures do not quite serve the climate and environment of this city. The panes of glass cannot keep out all the dust and smog from the heavy traffic outside, and the huge glass walls allow in so much sunlight without the escape of air that waiting in the lobby felt like being in a greenhouse.

Real estate is big business in Mumbai, both on and under the table. It has one of the heaviest cash flows of any element in the economy, and elements of violence do not remain strictly to the edges but are often an undercurrent through even fully legal transactions. Many of the poorer residents of colonies often spoke of the threat of goondas (thugs) being brought into conversations, especially when they had to do with forced evictions, a reality for most other city residents, especially those in informal settlements. Relative to private housing and especially to informal settlements, Parsis are little exposed to this kind of quotidian violence concerning their housing. It was quite a shock when one trustee I interviewed of a smaller trust even offered to show me the revolver he kept in his desk. He assured me that it was not for his safety but to intimidate other developers.

Meeting with Darius, the developer, gave me a more significant idea of Bombay's redevelopment landscape. Most of his clients were developers dealing in crores of rupees. They would recover their costs through the early sale of promised flats to overseas Indians or others looking for an investment opportunity. However, he was very interested in the community and often advised Parsi trusts on upcoming projects. He made clear that building new flats for charity recipients was untenable: "You must understand, poor housing is expensive," he exclaimed; how will the costs be recovered?

Many Parsi trusts had the advantage in these development projects as many had open plots on their vast lands, as we have seen in chapter 1 with Nowroze Baug, a scarce resource in Mumbai. I learned later that the aborted building at Godrej Baug had been planned around 2000 as a midrise housing unit intended to be ownership flats marketed toward nonresident Parsis. This was a dramatic move by the Punchayet because it signaled recognition of the reality of Mumbai again as a global city, which still held significant meaning for the worldwide Parsi-Zoroastrian diaspora—a new source for donations but also for potential beneficiaries. The legal category of the non-resident Indian (NRI), a person of Indian descent who is allowed to own property and do business in India, has created a new source of wealth and a possible constituency of diasporic Parsis for the Panchayat and other trusts. The profits from the sales of flats in the ownership building were intended to subsidize four hundred existing charity flats needing repairs or rebuilding as part of the cross-subsidy scheme.

Concerns from many sides, including the Alert Zoroastrian Association (AZA), were brought in front of the courts about the scheme. Sitting trustee Noshir Dadrawala, worried that this kind of fundraising (selling flats to gain liquidity) could be seen as a breach of the BPP, objected: "I may point out that due to the recent amendment to the Income Tax Act 1961, such a development on the Godrej Baug property and sale of flats for crores of rupees on ownership basis may result in withdrawal of the exemption . . . for our trust. This would result in the entire income of our trust, including revenue and corpus donations, being fully taxed. This may result in the trust being called upon to pay wealth tax on all its properties including the extensive Doongerwadi lands" (Noshir Dadrawala in a letter to the BPP quoted in "Building Standstill," *Parsiana*, May 21, 2011). Dadrawala was pushing back against the financial logic that had taken over the BPP, a charity now building housing as investment opportunities. While a few former trustees had questioned the enterprise of constructing new housing for a demographically declining community, the trustees under Dinshaw Mehta looked toward redevelopment not as an opportunity but as a necessity to maintain and inject liquidity into the trust's portfolios.

Due to intense in-fighting among the BPP trustees over the alleged misuse of flat allotments by the board's chairman, which was also brought before the charity commissioner's office, the building permits had been halted. Chairman Mehta was infamous for his pugilistic style of speaking as well as behaving. He was often referred to as a "street fighter" in a mildly appreciative way but also as a way to mark his working-class background in comparison to other trustees. In my brief meeting with Mehta in 2011, he insisted that the construction of the building was being held up as the BPP was awaiting a commencement certification from the Municipal Corporation to build more floors, as well as permission from the charity commissioner to sell the flats to Parsis. "We began the project over ten years ago! Now everything is blocked by the tunnel vision of some trustees," he shouted vehemently.

In my visit to Godrej Baug in 2018, years after this interview, the building was still incomplete, a grey shell now with significant decay, and no doubt, much of the internal infrastructure in complete disrepair. Without the injection of more funds, the BPP's project, burdened by municipal bureaucracy and the conflicting plans of its trustees, had been left as a concrete skeletal ruin in the heart of one of Mumbai's most sought-after neighborhoods. These solid properties can only survive if they attract liquid funds. This is a critical point about financial flows. They are often blocked or bottlenecked by legal stoppages. The Hong Kong Fund was also approached by the BPP and provided funding for some of the buildings, but the delays and difficulty dealing with the Punchayet board led many in Hong Kong to be wary of donating through this trust, with some refusing to donate to them altogether. Here it was the BPP's alleged improprieties that threatened its trust properties.

Eastward Destinies

While investment finance may hold the promise of being mobile, it may never actually achieve mobility (Rudden 1994), especially if held down by the weight of a dead hand and its obligations. But under a different regulatory frame, the constellations of capital and the law might lead to a different horoscope. In contrast to the older buildings of trusts in Mumbai, the Zoroastrian Building in Hong Kong has more of the style and décor of contemporary corporate offices, decorated in warm tones of grey and beige. In 2017, after meeting most of the trustees socially at a community lunch hosted by the Hong Kong Fund, I was then given the opportunity to meet with three of the trustees together on a separate floor to ask more specific questions. We sat in large comfortable chairs in the hall usually used for events, brightly illuminated by the large glass doors that led to a small terrace overlooking a street in Causeway Bay.

Perhaps due to the prominence of real estate investment and redevelopment in my conversations with trustees and managers in Mumbai, who were all wealthy in land but cash poor, I broached the same subject with the Hong Kong trustees. I asked if they had any projects for local real estate investment, and they each glanced at each other and quickly and, very vocally, balked. Communally, they had no desire to venture further into the highly competitive Hong Kong real estate market beyond the Leighton Road building, and there was no necessity to build communal housing for this relatively affluent community. Many fourth-generation families, who were involved mainly in the cotton and textile trade, had already redeveloped their old bungalows into profitable mid-rises, a few of these in very posh neighborhoods. The rest of the community was well housed in private flats and did not favor enclave living. Even with just 200 to 250 members, the trustees did not describe their community in terms of crisis. They mentioned that although endogamy was preferred, many would accept if their children or grandchildren might not marry another Parsi or Zoroastrian. When discussing the crisis rhetoric in India, they nodded, understanding that the sentiment was there, but noted that even small communities in North America, for example, were thriving. The mandate and objects of their communal management were not solely targeted at the ethnic survival of Parsis.

Regarding its global giving, the fund had two primary donation targets in 2017, beyond the local Hong Kong charities it supported. They explained how the trustees read through hundreds of individual letters and applications for donations. These leaned much more toward individual hardship cases for medical relief and education (with interest-free loans), which could be aided through liquid funds. The more significant concrete investments they now thought worthwhile were Zoroastrian temple building in the global diaspora. They had provided matching funds to new prayer halls and temples in California, New York, Houston, London, Toronto, and a few other cities. These were significantly different from real estate investments and were given more as top-up funds to projects currently underway by the local anjumans in those cities. This was not viewed as high-risk speculation to the Hong Kong trustees, as the projects were mostly built through the subscription of funds from local Parsis and were almost ready to be used.

Another significant factor in facilitating their liquidity was the relatively little oversight they received in Hong Kong as a charitable corporation. When I discussed the restrictions of annual accumulations and expenditures that the Charity Commission imposed on trusts in Mumbai, they were surprised. They assured me that aside from annual accounting, they were under no such restriction in Hong Kong. On many occasions, the infighting and litigation of Mumbai trusts and trustees were mentioned in contrast to the "harmony" of the community in Hong Kong. As a corporation, the Fund holds an annual general meeting, and projects are voted upon by members. It was critical, they insisted, that the beneficiaries of their largesse followed this path of harmony and was a factor in how they evaluated the donation appeals they received. They were keenly aware of their privilege in giving and their obligation to give and support their coreligionists, like Mr. Sodawala's trust, in Hong Kong and throughout the world.

Along with their liquidity, the Hong Kong community might be spreading its notions of Parsi propriety along with their property investments. The Hong Kong trustees quickly noted that they had a different outlook than Parsis in India. While many of the middle-aged Parsis in Hong Kong were dismayed but not surprised by the *Goolrukh Gupta* and *Kanga* cases that we discussed, which caused so much communal uproar and cost to the Indian Parsis, the younger generation I spoke with in Hong Kong was aghast at the prospect of such religious conservatism. While many were deeply committed to community traditions like tying the kusti, daily prayers, holy days, respect for elders, and charitable giving, they were not all convinced of the value of strict endogamy nor the expulsion of intermarried women and their children from the community. Board members further insisted that they were not accustomed to the "extra cash payments," as they euphemistically described bribes, necessary to gain permits and licenses in a timely manner in India and wanted to manage their Fund and community with prudence, guarding the gifts of their "ancestors." In a further move away from the concerns and controversies of Mumbai, a few members of the Hong Kong community have taken up critical roles in the Global Working Group, a committee brought together in 2011 of representatives of many of the large diaspora communities of Zoroastrians from all over the world.[17] The BPP is included in the group and has been present at the meetings since 2018, not in a leadership position but as a representative of India.

This perhaps *longue durée* approach to Parsi religious giving is an attempt to think through the movement from informal, immediate giving to customary endowments and eventually to formal and legal charitable trusts as a process of financialization. Key to this story is the role of urban real estate, which begins as personal and social equity and becomes a critical asset in communal investment. The trust's financial logic and perpetual nature reorganize religious giving into an intergenerational relation of obligation and accountability. From its inception, a trust is a financialized form of religious giving. Trustees are always thoroughly involved in accounting and investing procedures, as per their role as trust fiduciaries. As the BPP and other Mumbai trusts have gotten larger and more bureaucratized, their real estate has gotten older and more decaying. As financialization privileges movement and speed, it is no wonder they are now struggling to keep up with the velocity of circulation of more liquid funds. But as with all temporal logics, it runs against others: the perpetual nature of the trust alongside rent control laws, as I have shown, but much of this obligation is at risk. This risk is mitigated by a liquid inflow of investment from Hong Kong.

But these forms of giving are also intimately about how people relate to one another through things. Riles reminds us that finance "is a realm of explicit politics . . . a purposeful and stated compulsion, or 'regulation,' of self and others, a realm of must, shall, and will" and limited to certain temporalities (Riles 2010, 797). This accumulation and expenditure work in a different tense than the subjunctivity of the trust, which privileges the "should" and "as if." As they become more prominent funders of new projects and communal initiatives for Zoroastrians around the globe, the Hong Kong funders and the Global Working Group might slowly eclipse the influence and prominence of the Punchayet and perhaps even Mumbai as the central node of Parsi life.

CONCLUSION

An Unsettled (E)state

In the introduction, I discussed various ways of understanding the city, through infrastructure, housing, food, and other frames. After my field research, I have focused on one reading from Mr. Naik, who offered the horoscope, a way of seeing time in Bombay-Mumbai based on the arrangements of trusts in space, to guide my exploration. The trust directory, as a horoscope of the city, offers its own chronotope, a particular reading of the relation between time and space. By framing our understanding of the city in this way, I have argued why and how trusts matter. I have done so by showing how this econo-legal instrument is so deeply entangled in the history, urban space, kinship, reproduction, and death of a microminority in the city who use it ubiquitously. It is due to their use or overuse of this tenacious instrument, which congeals and selectively releases capital in space and time to promise immortality, that Parsis have been able to leave such a mark on Bombay-Mumbai.

Through the trust, Parsis were able to distribute charity, not just to their coreligionists but also through built spaces in the city and through time. It allowed this community to mark its minority spaces and preserve community codes through access to these spaces. Embedded in the purpose of the trust is the fulfillment of a particular intention to be carried out over time, but embedded in the practice of endowment itself are values as well of what constitutes good or proper relations with these assets. I have argued that the trust deed is a constitutional document, as it inaugurates and structures a social, legal, and fiduciary relation among its settlor, trustees, and beneficiaries. The trust document is the first instance of hinging an obligation to property. The written deed of a public charitable trust can be seen as an obligation not from one party to another but an object, a purpose, or an ideal. Obligation itself means to bind, just as the trust ties up and stops property. This makes giving through the trust distinct from immediate giving. With charitable trusts, this legal obligation is, fundamentally, also a moral obligation toward general public utility or toward a notion of "the good" (L. Vevaina 2018a). This dual obligation cannot be separated from the property once the trust is established, making the trust a technique of what the relationship should be between people and things.

We saw this relationship best through the connection between property and propriety, the relationship between ritual space and housing, and who is worthy of access to these benefits. The trust also sets up and conserves a very specific topography of proper religious practice. The deep entanglement of Parsi fortunes with their Zoroastrian faith and their very particular history of minorityhood has shaped the contours of the contemporary community. The various forms of proper Zoroastrian ritual practice and proper marriage are deeply concerned with specific topographies of real estate. But it is perhaps also this endurant technique that has constrained aspects of life for the community. For instance, the trust form has allowed a turn of the twentieth-century legal judgment to allow gender inequality to persist, even though marriage practices have now distinctly shifted. The trust's form has pushed for courts of law to become the ultimate arbiter for family disputes, disputes over correct ritual practice, and even the potential to have a proper funeral in Mumbai. The trusts' spatiality and the contested access to their use have become key to proper religious performance. For better or worse, the trust has hinged together forms of property with particular forms of propriety.

This book has shown how the trust, borne out of the private charitable intention of a settlor, becomes enmeshed in constantly oscillating spaces of public and private, the religious and secular, and productive and unproductive forms of capital. How these realms have overlapped unevenly with communal authority and civil law, and the contingencies between family property and municipal development present a crucible to understand the everyday life of Parsis as an ethnoreligious group with a dwindling population, the city they inhabit, and the postcolonial legal regime of India.

The Unsettled State

The trust is one of the few legal mechanisms to facilitate the ownership and management of property held in common. It allows for the immortality of the "body unincorporate" (Maitland, Runciman, and Ryan 2003, 52–61). It is a mechanism that allows for group life beyond the natural lives of its members. Even though called a settlement, "the trust maintains an unsettled state between the ideas of property and obligation" (Watt 2009, 118). This unsettled state often reverberates through the division of ownership between the trustees and the beneficiaries, whom I have shown have conflicting interests. This unsettled state of wobbly ownership and blurred obligations is felt throughout the relationships engendered by the trust. Most trustees that I met with were harried, pulled in different directions by the desires of their various constituents: both living beneficiaries, but also the wishes of dead settlors, as Mr. Sodawala lamented, "Maru bheja khaech!" ([beneficiaries] are eating my brains). If beneficiaries have the appetite of zombies, it is because they are inaugurated by a legal entity with a half-life, one that does not achieve personhood like a corporation but is still a corpus, a body to itself.

This unsettled state is a consequence of the legal form initiating social relationships and hinging various temporalities to them. The act of endowment by a settlor is the ultimate act of presentness; it only knows the now and acts as if it could prophesize the future. After this moment, the trust's outlook is both backward to the past and the settlor's wishes and forward to the future and all the beneficiaries to come. Then the trust's tripartite structure (settlor, trustee, beneficiary) creates obligations from the trustee to the trust, and from the trustee to the beneficiary. Obligations are owed to the dead and the unborn. With charitable trusts, these obligations are meant to endure in perpetuity. While the donor transfers their will into a future obligation for the trust, these obligations are bound together with legal forms for achieving those futures. These help to construct the trust's own chronotopes, which Bakhtin (1981) reminds, often have contradicting elements within them.

Chrono-Dissonance and the Trust as Hinge

In 2011, I was invited to meet former Bombai Parsi Puchayet (BPP) trustee "Mr. Ghadiali" at his home in one of the Wadia *baugs* after briefly being introduced to him at an election meeting at the same baug. At the meeting, he had sat toward the back with his arms crossed in resignation. Mr. Ghadiali's tenure was in the preelection batch of trustees, and he had actually fought hard in the courts to get the adult franchise scheme past. At the election meeting in 2011, where every adult Parsi could choose a trustee, he seemed disappointed by the loud vitriol of the candidates, who often made quite sharp personal attacks on one another, an outcome he had not foreseen as he advocated for adult franchise.

At his home, the front door opened into a large sitting room decorated with a lifetime's worth of curios and family photos; the room was also filled with clocks, which I inquired about. Mr. Ghadiali is an avid collector of antique clocks and proudly walked me around the room and showed me his collection. While we sat and chatted about his tenure at the BPP and his service as trustee to several other trusts that managed temples, I was often distracted by the constant metronymic swinging of pendulums large and small and the unsynchronized ticking of the analog clocks. When we had reached the hour, the whole room began to chime in low and high tones, which startled me. "Haha, I am used to it and also am half-deaf," he said with a giggle. He seemed to relish in my distraction, my unsettled state.

While Mr. Ghadiali joked that he was accustomed to the chrono-dissonance of the unsynchronized chiming of his multiple antique clocks, this book, in major part, has been an exploration of how the Parsis in Mumbai inhabit different chronotopes in the city within the frames of the trust instruments they have all around them. By understanding the various temporalities at play, we can see the kinds of time-work the trust is able to forge and accomplish. My insistence on including a significant component of the history of the present (Foucault 1979) in each chapter is not only to serve as contextual background to the contemporary ethnography but to show how we cannot view or understand a mechanism like the trust without acknowledging its historicity and its role as a hinge. The trust as a hinge, as a moveable joint, draws the wishes of a nineteenth-century donor into the present and, at the same time, constrains the potential and possibilities of the future. As a financial and legal device, the trust is not only future-oriented but continually collapses the past and the future, its birth, and its ends. It is a bearer of its own historicity, bringing its past forward while offering a prognosis for the future.

The trust as an instrument of accumulating and giving, therefore, engenders timely obligations because it changes the temporal structure of kin and communal relations. For example, Jerbai Wadia could have left her sons vast sums of money and extensive properties in Bombay to spend and use in their lifetimes. However, she broadened her giving to her coreligionists but left her sons and heirs the ability to manage this giving as trustees.

Instead of her properties being passed down linearly, she inaugurated a triangular structure, wherein beneficiaries of her giving, like Peshotan living in Nowroze Baug, could push back against the choices of her descendants to raze their homes and resettle them in high-rise buildings. Through trusts, the wealthy give over their ownership and tax liability while keeping the actual access to and utilization of the funds. They also relinquish their relationship to the state's distribution system. Trustees like the Wadia family are then able to indirectly accumulate funds for projects, be they circumscribed by the charity commission. They do not have any tax liability for these projects and avoid capital gains and inheritance tax since the transfer of ownership has already occurred: from Jerbai Wadia to the trust itself. By naming the trust and the physical properties after her kin, Wadia inscribed her family legacy throughout the city and in perpetuity. What the trust allows is "temporally stretched" giving (Riles 2010, 801), hinging the beneficence of a nineteenth-century merchant prince or wealthy widow with a young (Parsi) Mumbaiker today and a Parsi yet to be conceived.

Wadia's assets were once objects in property relations governed by subjects, which now, through the trust, become subjects themselves, assets with obligations. These obligations are legal, financial, and temporal relations. These forms of obligations make giving through the trust such a distinct social form. Unlike a corporation, the trust is not a legal entity and has no legal personality. One cannot sue a trust, but only the trustees, a definite group of people in any present moment. The trustees may also buy or sell assets, but only to further the objects of the trust and under the watchful eye of the charity commissioner. Yet, I argue that the trust, even if a nonentity under the law, intensely structures social, legal, and moral obligations and therefore acts *as if* it has a prominent legal personality. The trust's legal objects are not only managed but are given reign over the future intentions of imagined people as a means of caring for and enabling those future people.

The Subjunctive: As Near as Possible

The notion that the trust "does not work, yet cannot fail" led me to think about this paradox as a more significant issue of how the law allows capital to accumulate and be distributed in particular ways. As the trust comes out of the framework of Equity, it is an attempt to address the inflexibility that results from strict adherence to the law. Trusts, therefore, become an instrument to circumvent taxes, fund the public good, avoid strict inheritance, and even have a person's wishes fulfilled after death. "Equity cannot remove the force of the law, but it can moderate its impact. Equity does not break the rules but merely bends them" (Watt 2009, 3). This is the work of the subjunctive, the "as if," which is why the trust continually moves with a half-life, never entirely the dead hand, but never fully realized as mobile capital. Ironically, when a person settles a trust, they are decidedly against the subjunctive mode; they are trying to fix an obligation. But the trust, once settled, moves into the subjunctive mode, as it must travail a succession of trustees, the shifts of law, time, and the city itself. This subjunctive mode is in constant conflict with the legal obligation that the trust must fulfill its objects. The perpetual nature of the charitable trust in relation to urban space and communal history serves as a constraint on the space of a developing city and on the shifting gender and religious norms of a community. Thus, this instrument, borne out of fairness and flexibility, may result in profound inequalities.

The sole object or mandate of the trust is to maintain its tripartite structure (settlor, trustee, beneficiary) and continually fulfill its obligations. As we have seen, though, when the future of the trust is in question, the nearest possible substitute might be allowed with the cy près doctrine because the law does not allow the trust to fail. An unviable future, like no more liquid funds, forces the trust to put its solid assets into motion, a thoroughly financialized move and the only path for the viability of many older charities. We can understand this tenacity of law to force trusts to succeed only if they are providing for general public utility, for the good.

Parker Shipton (2009) writes that people have an attachment to land in Kenya through the dead protecting land for the unborn. As much as this book is about how past promises are entangled with their present purposes, the trust, as a device of timekeeping, is very much a future-oriented device. Ideas about succession and the transfer of property are held together with the inheritance of property from parents, grandparents, and, of course, the inheritance of obligations to trust property. This is keenly felt by Parsi parents in Mumbai, whose children are more upwardly mobile than they were and expect, usually around the time of marriage, to move to their own flats. Many of the young Parsis I spoke with had to navigate the immense privilege of the size of their natal homes in baugs to the loss of what could come after. While some rebelled against the surveillance and Parsi-*panu* of baug life, where older aunties continually look out windows and observe the goings-on, others were convinced that living within a Parsi enclave was the best way to maintain their Parsi-ness, what I described as their Parsi propriety.

Proper practice, especially proper marriage practice, becomes a keen focus as the reproduction of the community is assumed to be at stake. The majority of Parsi trusts in Mumbai recognize the rights of Parsi men who intermarry, as well as their children, provided they have a *navjote* initiation ceremony, while actively excluding women who do so. This custom was affirmed by a judgment over the succession of trustees and the rights of a French woman married to a Parsi man in 1908. Keeping young women married within the community becomes an intense matter when an out-marriage might result in eviction, in addition to her exclusion from much of Parsi public and religious life. Again, this tying of property to propriety is by design. Endogamy and building more housing become the only logical response to a community deemed to be in crisis.

Mr. Ghadiali is known in the community for his building expertise and his work toward universal franchise. He was also one of the few vocal critics of building more flats for the community to amend the demographics. He shared that as a trustee, he observed over and over that the waitlist was not a live document; hence, many applicants on that list were not presently worthy of flats. He also insisted that the change in municipal tenancy laws increased people moving around and created the supposed shortage of flats. But no one had listened to him. "Did you hear how they talk at these elections? The important characteristic of a trustee is that they be honest, open-minded, and able to adjust to the times." After shaking his head in exasperation, he proclaimed, "Parsis have survived fourteen hundred years only to see the [current] revival of Zoroastrianism, and we will perish by fighting amongst ourselves."

Mr. Ghadiali's tenure as trustee was plagued by disagreements with his fellow trustees, and they won out. The BPP, which is very literally tasked with nurturing Parsi communal life in Mumbai, shifted its focus from the poor and needy and invested (again, literally) in reproduction with its marriage bureaus, IVF clinics, and insistence on more communal housing. The BPP's obligations to distribute its assets to its beneficiaries could only be maintained perpetually if beneficiaries exist; therefore, reproducing its beneficiaries became the object itself. This is similar to English charities in the Victorian era, which began to be financialized, "helping only the deserving poor, i.e., those individuals whose behavior would represent a positive return on investment" (Maltby and Rutterford 2016, 265). The Punchayet's move toward biological reproduction is a symptom of its shift toward financialization. This trust would turn now to help the "deserving," those who could bear children, those now worthy of the trust's investment in them. The BPP shifted to monetizing children with its monthly payments to families who bore them.

Stepping outside of Mumbai, the mode of giving utilized by the Hong Kong Fund is also thoroughly financialized. The fund is keen to invest through interest-free loans in deserving cases of medical and educational needs. Although its trustees admit that they do not always see a monetary return on this investment, they still insist on this mode for all but medical recipients rather than giving out charity. Even its donations to temples and prayer halls in the diaspora are only through top-up funds, well evaluated against the risks that might befall the construction. While finance "is a realm of must, shall, and will" (Riles 2010, 797), this contrasts with the "should" and "as if," the subjunctivity of the trust. Yet the Mumbai trusts are slowly moving to this more indicative tense to address the needs of the demographic crisis, perhaps leaving behind their original obligations.

Remainders of Trust Matters

The book has been an exploration of people's relationship with a legal instrument that does not work yet cannot fail. While trusts are historical instruments, with sometimes exhausting endurance, their social lives—the ways people take them up, enjoy them, and contest them—are perpetually changing. As my research shows, housing trusts are very sensitive to legal interventions and changes in the real estate market, municipal laws, and of course, the social lives of their beneficiaries. Through the trust's spatial, legal, and ritual work, its entanglements have placed religious authority in trustees and spaces rather than priests and texts. Trust matters bring to the forefront how this legal mechanism structures the obligations of Parsi religious life and death in Mumbai. As a time-keeping device, the trust has also been pivotal as a mechanism of finance and communal connection.

Just as trust matters seem to spill over and exceed their original objects, so too can they exceed the scope of a book. I find studying trusts to be so fascinating for precisely this reason. These persistent instruments are all around us, guarding our sacred spaces, universities, and pension funds. Hence, it is critical to understand how they work and what they are doing to our material world and our social relations. Especially in this neoliberal moment, when much scholarship seems to focus on the individualizing tendencies of the economy, we must not forget that we deeply rely on mechanisms like trusts to manage our group lives. While the emergence of instruments like derivatives captures much attention, it is the relentless endurance of trusts, which preserve and accumulate assets over time, that has the potential to reveal the contradictions of contemporary capitalism.

INTRODUCTION: **Inheritances**

1. Throughout this work, I will use Bombay for the city pre-1995 and Mumbai post-1995, when the official name was changed.

2. I use the common orthography for Parsi, with the older spelling being Parsee.

3. The largest public landowner is the Mumbai Port Trust, which is owned by the government of India.

4. Industrialist Mukesh Ambani's twenty-seven-story high-rise in Mumbai is the world's most expensive private residence.

5. Fascinatingly explicated by Hans Vaihinger (2001) in his philosophy of the "as if," which he claims is central to human life. He argues that this mode is not useful because it is true but because it is a fiction. See also Riles (2011).

6. See also Hinnells (1985, 26). For a comprehensive analysis of various aspects of Zoroastrianism's historical and contemporary concepts and issues, see Stausberg and Y. Vevaina (2015).

7. For the Sasanian law of property and inheritance, see Macuch (2005, 125–33) and Jany (2004).

8. For more on the historical inheritance of the Zoroastrian foundation in the Islamic *waqf,* see Macuch (1994).

9. Even though the broad rules guiding charities in India did develop from English notions of charity from the sixteenth century, the concepts at their foundations are not the same, as both in Hindu and Muslim *waqf,* the property is vested in the deity or Almighty, respectively, and not in the trustee, for which, see Setalvad (2009, 234; Birla 2009).

10. Maitland held that trust laws were allowed to develop unhindered because they were not seen as a threat like corporations were. "Editor's Introduction" in Maitland (2003).

11. See Birla (2018) for a discussion on whether instruments of philanthropy, particularly corporate social responsibility (CSR), were indeed meant to be instruments of profit-making.

12. Maitland in *Equity* defines the role of a trustee as "when a person has rights which he is bound to exercise upon behalf of another, or for the accomplishment of some particular purpose he is said to have those rights in trust for that other or for that purpose he is called a trustee" (1913, 44).

13. As part of what Foucault et al. describe as a thoroughly modern arrangement of power wherein the task of political economy is to manage subjects as bodies and populations (1991).

14. In 1844, with the Companies Act, business groups could incorporate without a royal charter, and in 1855 with limited liability. These laws were consolidated into the English Companies Act in 1862.

15. The trust settlor no longer pays taxes on those assets as they are wholly divested.

16. While the main source of "object failure" in my research is due to the lack of beneficiaries, Moumtaz has shown the intense effects of regime change on the landscape of *waqf* in Beirut, with different property configurations during various empires as well as in the postcolonial era (2012, 2021).

17. See Ringer (2011) and Stewart (2012) for more on Zoroastrians in Iran.

18. Iranis are Zoroastrians who arrived in India from Iran in the nineteenth and twentieth centuries. They often speak Zoroastrian dialects of Persian and have some social distinctions. In terms of trust and other legal matters, they are included under the rubric of Parsis.

19. See the discussion in Cereti (1991).

20. This story has several different forms and is common lore among Parsis, but common to all versions is the contract between the settlers and the rajah regarding the low profile that the Parsis were to keep. For the oldest written source, see the *Qiṣṣe-ye Sanjān*, written in Persian couplets in 1599, with text and translation in Williams (2009).

21. See Kreyenbroek and Munshi (2001) and Luhrmann (2002) for more in-depth characterizations of contemporary Parsi religious categories, beliefs, and sects.

22. For instance, the works of Rohington Mistry (2001, 2010, 2011a, 2011b); Cyrus Mistry (2013); Gieve Patel (2008); and Thrity Umrigar (2001). For films, see *Shirin Farhad Ki Toh Nikal Padi*, Sehgal (2012); *Little Zizou*, Taraporevala (2008); *Being Cyrus*, Adajania (2006). For Parsi theater, see Gupta and Hansen (2005) and Nicholson (2021).

23. *Chawls* are residential buildings with small units and shared toilet and kitchen facilities. They were built to support working-class accommodations and often are found adjacent to factories or mill lands. A few Parsi colonies are built in *chawl* style and remain heavily subsidized for widows or very low-income Parsis. Most tenants pay only a ceremonial amount like a few rupees for the rent.

24. For more on the diverse Zoroastrian diaspora, see Hinnells (2005) and Hinnells and Williams (2007).

25. *Bawa* is a term used humorously and sometimes disparagingly to describe a Parsi.

26. Scholars like Asad (1993), Keane (2007), and Appadurai (2015) have remarked how this very notion has deep roots in Protestant thinking itself, having to do with issues of mediation between invisible and visible realms.

1. Refers to all communities.

2. The Directory of Public Charitable trusts is a document (soon to be digitized) that lists trust names, asset information, and current trustees. The information is split by region and religious community, with one section for cosmopolitan trusts. There are about three thousand Parsi public charitable trusts in the state of Maharashtra. Most are small endowments that deal with medical or educational welfare.

3. In other contexts, see Holston (1989) on Brasilia, Makdisi (1997) on Beirut, and Berman (1983) on New York.

4. For a complete list of the buildings that Murzban designed and constructed, see Murzban (1915).

5. See also Chopra's discussion of the network of Freemasonry that connected wealthy Parsis, and other prominent natives and the British in mutual obligation (92–100).

6. This chapter discusses public charitable trusts within the British Common Law. For more on trust-like instruments in ancient Zoroastrian law, see Jany (2004) and Macuch (1994).

7. The currency conversion through the text have used the historical conversion rate (INR-USD) at each instance.

8. Known as the "King of the Colonies," this twentieth-century Parsi colony is known for its large two- to three-bedroom flats, open verandas, and large green spaces.

9. While I agree with the former assessment, there is some evidence that segregated living was also quite prevalent in cities in Gujarat with the *pol* system (Doshi 1991).

10. For an in-depth discussion of this very critical historical moment of property development in Bombay, see Nikhil Rao (2013b).

11. It is essential to note that covenant agreements are not the same as trust deeds. While public charitable trusts are allowed to discriminate as to their beneficiaries because the latter still constitute a segment of the public, restrictive covenants are private contractual agreements. They are allowed to discriminate on these grounds. Hence, the "indefinite" public of trusts and the highly defined nature of two or more persons in a contract escape the antidiscrimination ethos in the Indian Constitution.

12. FSI—Floor Space Index—which refers to a building's total floor area indexed to the size of the plot of land it is built upon. In Mumbai, various ratios are fixed by the municipal government, in the development plan, onto specific wards of the city. So in this example, the buildings in the Parsi colony in Dadar were underdeveloped, having fewer floors than they potentially could have, making them prime areas for further development.

13. Parsi Central Association Housing Society representative quoted in "Dadar Parsi Colony to Stay 'Exclusive,'" by Nauzer Bharucha, TNN December 24, 2009.

14. The Transfer of Property Act ensures nondiscrimination to anyone who is allowed to form a contract.

15. As the Parsis gained much wealth and status during the colonial period from trade with China, many wealthy Parsis display antique Chinese vases and other interior décor.

16. This is not the case with private trusts, whose lifespans are usually only a few decades beyond the human lives of their beneficiaries.

17. Khoja Muslims are a distinct group that follow the leadership of the Aga Khan and have firm structures of Ismaili councils. The authority of the Aga Khan was established after an 1866 court decision in the Bombay High Court. While Mr. Vakil points to the Khojas as having firm communal authority, this itself is a function of litigation (Purohit 2012).

18. This is especially acute for older trusts and those that have received Heritage status from the city.

19. For a deeper discussion of the debates around legal fiction in law, see Riles (2017) and Fuller (1930). See Samuel (2004) for the status of fact in legal argument. For more on the epistemological basis of legal fictions, see Vaihinger (2001). Wagner (1986) thinks through Vaihinger's claims in relation to ethnography and fiction.

20. While related, these are not the same Petits of *Petit v. Jeejeebhoy*, the landmark case described in chapter 4.

21. In recent times, the hospital trust has also been running at a loss, and a huge donation has been pledged by a family in Hong Kong, although not without controversy, as the new building is meant to have cosmopolitan beneficiaries.

22. The hospital was once directly at the seaside, but the coastline was extended through large-scale reclamation projects throughout the western coast of south Bombay.

23. See L. Vevaina (2018a) and chapter 3 for a fuller account on the experience of one family living through this mobility.

24. Riles maintains that legal fictions are nonrepresentational speech, and therefore their meaning is not as important as their efficacy to produce action (2011, 173).

CHAPTER 2. **Presents and Futures**

Sections of this chapter have appeared in L. Vevaina (2018b).

1. All communities in India are governed by personal laws; these are civil law statutes on marriage, divorce, adoption, and inheritance that are specific to each community. In Parsi personal law all children inherit equally from their parents.

2. Children of intermarried Parsi women have varied status within the community in Mumbai, as to whether they are counted as Parsi and what benefits they may claim as such. This has been the source of several intense disputes that have been taken to court. This issue will be taken up further in the following chapters.

3. The settlor of a trust no longer pays taxes on those assets as they are completely divested of them.

4. See Friedman (2009, 125–39) for more on the rule against perpetuities.

5. The Wadia family descends from a family of shipbuilders who were the first builders to construct for the British Navy outside of England. They later moved into trade and cotton production with the still-successful Bombay Dyeing Corporation founded in 1879.

6. Cusrow Baug, Ness Baug, Rustom Baug, Jer Baug, and Nowroze Baug, with 1,545 flats in total.

7. Trust Settlement—The Nowrosjee Nusserwanjee Wadia Trust Buildings for Parsees. 16 August 1916, p. 3.

8. Trust Settlement—The Rustomji Nowrosjee Wadia Trust Building for Parsees. 10 November 1921, p. 5.

9. The Nowrosjee Nusserwanjee Wadia Trust Buildings for Parsees. 16 August 1916, p. 16.

10. Sir Ness's son, Neville Wadia, was given a navjote (a Zoroastrian initiation ritual) and "converted" back to Zoroastrianism (not without controversy) late in his life. He was married to Dinah Wadia, the daughter of Mohammed Ali Jinnah, and spearheaded the success of The Bombay Dyeing Corporation, one of India's largest textile concerns, until his death in 1996. Their son, Nusli, was also given a navjote. See Hinnells (2005, 129–35) for more details.

11. Discussed further in chapter 3, the BPP manages various types of housing, for example highly subsidized charity flat, leased flats, as well as those deemed to be "owned" by the tenant and are allowed to be resold under certain restrictions.

12. While Ardvan is making a point about Parsis and their relation to the BPP's welfare practices, I have heard from many young Parsis, especially those who would like to open a business, that they cannot even secure bank loans as they have no collateral to offer since they only rent their homes. There are organizations like the Zoroastrian Cooperative Bank and the funds through various groups that attempt to ameliorate this problem.

13. As we will see in chapter 4, it is this identity designation that has been so contentious.

14. See Appadurai (1988), Parry (1986), Raheja (1988), Laidlaw (1995, 2000), Copeman (2009, 2011), Banerjee and Copeman (2018), and Heim (2004).

15. These currency conversions are accurate to 2011; the value of the rupee to the US dollar has since dropped.

16. Parsi architect and developer Hafeez Contractor is said to have pioneered this scheme with slum redevelopment in Mumbai.

17. Currently at least one in three Parsi women in Mumbai marry out of the community. This high level of exogamy is one of the main issues the BPP addresses with its housing scheme.

18. The Maharashtra Housing and Development Authority (MHADA) is one of the governing bodies for housing and redevelopment issues in the city.

19. The scheme assigns priority for flat allotments; currently Parsi couples capable of bearing children are given priority. See chapter 3 for more.

20. Civic authorities insist upon this even though the green space is not open to the public but only to colony residents.

21. The scheme assured the current tenants of charity flats that their property taxes would be paid for twenty years after taking possession of their new ownership flats in the redevelopment.

22. Kozlowski (1985, 3–4) reminds us that trust deeds themselves are an act of preservation, expressing the values, fears, and objectives of the settlor.

23. See Birla (2018) for a discussion on whether instruments of philanthropy, particularly corporate social responsibility (CSR), were indeed meant to be instruments of profit making.

24. Each zone of the city is designated a certain ratio of built-up area. To encourage building in less developed zones, the city offers a transfer of development rights from more developed zones to less, in Mumbai from the island city in the south to the northern suburbs (Nainan 2008).

25. Dinshaw Mehta quoted in "Wadia Want Back Parsi Colonies Their Ancestors Developed" by Yogesh Sadhwani, *Mumbai Mirror*, May 20, 2014.

26. His father, Neville Wadia, was given a *navjote* (Zoroastrian initiation), turning away from his own father Ness Wadia's conversion to Christianity.

27. See also Luhrmann (1996), whose interlocutors saw the general decay of the community at the hands of so much charity.

CHAPTER 3. **No House, No Spouse**

Note on title: While the standard orthography in English is *panchayat*; I reproduce the spelling of the institution itself.

1. This periodical and the BPP website have not been published since mid-2017.

2. See BPP *Review*, October–November 2010.

3. See Sharafi (2015) for more details on this unique institution, one of the last vestiges of the jury system in India.

4. Critically it does not coordinate all Parsi charitable trusts in Mumbai, many of which operate and distribute charity independently.

5. Although there are Parsi trusts that manage more acreage, the BPP manages the most housing.

6. Amongst these are Hinnells (1985), Palsetia (2001; 2005), White (1991), and Writer (2016).

7. For much more detail on the intricacies of the case, including the analysis of unpublished papers, see Sharafi (2007).

8. Suzanne Briere took the Tata surname upon marriage and was henceforth known as Sooni, a Parsi first name meaning "gold."

9. P. A. Wadia, *Parsis Ere the Shadows Thicken*, Bombay (1949, 14), quoted in Hinnells (1985, 271).

10. See Sharafi (2014) for a fascinating and thorough analysis of legislation and case law in the colonial period and their relationship to the formation of Parsi communal identity. The 1908 case *Petit v. Jeejeebhoy*, and *Kanga v. The Funds and Properties of the BPP* (Bombay High Court, Appeal 256 of 2010) are just some examples of cases brought to court to interpret and delimit the functioning of the trust.

11. A. F. P. "The Parsi Crisis," *Newsweek Pakistan*, December 26, 2013, http://newsweekpakistan.com/the-parsi-crisis/, (accessed, April 6, 2014). M. Nair, "Dire Demographics of Parsi-Zoroastrians," DNA *Daily News and Analysis*, May 23, 2012, http://www.dnaindia.com/analysis/column-dire-demographics-of-parsi-zoroastrians-1692444, (accessed, January 28, 2016). B. Karkaria, "Why is India's wealthy Parsi Community Vanishing?" *B. B. C. News*, January 9, 2016, http://www.bbc.com/news/world-asia-india-35219331, (accessed January 28, 2016).

12. See Hinnells (2005) for a comprehensive overview of various diaspora communities worldwide.

13. The effect of intermarriage on Parsi women's communal membership is varied in the diaspora and even in India today. The community in Mumbai remains the strictest or most orthodox in its exclusion of intermarried women and their children. Chapter 4 will discuss this in more detail.

14. J. R. Patel (ed.), *Parsiana*, Parsiana Publications Pvt. Ltd., Bombay.

15. Last page of each issue.

16. See the timeline of trustees on www.bombayparsipunchayet.com.

17. Donors to the Punchayet still have their vote counted twice.

18. Trustee Dadi Engineer, quoted in Nauzer Bharucha, "Parsi Apex Body Seeks Universal Franchise," *The Times of India*, December 6, 2006.

19. Marzban Hathiram quoted in V. C. Sekhar, "No Room for Unwanted Neighbors," *Times of India* (Mumbai edition), April 25, 2005.

20. There is a much longer history within the community of racial thinking and even eugenics. For more, see Nicholson (2015) and Sharafi (2014).

21. N. Bharucha, "3125 New Flats for Parsis on the Anvil," *Times of India* (Mumbai edition), July 29, 2009.

22. *Times of India*, March 25, 2013, Nauzer Bharucha.

23. The opaque criteria and the high value of these flats make corruption allegations almost endemic to the system of allotment. A formal investigation was underway in 2014 as Rps. 210,000 (approx. US$3,500) were uncovered in the cupboard of the BPP CEO, who had recently died. Allegations also circulate frequently in the Parsi press and conversation about individual trustees and how much they have to gain from favorable flat allotments.

24. For example, Kamathipura is an area known for sex work and dance bars.

25. ParZor is a Delhi-based, UNESCO-funded, registered society, which aims to preserve and promote Zoroastrian and Parsi culture and heritage through various initiatives.

26. Ghildiyal, in *Times of India*, December 23, 2010.

27. Ministry of Minority Affairs. "Jiyo Parsi: Central Sector Scheme for Containing Population Decline of Parsis of India." Government of India, September 29, 2017.

28. All Phase I ads can be viewed at https://parsikhabar.net/news/jiyo-parsi -launches-a-brilliant-print-advertising-campaign/8813/.

29. Phase II ads can be viewed at https://parsikhabar.net/news/jiyo-parsi-phase-ii -launched-with-new-advertisement-campaign/15808/.

30. This refers to a two-bedroom, hall, and kitchen flat on Napean Sea Road, a high-end district of the city.

31. This interview was conducted in 2018. As the couple's identity is kept anonymous, and the regulations are kept quite vague about the Parsi status of the mother-to-be, it is unclear whether non-Parsi women married to Parsi men may avail of all the fertility assistance in the scheme.

CHAPTER 4. **The Beneficiary, the Law, and Sacred Space**

1. In L. Vevaina (2021), I examine how even Parsis with no professional legal expertise have become legal advocates for other Parsis.

2. There are several levels of Zoroastrian priests, with *vada dasturs*, or high priests, with the most training and religious education.

3. Letter from the high priests to the trustees of the Bombay Parsi Punchayet on August 29, 2009.

4. Justice D. Y. Chandrachud is from a very prominent legal family. His father, Y. V. Chandrachud, was the longest-serving chief justice of India. After serving on the Bombay and Allahabad High Courts, D. Y. Chandrachud was appointed to the Indian Supreme Court in 2016.

5. For more on the critical role of paper documents as evidence in South Asia, see Tarlo 2003; Hull 2003, 2012a, 2012b; N. Mathur 2016; and Suresh 2019.

6. Mirza has since become the primary priest at the Zoroastrian Prayer Hall cremation facility.

7. Khojeste Mistree runs several initiatives to educate Parsis on the principles of Zoroastrianism. He has fought to preserve the *dokhmenashini* practice at Doongerwadi through various campaigns and in the courts.

8. Since the early nineteenth century, the management of this temple has been under dispute between religious leaders in Odisha and the British and then the Indian state. The Shri Jagannath Temple Act, 1955 was challenged in a suit in the Indian Supreme Court by the appellant, who claimed to have the sole traditional and religious right to manage the temple and who had been removed from this management by the Act. The court affirmed that the Act did not interfere with religious affairs as the temple had two aspects, a religious and a secular one.

9. *Saklat v. Bella* (October 22, 1925) was a case in colonial Rangoon that decided on the rights of trustees to ban someone from Zoroastrian sacred spaces (Sharafi 2006).

10. Interestingly the justice is making a differentiation between judgments that are a result of their social and political presents like *Petit*, in contrast to the Constitution of India, which stands outside of historical time and should continue to have precedent.

11. Cities in India and abroad that do not have a tower of silence employ cemeteries or cremation to inter-Zoroastrians. More on this in the next chapter.

12. For more detailed analysis of this case, see L. Vevaina (2018b; forthcoming).

13. Here Gupta is referring to the Indian Constitution and not Parsi custom as the "law of the land."

14. (*Goolrukh Gupta v. Burjor Pardiwala, Valsad Anjuman Trust* 2012)

15. This is eerily reminiscent of a parallel process that Cohn (1996) describes in the early colonial British rush to the Indian textual tradition to understand native communities.

16. See Das Avecedo (2016) for the complex ways in which the Kerala High Court seeks both to reform and restrain itself in reforming practices surrounding the Sabarimala Temple.

CHAPTER 5. **From Excarnation to Ashes**

1. The 2011 Census has shown the number of Parsi Zoroastrians dropping even after several initiatives have been in place to stem demographic decline. For more details on Parsi demography, see Axelrod (1990), Gould (1972), Luhrmann (1996), Hinnells (2005), and chapter 3.

2. This was a *navjote* ceremony for children with a Zoroastrian mother and Hindu father. Only a few priests in Mumbai will conduct this ceremony.

3. According to Dobbin (1970), this was a long and contentious process.

4. In other parts of the world, this is often called sky burial.

5. *Nasa* (corpse) and *salar* (trustee), literally, trustees of the corpse. They can be viewed as an untouchable caste, especially to Parsis who observe all purity laws. Only recently have marriages, although extremely rare, between them and other Parsis been accepted (see Lueddeckens and Karanjia 2011 for more). Realizing their plight, the BPP and other trusts offer free housing and education, leading to the inevitable refusal of many of the next generation not wishing to continue bearing corpses. A recently published novel, *Chronicle of a Corpse Bearer* (2012) by Cyrus Mistry, explores the lives of *nasasalars* in contemporary Mumbai.

6. See the various cases detailed in Palsetia (2001), Desai (1977), Hinnells (2005), and Sharafi (2014).

7. In 2010, the Punchayet added another obstacle for intermarried women, who abrogate their rights if they take their husband's surnames upon marriage; for more on this issue, see chapter 4 and L. Vevaina (2018b).

8. See L. Vevaina (2013) for details on the Asia-wide extinction of vultures from environmental and pharmacological threat.

9. See http://www.heatherwick.com/projects/spaces/tower-of-silence/ for the design proposals for the tower of silence. Heatherwick has famously also designed the Vessel in New York City, and several other projects around the world.

10. Interview with former Punchayet trustee, January 2011.

11. Burjor Antia in http://www.nbcnews.com/id/14721606/ns/world_news-south _and_central_asia/t/zoroastrian-funeral-rites-arouse-anger-india/#.VdomK86_Ufo.

12. Little to no research has been done on the form and content of rituals associated with Zoroastrian burial in India, as most religious scholars focus on dokhme-nashini. Lueddeckens and Karanjia (2011), with its high level of detail of Parsi mortuary practices, does not mention cemeteries although it does discuss the cremation debates.

13. Then BPP Chairman Dinshaw Mehta, in Jyoti Shelar, "BMC Allots Land in Worli for Parsis Who Opt for Cremation," *Mumbai Mirror*, February 8, 2014.

14. The opening prayers in the Khordeh Avesta, Zoroastrian prayer book. The Ashem Vohu is believed to have a favorable influence on spiritual, physical, and mental health and is recited on many occasions (Lueddeckens and Karanjia 2011, 83).

15. Sandalwood is offered during ritual ceremonies, and *divos*, or oil candles, are lit for daily prayers and represent the soul of the dead.

16. During the COVID-19 pandemic, the government forced Doongerwadi to close, and for a time, all deceased Parsis in Mumbai had to be cremated.

17. The BPP does have a scheme to support full-time priests with trust funds. Since the ban, Madon does not receive this supplemental pay.

18. There is hierarchy among Zoroastrian priests as per their level of study and training. High priests are vada dasturs, followed by dasturs, and then mobeds, who have the title of Ervad.

19. Not to be confused with Ervad Framroz Mirza.

20. Lhendup G. Bhutia, *Open Magazine*, February 25, 2014.

21. Soli Arceivala, "Why I Opt for Cremation," *Parsiana*, March 7, 2014.

1. Some sections of this chapter have been published in L. Vevaina (2022a).

2. In England, laws prohibiting mortmain were implemented, but these laws did not transfer to India as they did to other colonies (L. Vevaina 2019).

3. Maria Graham, Selections from the Records of the Bombay Government, p. 44–45), referenced in Guha (1984, 127).

4. Frere quoted in Thampi and Saksena (2009, 83).

5. See Palsetia (2005) for details on the negotiation for the hospital.

6. Another powerful example of this is the construction of Cama Hospital by P. H. Cama, a Parsi philanthropist, in 1880. With his donation, Cama proposed a hospital for women with entirely female staff. With his largesse and charitable intention, he further showed that Parsis were a progressive community in terms of gender relations.

7. For a fascinating account of how the Tata family and firm have navigated through Indian history to become a global conglomerate, see Raianu (2021).

8. For more, see Patel and Masselos (2003), V. Rao (2007), and Nijman (2000).

9. Currently an enormous redevelopment project in central Mumbai is also being undertaken by the Bohra Muslim community through the Saifee Burhani Upliftment Trust.

10. Quoted in George Beer Endacott, *A History of Hong Kong*, 1973.

11. It had become a pattern in the Parsi-Zoroastrian diaspora until the latter half of the twentieth century that settlers would first construct a tower of silence or a cemetery for the disposal of the dead (Hinnells 2005).

12. In Southeast Asia there is also a small community in Singapore represented by the Parsi Zoroastrian Association of Singapore (PZAS), which is the umbrella group for Parsis in Malaysia, Thailand, Indonesia, and Brunei. There is little trace of the small community in Yangon, Myanmar.

13. Roxan Jokhi quoted in Parinaz M. Gandhi, "Profitability with Philanthropy," *Parsiana*, November 21, 2011.

14. Several of the Parsis I interviewed also donated substantial funds to India through a personal capacity or their own endowments. Most wished to remain anonymous.

15. The foundation was established in 1972 and owns one-third of the shares of the holding company Godrej & Boyce. The dividend income is sued for promoting the trust's objects, which include medical relief, education, and disaster relief.

16. This later turned sour as Naoroji Godrej resigned from the BPP board in frustration after he was accused of seeking profit from the donation to the baug.

17. The group's mandate is to strengthen identity and ties of Parsi-Irani Zoroastrians around the globe, increase youth participation, and to integrate the various communities through a common database.

Adajania, Homi, dir. 2006. *Being Cyrus*. Mumbai: Miracle CineFilms.

Adarkar, Necra, ed. 2011. *The Chawls of Mumbai: Galleries of Life*. Gurgaon: imprintOne.

Agnes, Flavia. 1999. *Law and Gender Inequality: The Politics of Women's Rights in India*. New York: Oxford University Press.

Alexander, Gregory S. 1998. "Property as Propriety." *Neb. L. Rev.* 77: 667–702.

Alexander, Gregory S. 2008. *Commodity and Propriety: Competing Visions of Property in American Legal Thought, 1776–1970*. Chicago: University of Chicago Press.

Anand, Nikhil. 2017. *Hydraulic City: Water and the Infrastructures of Citizenship in Mumbai*. Durham, NC: Duke University Press.

Anand, Nikhil, and Anne Rademacher. 2011. "Housing in the Urban Age: Inequality and Aspiration in Mumbai." *Antipode* 43 (5): 1748–72.

Anjaria, Jonathan. 2016. *The Slow Boil: Street Food, Rights and Public Space in Mumbai*. Stanford, CA: Stanford University Press.

Appadurai, Arjun. 1977. "Kings, Sects and Temples in South India, 1350–1700 A.D." *The Indian Economic and Social History Review* 14 (1): 47–73.

Appadurai, Arjun. 1981. *Worship and Conflict under Colonial Rule: A South Indian Case*. New York: Cambridge University Press.

Appadurai, Arjun. 1988. "Introduction: Commodities and the Politics of Value." In *The Social Life of Things: Commodities in Cultural Perspective*, edited by Arjun Appadurai, 3–63. Cambridge: Cambridge University Press.

Appadurai, Arjun. 2000. "Spectral Housing and Urban Cleansing: Notes on Millennial Mumbai." *Public Culture* 12 (3): 627–51.

Appadurai, Arjun. 2004. "The Capacity to Aspire: Culture and the Terms of Recognition." In *Culture and Public Action*, edited by Vijayendra Rao and Michael Walton, 59–84. Stanford, CA: Stanford University Press.

Appadurai, Arjun. 2015. "Mediants, Materiality, Normativity." *Public Culture* 27 (2): 221–37.

Appadurai, Arjun, and Carol Appadurai Breckenridge. 1976. "The South Indian Temple: Authority, Honour and Redistribution." *Contributions to Indian Sociology* 10 (2): 187–211.

Asad, Talal. 1993. *Genealogies of Religion: Discipline and Reasons of Power in Christianity and Islam*. Baltimore: Johns Hopkins University Press.

Asad, Talal. 2003. *Formations of the Secular: Christianity, Islam, Modernity*. Stanford, CA: Stanford University Press.

Axelrod, Paul. 1990. "Cultural and Historical Factors in the Population Decline of the Parsis of India." *Population Studies* 44 (3): 401–19.

Bakhtin, Mikhail M. 1981. *The Dialogic Imagination: Four Essays*. Translated by Caryl Emerson and Michael Holquist. Austin: University of Texas Press.

Banerjee, Dwaipayan, and Jacob Copeman. 2018. "Ungiven: Philanthropy as Critique." *Modern Asian Studies* 52 (1): 325–50.

Basu, Srimati. 1999. *She Comes to Take Her Rights: Indian Women, Property, and Propriety*. Albany: State University of New York Press.

Bear, Laura. 2015. *Navigating Austerity: Currents of Debt along a South Asian River*. Stanford, CA: Stanford University Press.

Bear, Laura. 2016. "Time as Technique." *Annual Review of Anthropology* 45 (1): 487–502.

Bear, Laura. 2020. "Speculation: A Political Economy of Technologies of Imagination." *Economy and Society* 49 (1): 1–15.

Bear, Laura, Ritu Birla, and Stine Simonsen Puri. 2015. "Speculation: Futures and Capitalism in India." *Comparative Studies of South Asia, Africa and the Middle East* 35 (3): 387–91.

Becci, Irene, Marian Burchardt, and José Casanova, eds. 2013. *Topographies of Faith: Religion in Urban Spaces*. Leiden, The Netherlands: Brill.

Benjamin, Solomon. 2008. "Occupancy Urbanism: Radicalizing Politics and Economy Beyond Policy and Programs." *International Journal of Urban and Regional Research* 32 (3): 719–29.

Berman, Marshall. 1983. *All That Is Solid Melts into Air: The Experience of Modernity*. New York: Verso.

Beverley, Eric Lewis. 2011. "Property, Authority and Personal Law: Waqf in Colonial South Asia." *South Asia Research* 31 (2): 155–82.

Beverley, Eric Lewis. 2018. "Territoriality in Motion: Waqf and Hyderabad State." *The Muslim World* 108 (4): 630–51.

Bhabha, Homi K. 2013. "The Sethias and Soft Power." In *Across Oceans and Flowing Silks*, edited by Pheroza Godrej. Mumbai: Spenta Multimedia.

Bhandar, Brenna. 2018. "Colonial Lives of Property." Durham, NC: Duke University Press.

Bhargava, Rajeev, ed. 1998. *Secularism and Its Critics*. Oxford: Oxford University Press.

Bhargava, Rajeev. 2007. "The Distinctiveness of Indian Secularism." In *The Future of Secularism*, edited by T. N. Srinivasan. Oxford: Oxford University Press.

Bharucha, Nauzer K. 2013. "Nowroz Baug May Turn into Luxury Towers." *The Times of India*, March 25, 2013. https://timesofindia.indiatimes.com/city/mumbai/nowroz-baug-may-turn-into-luxury-towers/articleshow/19180221.cms.

Bhattacharyya, Debjani. 2018. *Empire and Ecology in the Bengal Delta: The Making of Calcutta*. Cambridge: Cambridge University Press.

Bhattacharyya, Debjani. 2020. "Speculation." *Comparative Studies of South Asia, Africa and the Middle East* 40 (1): 51–56.

Bhuwania, Anuj. 2017. *Courting the People: Public Interest Litigation in Post-Emergency India*. Cambridge: Cambridge University Press.

Biagioli, Mario. 2006. "Documents of Documents: Scientists' Names and Scientific Claims." *Documents: Artifacts of Modern Knowledge*, edited by Annelise Riles, 127–57. Ann Arbor: University of Michigan Press.

Birla, Ritu. 1999. "Hedging Bets: The Politics of Commercial Ethics in Late Colonial India." New York: Columbia University.

Birla, Ritu. 2009. *Stages of Capital: Law, Culture, and Market Governance in Late Colonial India*. Durham, NC: Duke University Press.

Birla, Ritu. 2012. "Law as Economy: Convention, Corporation, Currency." *UC Irvine L. Rev.* 1: 1015–37.

Birla, Ritu. 2015. "Speculation Illicit and Complicit: Contract, Uncertainty, and Governmentality." *Comparative Studies of South Asia, Africa and the Middle East* 35 (3): 392–407.

Birla, Ritu. 2018. "C = f (P): The Trust, 'General Public Utility,' and Charity as a Function of Profit in India." *Modern Asian Studies* 52 (1): 132–62.

Biruk, Crystal. 2018. *Cooking Data: Culture and Politics in an African Research World*. Durham, NC: Duke University Press.

Björkman, Lisa. 2015. *Pipe Politics, Contested Waters: Embedded Infrastructures of Millennial Mumbai*. Durham, NC: Duke University Press.

Bornstein, Erica. 2012. *Disquieting Gifts: Humanitarianism in New Delhi*. Stanford, CA: Stanford University Press.

Breckenridge, Carol Appadurai. 1976. "The Sri Minaksi Sundaresvarar Temple: Worship and Endowments in South India, 1833 to 1925." Madison: University of Wisconsin. Madison ProQuest Dissertations Publishing.

Cantera, Alberto. 2015. "Ethics." In *The Wiley Blackwell Companion to Zoroastrianism*, edited by Michael Stausberg and Yuhan S. D. Vevaina. West Sussex: John Wiley and Sons, Ltd.

Cereti, Carlo. 1991. *An Eighteenth Century Account of Parsi History: The Qesse-Ye-Zartostian-e Hindustan*. Naples: Instituto Universitario Orientale Dipartimento di Studi Asiatici.

Chatterjee, Partha. 2004. *The Politics of the Governed: Reflections on Popular Politics in Most of the World*. New York: Columbia University Press.

Chhabria, Sheetal. 2018. "The Aboriginal Alibi: Governing Dispossession in Colonial Bombay." *Comparative Studies in Society and History* 60 (4): 1096–126.

Chhabria, Sheetal. 2019. *Making the Modern Slum: The Power of Capital in Colonial Bombay*. Seattle: University of Washington Press.

Chopra, Preeti. 2011a. *A Joint Enterprise: Indian Elites and the Making of British Bombay*. Minneapolis: University of Minnesota Press.

Chopra, Preeti. 2011b. "A Joint Enterprise: The Creation of a New Landscape in British Bombay." In *Mumbai Reader '10*. Urban Design Research Institute.

Clifford, James. 1999. *The Predicament of Culture*. Cambridge, MA: Harvard University Press.

Cohn, Bernard S. 1996. *Colonialism and Its Forms of Knowledge: The British in India.* Princeton, NJ: Princeton University Press.

Coombe, Rosemary, and Andrew Herman. 2000. "Trademarks, Property, and Propriety: The Moral Economy of Consumer Politics and Corporate Accountability on the World Wide Web." *DePaul L. Rev.* 50: 597.

Copeman, Jacob. 2009. *Veins of Devotion: Blood Donation and Religious Experience in North India.* New Brunswick, NJ: Rutgers University Press.

Copeman, Jacob. 2011. "The Gift and Its Forms of Life in Contemporary India." *Modern Asian Studies* 45 (05): 1051–94.

Das Acevedo, Deepa. 2013. "Secularism in the Indian Context." *Law and Social Inquiry* 38 (1): 138–67.

Das Acevedo, Deepa. 2016. "Divine Sovereignty, Indian Property Law, and the Dispute over the Padmanabhaswamy Temple." *Modern Asian Studies* 50 (3): 841–65.

Das Acevedo, Deepa. 2018. "Gods' Homes, Men's Courts, Women's Rights." *International Journal of Constitutional Law* 16 (2): 552–73.

Das, Veena. 1995. *Critical Events: An Anthropological Perspective on Contemporary India.* Oxford: Oxford University Press.

Davar, S. P. 1949. *The History of the Parsi Punchayet of Bombay.* Jalandhar, India: New Book Co.

De Goede, Marieke. 2005. *Virtue, Fortune, and Faith: A Genealogy of Finance.* Vol. 24. Borderlines. Minneapolis: University of Minnesota Press.

Derrett, J. D. M. 1968. *Religion, Law and the State in India.* London: Faber and Faber.

Dery, David. 1998. "'Papereality' and Learning in Bureaucratic Organizations." *Administration and Society* 29 (6): 677–89.

Desai, Berjis. 2019. *The Bawaji.* Chennai, India: Zero Degree Publishing.

Desai, Sapur Faredun. 1940. *Parsis and Eugenics.* The Author.

Desai, Sapur Faredun. 1977. *History of the Bombay Parsi Punchayet, 1860–1960.* Mumbai: Trustees of the Parsi Punchayet Funds and Properties.

Dharia, Namita Vijay. 2022. *The Industrial Ephemeral: Labor and Love in Indian Architecture and Construction.* Oakland: University of California Press.

D'Monte, Darryl. 2002. *Ripping the Fabric: The Decline of Mumbai and Its Mills.* New York: Oxford University Press.

Dobbin, Christine E. 1970. "The Parsi Panchayat in Bombay City in the Nineteenth Century." *Modern Asian Studies* 4 (2): 149–64.

Dobbin, Christine E. 1972. *Urban Leadership in Western India: Politics and Communities in Bombay City, 1840–1885.* Oxford: Oxford University Press.

Doshi, Harish. 1991. "Traditional Neighbourhood in Modern Ahmedabad: The Pol." In *A Reader in Urban Sociology,* edited by MSA Rao et al., 179–208. New Delhi, India: Orient Longman.

Dossal, Mariam. 2010. *Theatre of Conflict, City of Hope: Mumbai 1660 to Present Times.* Mumbai: Oxford University Press.

Endacott, George Beer. 1973. *A History of Hong Kong.* Oxford: Oxford University Press.

Farooqui, Amar. 2006. *Opium City: The Making of Early Victorian Bombay.* Three Essays Collective. Gurgaon: Three Essays Press.

Finkelstein, Maura. 2018. "Ghosts in the Gallery: The Vitality of Anachronism in a Mumbai Chawl." *Anthropological Quarterly* 91 (3): 937–68.

Finkelstein, Maura. 2019. *The Archive of Loss: Lively Ruination in Mill Land Mumbai.* Durham, NC: Duke University Press.

Foucault, Michel. 1979. *Discipline and Punish.* New York: Random House.

Foucault, Michel, Graham Burchell, Colin Gordon, and Peter Miller. 1991. *The Foucault Effect: Studies in Governmentality.* Chicago: University of Chicago Press.

Friedman, Lawrence. 2009. *Dead Hands: A Social History of Wills, Trusts, and Inheritance Law.* Stanford, CA: Stanford University Press.

Fuller, Lon L. 1930. "Legal Fictions." *Illinois Law Review* 25 (4): 363–99.

Gandhi, Ajay, Barbara Harriss-White, Douglas E. Haynes, and Sebastian Schwecke. 2020. *Rethinking Markets in Modern India: Embedded Exchange and Contested Jurisdiction.* Cambridge: Cambridge University Press.

Gell, A., 2021. *The Anthropology of Time: Cultural Constructions of Temporal Maps and Images.* New York: Routledge. Getzler, Joshua. 2016. "Frederic William Maitland-Trust and Corporation." *U. Queensland Law Journal* 35: 171.

Ghosh, Amitav. 2013. "Parsis and the China Trade." In *Across Oceans and Flowing Silks,* edited by Pheroza Godrej, 52–61. Mumbai: Spenta Multimedia.

Ghosh, Amitav. 2019. *Ibis Trilogy.* Gurgaon, India: Penguin Random House India Private Limited.

Gilsenan, Michael. 2011. "Translating Colonial Fortunes: Dilemmas of Inheritance in Muslim and English Laws across a Nineteenth-Century Diaspora." *Comparative Studies of South Asia, Africa and the Middle East* 31 (2): 355–71.

Glover, William Jack. 2007. *Making Lahore Modern: Constructing and Imagining a Colonial City.* Minneapolis: University of Minnesota Press.

Godrej, Pheroza, and Firoza Punthakey Mistree. 2002. *A Zoroastrian Tapestry: Art, Religion and Culture.* Ahmedabad, India: Mapin.

Godrej, Pheroza, Firoza Punthakey Mistree, Sudha Seshadri, Ranjit Hoskote, and Nancy Adajania. 2013. *Across Oceans and Flowing Silks: From Canton to Bombay 18th-20th Centuries.* Mumbai: Spenta Multimedia.

Goh, Daniel P. S., and Peter Van der Veer. 2016. *Introduction: The Sacred and the Urban in Asia.* London: SAGE Publications Sage UK.

Goldman, Michael, Vinay Gidwani, and Carol Upadhya. 2017. "Bangalore's 'Great Transformation'—The Problem." *Seminar* 694: 12–16.

Good, Byron J., Mary-Jo Del Vecchio Good, Isenbike Togan, Zafer Ilbars, A. Güvener, and Ilker Gelişen. 1994. "In the Subjunctive Mode: Epilepsy Narratives in Turkey." *Social Science and Medicine* 38 (6): 835–42.

Goolrukh Gupta v. Burjor Pardiwala, Valsad Anjuman Trust. 2012. High Court of Gujarat at Ahmedabad.

Gould, Ketayun H. 1972. "Parsis and Urban Demography: Some Research Possibilities." *Journal of Marriage and the Family* 34 (2): 345–52.

Graeber, David, Laura Bear, and Nayanika Mathur. n.d. Discussing a New Anthropology of Bureaucracy. Accessed June 3, 2021. https://soundcloud.com/berghahn-books/sets/discussing-a-new-anthropology.

Greenhouse, Carol J. 1989. "Just in Time: Temporality and the Cultural Legitimation of Law." *Yale Law Journal* 98 (8): 1631–51.

Greenhouse, Carol J. 1996. *A Moment's Notice: Time Politics across Cultures*. Ithaca, NY: Cornell University Press.

Guha, Amalendu. 1984. "More about the Parsi Seths: Their Roots, Entrepreneurship and Comprador Role, 1650–1918." *Economic and Political Weekly*, 117–32.

Gupta, Akhil. 2012. *Red Tape: Bureaucracy, Structural Violence, and Poverty in India*. Durham, NC: Duke University Press.

Gupta, Somanātha, and Kathryn Hansen. 2005. *The Parsi Theatre: Its Origins and Development*. Kolkata, India: Seagull Books.

Guyer, Jane I. 2007. "Prophecy and the Near Future: Thoughts on Macroeconomic, Evangelical, and Punctuated Time." *American Ethnologist* 34 (3): 409–21.

Guyer, Jane I. 2012. "Obligation, Binding, Debt and Responsibility: Provocations about Temporality from Two New Sources." *Social Anthropology* 20 (4): 491–501.

Guyer, Jane I. n.d. "Gifts: A Study in Comparative Law by Richard Hyland." *American Ethnologist* 38 (3): 607–8.

Hann, C. M. 1998. *Property Relations: Renewing the Anthropological Tradition*. Cambridge: Cambridge University Press.

Hann, Chris. 2006. "The Gift and Reciprocity: Perspectives from Economic Anthropology." *Handbook on the Economics of Giving, Reciprocity and Altruism* 1: 207–23.

Hanson, John H. 2015. "The Anthropology of Giving: Toward a Cultural Logic of Charity." *Journal of Cultural Economy* 8 (4): 501–20.

Hardin, Jessica. 2021. "Life before Vegetables: Nutrition, Cash, and Subjunctive Health in Samoa." *Cultural Anthropology* 36 (3): 428–57.

Harding, Vanessa. 2002. "Space, Property, and Propriety in Urban England." *Journal of Interdisciplinary History* 32 (4): 549–69.

Haynes, Douglas E. 1987. "From Tribute to Philanthropy: The Politics of Gift Giving in a Western Indian City." *The Journal of Asian Studies* 46 (02): 339–60.

Heim, Maria. 2004. *Theories of the Gift in South Asia: Hindu, Buddhist, and Jain Reflections on Dana*. New York: Routledge.

Heitzman, James. 2008. *The City in South Asia*. London: Routledge.

Hertz, Ellen. 2010. "Comment on Riles 'Collateral Expertise.'" *Current Anthropology* 51 (6): 807–8.

Hinnells, John R. 1985. "The Flowering of Zoroastrian Benevolence: Paris Charities in the 19th and 20th Centuries." In *Papers in Honour of Professor Mary Boyce, Hommages et Opera Minora*. Leiden, The Netherlands: Brill.

Hinnells, John R. 2005. *The Zoroastrian Diaspora: Religion and Migration: Religion and Migration*. Oxford: Oxford University Press.

Hinnells, John R., and Alan Williams, eds. 2007. *Parsis in India and the Diaspora*. London: Routledge.

Ho, Engseng. 2006. *The Graves of Tarim: Genealogy and Mobility across the Indian Ocean*. Vol. 3. Oakland: University of California Press.

Ho, Engseng. 2014. "Afterword: Mobile Law and Thick Transregionalism." *Law and History Review* 32 (4): 883–89.

Hoag, Colin. 2011. "Assembling Partial Perspectives: Thoughts on the Anthropology of Bureaucracy." *PoLAR: Political and Legal Anthropology Review* 34 (1): 81–94.

Hoag, Colin. 2014. "Dereliction at the South African Department of Home Affairs: Time for the Anthropology of Bureaucracy." *Critique of Anthropology* 34 (4): 410–28.

Holston, James. 1989. *The Modernist City: An Anthropological Critique of Brasilia*. Chicago: University of Chicago Press.

Hull, Matthew S. 2003. "The File: Agency, Authority, and Autography in an Islamabad Bureaucracy." *Language and Communication* 23 (3–4): 287–314.

Hull, Matthew S. 2012a. "Documents and Bureaucracy." *Annual Review of Anthropology* 41: 251–67.

Hull, Matthew S. 2012b. *Government of Paper: The Materiality of Bureaucracy in Urban Pakistan*. Berkeley: University of California Press.

Huyssen, Andreas. 2003. *Present Pasts: Urban Palimpsests and the Politics of Memory*. Stanford, CA: Stanford University Press.

Jamsheed Kanga and Anr. v. Parsi Punchayet Funds and Properties and Ors. 2011. High Court of Judicature at Bombay.

Jany, János. 2004. "The Idea of a Trust in Zoroastrian Law." *Journal of Legal History* 25 (3): 269–86.

"Judgments: Petit v. Jeejeebhoy 1908 and Saklat v. Bella 1925." 2010. Mumbai: Parsiana Publications.

Karaka, D. F. 2000. *History of the Parsis: Including Their Manners, Customs, Religion, and Present Position*. London: Elibron Classics.

Karkaria, Bachi. 2016. "Why Is India's Wealthy Parsi Community Vanishing?" BBC News, January 9, 2016, sec. India. https://www.bbc.com/news/world-asia-india-35219331.

Keane, Webb. 2007. *Christian Moderns*. Oakland: University of California Press.

Khorakiwala, Rahela. 2020. *From the Colonial to the Contemporary: Images, Iconography, Memories, and Performances of Law in India's High Courts*. New Delhi, India: Bloomsbury Publishing.

Kidambi, Prashant, Manjiri Kamat, and Rachel Dwyer. 2019. *Bombay Before Mumbai: Essays in Honour of Jim Masselos*. Oxford: Oxford University Press.

Klaits, Frederick. 2017. *The Request and the Gift in Religious and Humanitarian Endeavors*. New York: Springer.

Kozlowski, G. C. 1985. *Muslim Endowments and Society in British India*. Cambridge: Cambridge University Press.

Kreyenbroek, Philip G., and Shehnaz Neville Munshi. 2001. *Living Zoroastrianism: Urban Parsis Speak about Their Religion*. Oxford: Psychology Press.

Krishnan, Shekhar. 2013. "Empire's Metropolis: Money Time and Space in Colonial Bombay, 1870–1930." PhD Dissertation, Massachusetts Institute of Technology, Cambridge, MA.

Kurie, Peter. 2018. *In Chocolate We Trust: The Hershey Company Town Unwrapped*. Philadelphia: University of Pennsylvania Press.

Laidlaw, James. 1995. *Riches and Renunciation: Religion, Economy, and Society among the Jains*. Oxford: Clarendon Press.

Laidlaw, James. 2000. "A Free Gift Makes No Friends." *Journal of the Royal Anthropological Institute* 6 (4): 617–34.

Latour, Bruno. 2010. *The Making of Law: An Ethnography of the Conseil d'État.* Boston: Polity.

Lepaulle, Pierre. 1927. "Civil Law Substitutes for Trusts." *Yale Law Journal* 36 (8): 1126–47.

Lueddeckens, Dorothea, and Ramiyar Karanjia. 2011. *Days of Transition: The Parsi Death Rituals.* Goettingen: Wallstein Verlag.

Luhrmann, Tanya. 1996. *The Good Parsi: The Fate of a Colonial Elite in a Postcolonial Society.* Cambridge, MA: Harvard University Press.

Luhrmann, Tanya M. 2002. "Evil in the Sands of Time: Theology and Identity Politics among the Zoroastrian Parsis." *Journal of Asian Studies* 61 (3): 861–89.

Macuch, Maria. 1991. "Charitable Foundations." *Encyclopaedia Iranica* V (4): 380–85.

Macuch, Maria. 1994. "Die Sasanidishe Stiftung." In *Iranian and Indo-European Studies: Memorial Volume of Otakar Klima*, edited by Otakar Klima and Petr Vavroušek. Prague: Enigma Corporation.

Macuch, Maria. 2004. "Pious Foundations in Byzantine and Sasanian Law." *Atti Dei Convegni Lincei-Accademia Nazionale Dei Lincei* 201: 181.

Macuch, Maria. 2005. "The Hērbedestān as a Legal Source: A Section on the Inheritance of a Convert to Zoroastrianism." *Bulletin of the Asia Institute* 19: 91–102.

Macuch, Maria. 2015. "Law in Pre-Modern Zoroastrianism." In *The Wiley Blackwell Companion to Zoroastrianism*, 289–98.

Mahajan, Nidhi. 2021. "Notes on an Archipelagic Ethnography: Ships, Seas, and Islands of Relation in the Indian Ocean." *Island Studies Journal* 16 (1).

Maitland, Frederic William. 1913. *Equity Also the Forms of Action at Common Law.* Cambridge University Press Archive.

Maitland, Frederic William, David Runciman, and Magnus Ryan. 2003. *Maitland: State, Trust and Corporation.* Cambridge: Cambridge University Press.

Makdisi, Saree. 1997. "Laying Claim to Beirut: Urban Narrative and Spatial Identity in the Age of Solidere." *Critical Inquiry* 23 (3): 661–705.

Maltby, Josephine, and Janette Rutterford. 2016. "Investing in Charities in the Nineteenth Century: The Financialization of Philanthropy." *Accounting History* 21 (2–3): 263–80.

Mankekar, Purnima, and Akhil Gupta. 2017. "Future Tense: Capital, Labor, and Technology in a Service Industry: The 2017 Lewis Henry Morgan Lecture." *Journal of Ethnographic Theory* 7 (3): 67–87.

Marcus, George E., and Peter Dobkin Hall. 1992. *Lives in Trust: The Fortunes of Dynastic Families in Late Twentieth-Century America.* Boulder, CO: Westview Press.

Mathur, Nayanika. 2016. *Paper Tiger.* Cambridge: Cambridge University Press.

Mathur, Saloni. 2000. "History and Anthropology in South Asia: Rethinking the Archive." *Annual Review of Anthropology* 29 (1): 89–106.

Mattingly, Cheryl. 2014. *Moral Laboratories: Family Peril and the Struggle for a Good Life.* Berkeley: University of California Press.

Maurer, Bill. 2002. "Anthropological and Accounting Knowledge in Islamic Banking and Finance: Rethinking Critical Accounts." *Journal of the Royal Anthropological Institute* 8 (4): 645–67.

Maurer, Bill. 2005. *Mutual Life, Limited: Islamic Banking, Alternative Currencies, Lateral Reason*. Princeton, NJ: Princeton University Press.

Maurer, Bill. 2006. *Pious Property: Islamic Mortgages in the United States*. New York: Russell Sage Foundation.

Mauss, Marcel. 1990. *The Gift: The Form and Reason for Exchange in Archaic Societies*. Translated by W. D. Halls. New York: Norton.

Mawani, Renisa. 2014. "Law as Temporality: Colonial Politics and Indian Settlers." UC *Irvine Law Review* 4: 65.

Ministry of Minority Affairs. 2017. Government of India. September 29, 2017. "Jiyo Parsi" Central Sector Scheme for Containing Population Decline of Parsis in India. https://www.jiyoparsi.org/.

Mistry, Cyrus. 2013. *Chronicle of a Corpse Bearer*. New Delhi: Aleph Book Company.

Mistry, Rohinton. 2001. *A Fine Balance*. New York: Faber and Faber.

Mistry, Rohinton. 2010. *Such a Long Journey*. New York: Random House.

Mistry, Rohinton. 2011a. *Family Matters*. New York: Random House.

Mistry, Rohinton. 2011b. *Tales from Firozsha Baag*. London: Random House.

Mosse, David. 2020. "The Modernity of Caste and the Market Economy." *Modern Asian Studies* 54 (4): 1225–71.

Moumtaz, Nada. 2012. "Modernizing Charity, Remaking Islamic Law." PhD Dissertation, City University of New York, NY.

Moumtaz, Nada. 2021. *God's Property: Islam, Charity, and the Modern State*. Berkeley: University of California Press.

Mukherji, Anahita. 2017. "Asking Parsis to Have More Kids, in the Most Regressive and Patriarchal Way." *The Wire*. August 7, 2017. https://thewire.in/society/jiyo-parsi -phase-ii-parsi-panchayat-khap-panchayat.

Munn, Nancy D. 1992. "The Cultural Anthropology of Time: A Critical Essay." *Annual Review of Anthropology* 21 (1): 93–123.

Murphy, Tim. 2004. "Legal Fabrications and the Case of 'Cultural Property.'" In *Law, Anthropology, and the Constitution of the Social: Making Persons and Things*, edited by Martha Mundy. Cambridge: Cambridge University Press.

Murzban Muncherji Murzbanji. 1915. *Leaves from the Life of Muncherji Cowasji Murzban*. Bombay: F.B. Marzban and Co.'s Printing Press.

Nainan, Navtej. 2008. "Building Boomers and Fragmentation of Space in Mumbai." *Economic and Political Weekly* 43 (21): 29–34.

Nair, Manoj R. 2012. "Dire Demographics of Parsi-Zoroastrians." DNA *India*. May 23, 2012. https://www.dnaindia.com/analysis/column-dire-demographics-of-parsi -zoroastrians-1692444.

Narayan, Kirin. 1993. "How Native Is a 'Native' Anthropologist?" *American Anthropologist* 95 (3): 671–86.

Nicholson, Rashna Darius. 2015. "Corporeality, Aryanism, Race: The Theatre and Social Reform of the Parsis of Western India." *South Asia: Journal of South Asian Studies* 38 (4): 613–38.

Nicholson, Rashna Darius. 2021. *The Colonial Public and the Parsi Stage: The Making of the Theatre of Empire (1853–1893)*. New York: Springer Nature.

Nijman, Jan. 2000. "Mumbai's Real Estate Market in 1990s: De-Regulation, Global Money and Casino Capitalism." *Economic and Political Weekly* 35 (7): 575–82.

Nijman, Jan. 2007. "Mumbai since Liberalisation: The Space-Economy of India's Gateway." In *Indian Cities in Transition*, edited by Annapurna Shaw, 238–59. Hyderabad: Orient Blackswan.

Osella, Filippo. 2018. "Charity and Philanthropy in South Asia: An Introduction." *Modern Asian Studies* 52 (1): 4–34.

Palsetia, Jesse S. 2001. *The Parsis of India: Preservation of Identity in Bombay City*. Vol. 17. Leiden, The Netherlands: Brill.

Palsetia, Jesse S. 2005. "Merchant Charity and Public Identity Formation in Colonial India: The Case of Jamsetjee Jejeebhoy." *Journal of Asian and African Studies* 40 (3): 197–217.

Palsetia, Jesse S. 2008. "The Parsis of India and the Opium Trade in China." *Contemporary Drug Problems* 35: 647.

Palsetia, Jesse S. 2017. "Parsi Charity: A Historical Perspective on Religion, Community, and Donor-Patron Relations among the Parsis of India." In *Holy Wealth: Accounting for This World and The Next in Religious Belief and Practice*, edited by Almut Hintze and Alan Williams, 175–92. Festschrift for John R. Hinnells. Wiesbaden, Germany: Harrassowitz Verlag.

Parry, Jonathan. 1986. "The Gift, the Indian Gift and the 'Indian Gift.'" *Man* 21 (3): 453–73.

Patel, Bomanji Byram. 1888. *A Record of Important Events of the Parsi Community in India Chronologically Arranged from the Date of Their Immigration into India to 1860*. Bombay: Duftar Ashkara Press.

Patel, Gieve. 2008. *Mister Behram and Other Plays*. Calcutta: Seagull Books.

Patel, Sujata, and Jim Masselos. 2003. *Bombay and Mumbai: The City in Transition*. New Delhi: Oxford University Press.

Pathak, V. K. 2008. "Developing Land and Real Estate Markets." In *Mumbai Reader '07*. Mumbai: Urban Design Research Institute.

Pedersen, Morten Axel, and Morten Nielsen. 2013. "Trans-Temporal Hinges: Reflections on an Ethnographic Study of Chinese Infrastructural Projects in Mozambique and Mongolia." *Social Analysis* 57 (1): 122–42.

Piketty, Thomas. 2018. *Capital in the Twenty-First Century*. Cambridge, MA: Harvard University Press.

Pistor, Katharina. 2019. *The Code of Capital: How the Law Creates Wealth and Inequality*. Princeton, NJ: Princeton University Press.

Pocock, John GA. 1981. "Virtues, Rights, and Manners: A Model for Historians of Political Thought." *Political Theory* 9 (3): 353–68.

Poovey, Mary. 1998. *A History of the Modern Fact: Problems of Knowledge in the Sciences of Wealth and Society*. Chicago: University of Chicago Press.

Povinelli, Elizabeth A. 2002. *The Cunning of Recognition: Indigenous Alterities and the Making of Australian Multiculturalism*. Durham, NC: Duke University Press.

Presler, Franklin A. 1987. *Religion under Bureaucracy: Policy and Administration for Hindu Temples in South India*. Cambridge: Cambridge University Press.

Purohit, Teena. 2012. *The Aga Khan Case*. Cambridge, MA: Harvard University Press.

Qadir, Abdul. 2004. *Waáqf : Islamic Law of Charitable Trust.* New Delhi: Global Vision Publishing House.

Raheja, Gloria Goodwin. 1988. *The Poison in the Gift: Ritual, Prestation, and the Dominant Caste in a North Indian Village.* Chicago: University of Chicago Press.

Raianu, Mircea. 2021. *Tata: The Global Corporation That Built Indian Capitalism.* Cambridge, MA: Harvard University Press.

Rajaratnam, S., M. Natarajan, and C. P. Thangaraj. 2010. *Law and Procedure on Charitable Trusts and Religious Institutions.* 10th ed. Mumbai: Snow White Publications.

Raman, Bhavani. 2012. *Document Raj: Writing and Scribes in Early Colonial South India.* Chicago: University of Chicago Press.

Ranganathan, Murali. 2019. "Mohammad Ali Rogay: Life and Times of a Bombay Country Trader." In *Bombay Before Mumbai: Essays in Honour of Jim Masselos,* edited by Prashant Kidambi, Manjiri Kamat, and Rachel Dwyer, 15–33. New York: Oxford University Press.

Rao, Nikhil. 2013a. "Community, Urban Citizenship and Housing in Bombay, ca. 1919–1980." *South Asia: Journal of South Asian Studies* 36 (3): 415–33.

Rao, Nikhil. 2013b. *House, But No Garden: Apartment Living in Bombay's Suburbs, 1898–1964.* Minneapolis: University of Minnesota Press.

Rao, Vyjayanthi. 2007. "Proximate Distances: The Phenomenology of Density in Mumbai." *Built Environment* 33 (2): 227–48.

Richland, Justin. 2013. "Jurisdiction: Grounding Law in Language." *Annual Review of Anthropology* 42: 209–26.

Richland, Justin B. 2008. "Sovereign Time, Storied Moments: The Temporalities of Law, Tradition, and Ethnography in Hopi Tribal Court." *PoLAR: Political and Legal Anthropology Review* 31 (1): 8–27.

Richland, Justin B. 2012. "Perpetuities against Rules: Law, Ethnography and the Measuring of Lives." *Law, Culture and the Humanities* 8 (3): 433–47.

Riles, Annelise. 2004. "Property as Legal Knowledge: Means and Ends." *Journal of the Royal Anthropological Institute* 10 (4): 775–95.

Riles, Annelise. 2006. *Documents: Artifacts of Modern Knowledge.* Ann Arbor: University of Michigan Press.

Riles, Annelise. 2010. "Collateral Expertise." *Current Anthropology* 51 (6): 795–818.

Riles, Annelise. 2011. *Collateral Knowledge—Legal Reasoning in the Global Financial Markets.* Chicago: University of Chicago Press.

Riles, Annelise. 2017. "Is the Law Hopeful?" In *The Economy of Hope,* edited by Hirokazu Miyaaki and Richard Swedberg, 126–46. Philadelphia: University of Philadelphia Press.

Ring, Laura A. 2006. *Zenana: Everyday Peace in a Karachi Apartment Building.* Bloomington: Indiana University Press.

Ringer, Monica M. 2011. *Pious Citizens: Reforming Zoroastrianism in India and Iran.* Syracuse, NY: Syracuse University Press.

Roitman, Janet. 2013. *Anti-Crisis.* Durham, NC: Duke University Press.

Rose, Carol M. 1994. *Property and Persuasion: Essays on the History, Theory, and Rhetoric of Ownership.* Boulder, CO: Westview Press.

Rosen, Matthew. 2018. "Accidental Communities: Chance Operations in Urban Life and Field Research." *Ethnography* 19 (3): 312–35.

Roy, Ananya. 2005. "Urban Informality: Toward an Epistemology of Planning." *Journal of the American Planning Association* 71 (2): 147–58.

Roy, Ananya. 2009. "Why India Cannot Plan Its Cities: Informality, Insurgence and the Idiom of Urbanization." *Planning Theory* 8 (1): 76–87.

Roy, Thirankar. 2013. "Embracing the World: Parsis after China Trade." In *Across Oceans and Flowing Silks*, edited by Pheroza Godrej. Mumbai: Spenta Multimedia.

Rudden, Bernard. 1994. "Things as Thing and Things as Wealth." *Oxford J. Legal Stud.* 14: 81.

Rudnyckyj, Daromir. 2011. *Spiritual Economies. Spiritual Economies*. Ithaca, NY: Cornell University Press.

Sadhwani, Yogesh. 2014. "Wadias Want Back Parsi Colonies Their Ancestors Developed." *Mumbai Mirror*, May 20, 2014. https://mumbaimirror.indiatimes.com /mumbai/cover-story/wadias-want-back-parsi-colonies-their-ancestors-developed /articleshow/35352722.cms.

Samuel, Geoffrey. 2004. "Epistemology and Comparative Law: Contributions from the Sciences and Social Sciences." In *Epistemology and Methodology of Comparative Law*, edited by M. V. Hoeke, 35–78. Oxford: Hart Publishing.

Sanchez, Andrew, James G. Carrier, Christopher Gregory, James Laidlaw, Marilyn Strathern, Yunxiang Yan, and Jonathan Parry. 2017. "'The Indian Gift': A Critical Debate." *History and Anthropology* 28 (5): 553–83.

Scheffler, Karl. 1910. *Berlin, Ein Stadtschicksal*. Berlin: E. Reiss.

Scherz, China. 2013. "Let Us Make God Our Banker: Ethics, Temporality, and Agency in a Ugandan Charity Home." *American Ethnologist* 40 (4): 624–36.

Searle, Llerena Guiu. 2016. *Landscapes of Accumulation: Real Estate and the Neoliberal Imagination in Contemporary India*. Chicago: University of Chicago Press.

Sehgal, Bela Bhansali, dir. 2012. *Shirin Farhad Ki Toh Nikal Padi*. Mumbai: Eros International.

Setalvad, Atul M. 2009. *Law of Trusts and Charities*. Delhi: Universal Law Publishing.

Shaikh, Juned. 2021. *Outcaste Bombay: City Making and the Politics of the Poor*. Seattle: University of Washington Press.

Sharafi, Mitra. 2006. "Bella's Case: Parsi Identity and the Law in Colonial Rangoon, Bombay and London, 1887–1925." PhD Dissertation. Princeton, NJ: Princeton University.

Sharafi, Mitra. 2007. "Judging Conversion to Zoroastrianism: Behind the Scenes of the Parsi Panchayat Case (1908)." In *Parsis in India and the Diaspora*, edited by John R. Hinnells and Alan Williams. London: Routledge.

Sharafi, Mitra. 2010. *Colonial Parsis and Law: A Cultural History. Government Research Fellowship Lectures 2009–2010*. Mumbai: K. R. Cama Oriental Institute.

Sharafi, Mitra. 2014. *Law and Identity in Colonial South Asia: Parsi Legal Culture, 1772–1947*. New York: Cambridge University Press.

Sharafi, Mitra. 2015. "Law and Modern Zoroastrians." In *The Wiley Blackwell Companion to Zoroastrianism*, edited by Michael Stausberg and Yuhan Vevaina. Cambridge: Blackwell.

Sharma, R. N. 2010. "Mega Transformation of Mumbai: Deepening Enclave Urbanism." *Sociological Bulletin* 59 (1): 69–91.

Shipton, Parker MacDonald. 2009. *Mortgaging the Ancestors: Ideologies of Attachment in Africa*. New Haven, CT: Yale University Press.

Silbey, Susan S. 2005. "After Legal Consciousness." *Annual Review of Law and Social Science* 1: 323–68.

Srinivas, Smriti, Bettina Ng'weno, and Neelima Jeychandran. 2020. *Reimagining Indian Ocean Worlds*. London: Routledge.

Stausberg, Michael. 2004a. "Monday-Nights at the Banaji, Fridays at the Aslaji: Ritual Efficacy and Transformation in Bombay City." In *Zoroastrian Rituals in Context*, edited by Michael Stausberg, 653–718. Leiden, The Netherlands: Brill.

Stausberg, Michael. 2004b. *Zoroastrian Rituals in Context*. Vol. 102. Leiden, The Netherlands: Brill.

Stausberg, Michael, and Yuhan S. D. Vevaina, eds. 2015. *The Wiley Blackwell Companion to Zoroastrianism*. West Sussex: John Wiley and Sons.

Stebbings, Chantal. 1989. "The Commercial Application of the Law of Mortmain." *Journal of Legal History* 10 (1): 37–44.

Stewart, Sarah. 2012. "The Politics of Zoroastrian Philanthropy and the Case of Qasr-e Firuzeh." *Iranian Studies* 45 (1): 59–80.

Stewart, Sarah, Ursula Sims-Williams, and Firoza Punthakey Mistree. n.d. "Everlasting Flame." Exhibition at the National Museum, Delhi, March–May 2016.

Strohl, David James. 2019. "Love Jihad in India's Moral Imaginaries: Religion, Kinship, and Citizenship in Late Liberalism." *Contemporary South Asia* 27 (1): 27–39.

Sullivan, Winnifred Fallers. 2017. "'Going to Law': Reflections on Law, Religion, and Mitra Sharafi's Law and Identity in Colonial South Asia." *Law and Social Inquiry* 42 (4): 1231–39.

Suresh, Mayur. 2019. "The 'Paper Case': Evidence and Narrative of a Terrorism Trial in Delhi." *Law and Society Review* 53 (1): 173–201.

Swan, Gerry E., Richard Cuthbert, Miguel Quevedo, Rhys E. Green, Deborah J. Pain, Paul Bartels, Andrew A. Cunningham, et al. 2006. "Toxicity of Diclofenac to Gyps Vultures." *Biology Letters* 2 (2): 279–82.

Taraporevala, Sooni, dir. 2008. *Little Zizou*. Mumbai: Jigri Dost Productions.

Tarlo, Emma. 2003. *Unsettling Memories: Narratives of India's Emergency*. Berkeley: University of California Press.

Thampi, Madhavi, and Shalini Saksena. 2009. *China and the Making of Bombay*. K. R. Cama Oriental Institute, Mumbai.

Throop, C. Jason. 2014. "Moral Moods." *Ethos* 42 (1): 65–83.

"Trust Settlement—The Nowrosjee Nusserwanjee Wadia Trust Buildings for Parsees." 1916.

Umrigar, Thrity. 2001. *Bombay Time*. New York: Il Saggiatore.

Upadhya, Carol. 2020. "Assembling Amaravati: Speculative Accumulation in a New Indian City." *Economy and Society* 49 (1): 141–69.

Upton, Dell. 1996. "Lancasterian Schools, Republican Citizenship, and the Spatial Imagination in Early Nineteenth-Century America." *Journal of the Society of Architectural Historians* 55 (3): 238–53.

Vaihinger, Hans. 2001. *The Philosophy of "as If": A System of the Theoretical, Practical and Religious Fictions of Mankind*. London: Routledge.

Valverde, Mariana. 2015a. *Chronotopes of Law: Jurisdiction, Scale and Governance*. London: Routledge.

Valverde, Mariana. 2015b. "On Chronotopes of Law." *Feminist Legal Studies* 23 (3): 349–52.

Valverde, Mariana. 2019. "Spacetime in/and Law." In *The Oxford Handbook of Law and Humanities*, by Mariana Valverde, edited by Simon Stern, Maksymilian Del Mar, and Bernadette Meyler, 217–34. New York: Oxford University Press.

Van der Veer, Peter, ed. 2015. *Handbook of Religion and the Asian City: Aspiration and Urbanization in the Twenty-First Century*. Oakland: University of California Press.

Van der Zwan, Natascha. 2014. "Making Sense of Financialization." *Socio-Economic Review* 12 (1): 99–129.

Vanaik, Anish. 2015. "Representing Commodified Space: Maps, Leases, Auctions and 'Narrations' of Property in Delhi, c. 1900–47." *Historical Research* 88 (240): 314–32.

Vanaik, Anish. 2019. *Possessing the City: Property and Politics in Delhi, 1911–1947*. London: Oxford University Press.

Verdery, Katherine. 2003. *The Vanishing Hectare: Property and Value in Postsocialist Transylvania*. Ithaca, NY: Cornell University Press.

Verdery, Katherine, and Caroline Humphrey. 2004. *Property in Question: Value Transformation in the Global Economy*. Oxford: Berg Publishers.

Vevaina, Leilah. 2013. "Excarnation and the City: The Tower of Silence Debates in Mumbai." In *Topographies of Faith: Religion in Urban Space*, 73–95. Leiden, The Netherlands: Brill.

Vevaina, Leilah. 2014. "Trust Matters: Parsis and Property in Mumbai." PhD Dissertation, The New School for Social Research, New York.

Vevaina, Leilah. 2015. "Good Thoughts, Good Words, and Good (Trust) Deeds: Parsis, Risk, and Real Estate in Mumbai." In *Handbook of Religion and the Asian City: Aspiration and Urbanization in the Twenty-First Century*, 152–67. Berkeley: University of California Press.

Vevaina, Leilah. 2018a. "Good Deeds: Parsi Trusts from 'the Womb to the Tomb.'" *Modern Asian Studies* 52 (1): 238–65.

Vevaina, Leilah. 2018b. "She's Come Undone: Parsi Women's Property and Propriety under the Law." *PoLAR: Political and Legal Anthropology Review* 41 (1): 44–59.

Vevaina, Leilah. 2019. "Adjudicating the Sacred: The Fates of 'Native' Religious Endowments in India and Hong Kong." In *The Secular in South, East, and Southeast Asia*, 261–85. New York: Springer.

Vevaina, Leilah. 2021. "Farhad 'Sue Maker.'" In *Bombay Brokers*, edited by Lisa Björkman, 154–62. Durham, NC: Duke University Press.

Vevaina, Leilah. 2022a. "Trusts on the Monsoon Winds: Parsi Transnational Religious Philanthropy." *Ethnography*. Published ahead of print, October 25, 2022. https://doi.org/10.1177/14661381221134414.

Vevaina, Leilah. 2022b. "Two Fire Temples and a Metro: Contesting Infrastructures in Mumbai." *Space and Culture* 26 (2). https://doi.org/10.1177/12063312221130245.

Vevaina, Leilah. 2023. "Mergers and Legal Fictions: Coverture and Intermarried Women in India." *Law and History Review* 1–18.

Vevaina, Yuhan S. D. 2015. "Theologies and Hermeneutics." In *The Wiley Blackwell Companion to Zoroastrianism*, 211–34. West Sussex: John Wiley and Sons.

Visaria, L. 1974. "Demographic Transition among Parsis: 1881–1971: III: Fertility Trends." *Economic and Political Weekly* 9 (41): 1828–32.

Visaria, Leela, and Rajani R. Ved. 2016. *India's Family Planning Programme: Policies, Practices and Challenges*. London: Routledge.

von Benda-Beckmann, Franz, Keebet von Benda-Beckmann, and Melanie Wiber. 2006. "The Properties of Property." In *Changing Properties of Property*, edited by Franz von Benda-Beckmann, Keebet von Benda-Beckmann, and Melanie Wiber, 1–39. Oxford: Berghahn Books.

von Benda-Beckmann, Keebet. 2014. *Trust and the Temporalities of Law*. Abingdon, UK: Taylor and Francis.

Wadia, Arzan S. 2017. "Asking Parsis to Have More Kids, in the Most Regressive and Patriarchal Way." *Parsi Khabar* (blog), August 8, 2017. https://parsikhabar.net/issues/asking-parsis-to-have-more-kids-in-the-most-regressive-and-patriarchal-way/15861/.

Wadia, Pestonji Ardesir. 1949. *Parsis Ere the Shadows Thicken*. Bombay: P. A. Wadia.

Wadia, Rusheed. 2008. "Bombay Parsi Merchants in the Eighteenth and Nineteenth Centuries." In *Parsis in India and the Diaspora*, edited by J. R. Hinnells and Alan Williams. London: Routledge.

Wagner, Roy. 1986. *Symbols That Stand for Themselves*. Chicago: University of Chicago Press.

Walthert, Rafael. 2010. "Problematisierte Patrilinearität Bei Den ParsInnen in Mumbai." *GENDER–Zeitschrift Für Geschlecht, Kultur Und Gesellschaft* 2 (1): 9–27.

Watt, Gary. 2009. *Equity Stirring: The Story of Justice Beyond Law*. London: Bloomsbury Publishing.

Weber, Max. 2002. *The Protestant Ethic and the "Spirit" of Capitalism and Other Writings*. Translated and edited by Gordon C. Wells, and Peter R. Baehr. London: Penguin Classics.

Weil, Shalva. 2019. *The Baghdadi Jews in India: Maintaining Communities, Negotiating Identities and Creating Super-Diversity*. London: Routledge.

Weiner, Annette B. 1992. *Inalienable Possessions: The Paradox of Keeping-While-Giving*. Berkeley: University of California Press.

Weinstein, Liza. 2008. "Mumbai's Development Mafias: Globalization, Organized Crime and Land Development." *International Journal of Urban and Regional Research* 32 (1): 22–39.

White, David. 1987. "Parsis in the Commercial World of Western India, 1700–1750." *Indian Economic and Social History Review* 24 (2): 183–203.

White, David. 1991. "From Crisis to Community Definition: The Dynamics of Eighteenth-Century Parsi Philanthropy." *Modern Asian Studies* 25 (2): 303–20.

Williams, Alan. 2009. *The Zoroastrian Myth of Migration from Iran and Settlement in the Indian Diaspora: Text, Translation and Analysis of the 16th Century Qesse-Ye Sanjān 'The Story of Sanjan.'* Leiden, The Netherlands: Brill.

Writer, Rashna. 2016. "Charity as a Means of Zoroastrian Self-Preservation." *Iranian Studies* 49 (1): 117–36.

Yahaya, Nurfadzilah. 2020. *Fluid Jurisdictions*. Ithaca, NY: Cornell University Press.

Yan, Yunxiang. 2020. "Gifts." *The Open Encyclopedia of Anthropology*, July 2020. http://doi.org/10.29164/20gifts.

Note: Page numbers in italics refer to figures.

gendered issues, 102–4, 184n6

ghambars (communal feasts), 8, 47, 80

Ghosh, Amitav, 149, 150

gifts, 7, 21, 61, 72–73, 100, 165

Gilder Lane Colony, 33–34, *34*, 37–38, 91

giving: accumulation and, 147, 148, 170; communal, 14, 30; definition of charity and, 35–36; early practices of, 7–9, 80, 132, 150, 152; financialization of, 173–74; global, 164, 166; legal regulations on, 11; perpetual and direct, 53, 80, 165; privilege and, 96; and receiving binary, 24, 54, 61, 72–73; temporality of, 24–25; traces of, 154. *See also* reciprocity

Godrej, Naoroji, 158, 184n16

Godrej Baug, 46, 142, 158–63, *160*

Godrej & Boyce Manufacturing Company Ltd., 158, 184n15

governance, 2, 59, 75, 81, 131, 132

Gujarat, 155; early Parsi settlement, 15–16, 18, 80, 149; migration to Bombay, 16, 31, 57, 59, 80–81, 149; Navsari, 130, 131, 156, 159

Gujarat High Court, 123

Gupta, Goolrukh (*"Gupta* case"), 123–27, 133, 165, 182n13

Guyer, 43

gymkhana (community center), 38–39

Hafeez Contractor, 67, 179n16

Haynes, Douglas E., 11

Heatherwick, Thomas, 136, 183n9

Heim, Maria, 73

heritage status, 46, 48, 178n18

high-rises, 2, 45, 66, 136, 159, 175n4; Hilla Towers, 64–65, *65*, 92; Petit Towers, 49–50

Hindu Undivided Family, 35

hinge function, 13–14, 22, 23, 148; of trusts, 24, 50–51, 108, 109, 168, 170–71

Hoag, Colin, 90, 96

Hong Kong, 5, 12, 145, 149; Parsi settlement in, 147, 155–58; trust and

donations, 26, 154, 159, 163–65, 173–74, 178n21; Zoroastrian building in, 163

horoscope, 50, 145, 163; of Mumbai, 4, 24, 32, 149; time and, 14, 30; trust directory as, 4, 5, 10, 29, 30

hospitals, 152, 157, 184n6; Parsi General, 44–48, 128, 156

housing colonies, 16, 17–18, 89, 150; BPP, 60, 70–71, 78, 179n11; bungalow architecture and, 157–58; Dadar, 38–42, 100, *101*, 177n12; Gilder Lane, 33–34, *34*, 37–38, 91; Khareghat, 38; managing and funding, 27–28, 154–55; plaques adorning, 154; violence and, 161. *See also baugs*; sanatoria

Hull, Matthew, 112

identity, 80, 83, 123, 133, 153, 184n17; ethnic group, 103, 104; feistiness and, 106–7; historical, 14–15, 176n18; lineage and, 108; minority, 167, 168

Income Tax Act, 36, 162

Incorporated Zoroastrian Charity Funds of Hong Kong, 156

Indian Constitution, 116, 121, 123–24, 127, 177n11, 182n10

Indian Contract Act, 40, 111

inheritances: family heirlooms, 99–100; historical practices, 7–11, 35; lack of trust and, 52–53, 68; of property, 30, 102, 172; religious conversion and, 57–58; tax, 171; tenancy claims and, 60

inter-Asia, 149, 151, 153, 154

intermarriage, 19, 64, 101–2, 164, 165; access to sacred spaces and, 108, 123, 125–26, 134; claims to trust benefits and, 82–83, 84, 178n2; cremation ceremonies and prayers for, 109–10, 115, 120, 126, 134, 142; exclusion of women and children and, 84, 89, 173, 180n13; rate of, 142, 179n17; surnames and, 183n7

in vitro fertilization (IVF), 25, 86, 97–98, 103–4, 173, 181n31

shareholders, 10, 157

shipbuilding, 16, 147, 150, 151, 178n5

Shipton, Parker, 172

Shri Jagannath Temple Act, 119, 182n8

social class, 17–18, 68

social relations, 7, 54, 72, 80, 107–8, 169, 174; communal, 93

Societies Act, 40, 44

soft power, 152

space: authority in, 126; communal, 130; green, 66, 67, 92, 177n8, 179n20; living, 84; Parsi, 82, 89–90; philanthropic, 152; religious, 111, 120, 122; time and, 7, 30, 108, 167; trust, 3, 44, 125–26, 167; urban, 4, 5, 23, 24, 53, 144, 172. See also sacred spaces

Special Marriages Act, 123, 125

speculation, 23

stereotypes, 19, 98, 100, 102

subjunctive mode, 4–5, 22, 23, 96, 171–74

succession laws, 9, 53, 58, 68, 173

sugar in the milk myth, 15, 100, 103, 176n20

Supreme Court of India, 88, 119, 122, 126, 127, 182n4, 182n8

Surat, 80, 150, 155

Tata, Ratanji Dadabhoy (and family), 82–83, 100, 108, 180n8, 184n7

tax-exemption status, 2, 13, 36, 54, 81, 178n3; potential loss of, 63, 162

tax liability, 171

temples, 8, 19, 22, 125–26, 150, 156; fire, 17, 38, 82, 100, 130, 134, 146, 159; global diaspora, 164, 174; Jagannath, 119, 182n8

temporality, 2, 11, 26, 166, 169; of bureaucracy, 79, 94, 96; future-focused, 108, 170, 172; horoscope and, 4, 14, 30, 167; housing priorities and, 95–96; of obligations, 25, 54, 72, 170; of trusts, 12, 24, 43, 170–71; uncertainty and, 23, 85. See also meantime

text, rush to, 124–25, 182n15

textile industry, 30, 63, 83, 164, 179n10

time. See meantime; temporality

Towers of Silence, 82, 108, 110, 123, 125, 184n11; construction of the first, 130–31, 132. See also Doongerwadi

trade. See China trade; cotton trade

transfer development rights (TDR), 70, 179n24

transfer fees, pugree, 60, 62, 69, 70, 74, 148, 155

Transfer of Property Act, 41, 177n14

trust directory. See Directory of Public Trusts

trustees, role of, 2, 10, 13, 165, 173, 176n12; assets and, 148; authority and, 82, 109, 118, 119, 174; beneficiaries and, 36–37, 108, 169; of BPP, 75–79, 86–87; deeds and, 119–20; of Hong Kong, 163–66; infighting and improprieties and, 162–63; for Petit trust, 44–48; rights and, 116, 182n9; and temples, 110; for Wadia trust, 55–59

trust form. See charitable trusts; hinge function

trust laws, 7, 9–10, 36, 82, 175n10

trust objects, 7, 25, 144, 145; assets as, 22, 36–37, 148, 171; becoming subjects, 147, 171; beneficiaries as, 104, 117; cy près and, 24, 42, 49, 66; obligation and, 13, 36, 54, 57, 68, 71, 96, 171–72; original, 10, 43, 44, 51, 68, 69, 71, 174; structure, 104, 147, 168–69

Universal Adult Franchise (UAF), 87–88, 107

unsettled state, 6, 17, 169, 170

urban planning, 29, 39–40. See also redevelopment projects

uthamna ceremony, 129, 138

Vaihinger, Hans, 175n5, 178n19

vulture population, 108, 132, 134, 135–37, 183n8

Wadia, Hormusji and Pestonji, 151

Wadia, Jerbai, 24, 61, 67; founding wish
and obligation, 70–72, 73–74; trust
deeds and trustees, 55–59, 170–71

Wadia, Lowji, 150

Wadia, Nowrosjee Nusserwanjee, 55, 65,
178n5

Wadia, Nusli and Ness, 67, 68, 70, 71, 85

Wadia, Sir Ness, 57, 59, 179n10, 180n26

Wadia Building Trust Fund, 55, 59,
66, 70

Wadia Committee of Management, 57,
65–66, 69, 71

waqif/waqf, 9, 10, 79, 175n9, 176n16

wealth, 16, 60, 106, 155, 162; accumulation and distribution of, 7, 22, 131,
148; antiques and, 41, 177n15; tax,
162; trade and, 147, 149, 156; urban
real estate investment and, 151–53;
widows and, 52–53, 171. *See also*
philanthropy

White, David, 80

widows: *chawl* housing for, 20, 37, 176n23;
trusts established by, 52–53, 55–59

World Alliance of Parsi Irani Zarthoshtis
(WAPIZ), 86–87, 110

World Zoroastrians Organization (WZO),
86

Worli municipal crematorium, 139, 140, 145

Yahaya, Nurfadzilah, 152

Zoroastrianism: charitable giving practices, 8–9, 11, 35; cultural preservation,
103; diaspora, 14–15, 16, 21, 176n18;
family lineages, 18, 108; funerary
practice, 25, 108, 121, 129–30, 131–32, 137,
183n12; global initiatives, 164, 165, 166;
madressas (seminaries), 39; *nasasalars*,
132, 133–34, 183n5; *navjote* (initiation
ceremony), 82, 108, 119, 129, 173, 179n10,
182n2; purity laws, 129, 131, 132, 139,
183n5; revival, 173; *sudreh* (holy vest),
47. See also *dokhmenashini*